LESSONS

from the TOP

PARALEGAL

EXPERTS

*The 15 Most Successful Paralegals in America
and What You Can Learn from Them*

D0872967

LESSONS

from the TOP

PARALEGAL

EXPERTS

*The 15 Most Successful Paralegals in America
and What You Can Learn from Them*

CAROLE A. BRUNO

Paralegal Author and pioneer in defining
the paralegal profession

DELMAR
CENGAGE Learning

Australia Canada Mexico Singapore Spain United Kingdom United States

DELMAR
CENGAGE Learning™

Lessons from the Top Paralegal Experts, First Edition
Carole A. Bruno

Vice President:
Dawn Gerrain

Director of Learning Solutions: John Fedor

Acquisitions Editor:
Shelley Esposito

Developmental Editor:
Anne Orgren

Editorial Assistant:
Melissa Zaza

Director of Production:
Wendy A. Troeger

Content Project Manager:
Steven S. Couse

Director of Marketing:
Wendy Mapstone

Marketing Manager:
Gerard McAvey

Marketing Coordinator:
Jonathan Sheehan

Art Director:
Joy Kocsis

Cover Design:
Kathryn Sky-Peck

Cover Image:
© Getty Images, Inc.

For product information and technology assistance, contact us at
Professional & Career Group Customer Support, 1-800-648-7450

For permission to use material from this text or product,
submit all requests online at **www.cengage.com/permissions**
Further permissions questions can be emailed to
permissionrequest@cengage.com

ExamView® and ExamView Pro® are registered trademarks of FSCreations, Inc. Windows is a registered trademark of the Microsoft Corporation used herein under license. Macintosh and Power Macintosh are registered trademarks of Apple Computer, Inc. Used herein under license.

© 2008 Cengage Learning. All Rights Reserved. Cengage Learning WebTutor™ is a trademark of Cengage Learning.

Library of Congress Control Number: 2007942792

ISBN-13: 978-1-4018-8921-0

ISBN-10: 1-4018-8921-2

Delmar Cengage Learning
5 Maxwell Drive
Clifton Park, NY 12065-2919
USA

Cengage Learning products are represented in Canada by Nelson Education, Ltd.

For your lifelong learning solutions, visit **delmar.cengage.com**

Visit our corporate website at **www.cengage.com**

Notice to the Reader

Publisher does not warrant or guarantee any of the products described herein or perform any independent analysis in connection with any of the product information contained herein. Publisher does not assume, and expressly disclaims, any obligation to obtain and include information other than that provided to it by the manufacturer. The reader is expressly warned to consider and adopt all safety precautions that might be indicated by the activities described herein and to avoid all potential hazards. By following the instructions contained herein, the reader willingly assumes all risks in connection with such instructions. The publisher makes no representations or warranties of any kind, including but not limited to, the warranties of fitness for particular purpose or merchantability, nor are any such representations implied with respect to the material set forth herein, and the publisher takes no responsibility with respect to such material. The publisher shall not be liable for any special, consequential, or exemplary damages resulting, in whole or part, from the readers' use of, or reliance upon, this material.

Printed in the United States of America

1 2 3 4 5 X X X 11 10 09 08 07

DEDICATION

To My Brothers,

Jimmy and John,

Without Whose Love,

I Could Not Have Written This Book

CONTENTS

PREFACE

CONCEPT—BEYOND EDUCATION AND EXPERIENCE—MENTORING, A QUICKER WAY OF LEARNING

You use textbooks to learn in paralegal school, but have you found a book that is a conspectus of others' hands-on experience? The primary purpose of *LESSONS from the Top Paralegal Experts (LESSONS)* is to give you that kind of book—*a book like no other*—*a book that will let you peek into the world of successful top-producing, effective, and well-paid paralegals, working in various paralegal specialties in law firms, businesses, and government offices through the nation. You will have the rare opportunity of delving into the minds of these creative thinkers and taking what they know, their experience and wisdom, and applying it to your job, or the job you are seeking. You will have your personal mentors—in the rare book in your hand—LESSONS that you can call on when you need them.*

MENTORS SHORTEN THE LEARNING CURVE

On the job many paralegals often find themselves left alone to figure things out; their attorneys are busy and have little time to explain assignments; and other paralegals are overwhelmed with work. It is hard to admit what you do not know to your colleagues in the office. Often, paralegals can call other paralegals with their questions, or subscribe to a ListServ (a computerized bulletin board like Legal Assistant Today magazine[1] sponsors) and post their query. Their answer will come from their peers, instructors, or others visiting the ListServ. The answer may come immediately, in an hour, or never. Mentors simply are not available, especially experienced paralegals, or even the attorneys for whom they work. Seldom is on-the-job training available. Seminars often do

---

[1]See www.legalassistanttoday.com to join.

not fill this void because they usually are narrowly focused and more basic in content.

The formula of *LESSONS* is simple: Interview the experienced *movers and shakers* in the paralegal profession to glean their hidden secrets. Put the organizational tips, techniques, and methods that these creative leaders use in their daily work into a compendium of useful ideas, codified into an easy-to-use reference book. Readers will see how these paralegal pathfinders approach their work and strategize their complex projects. Aspiring paralegals may apply these proven creative solutions pulled from the minds of these forward-thinking leaders. This innovative mentoring process helps growing paralegals avoid the trials and tribulations that these experienced paralegal experts had to suffer before they figured it out.

THE EMPLOYER BENEFITS FROM PARALEGALS USING *LESSONS*

Ultimately, the employer directly benefits from their paralegals having a book like *LESSONS* on their desk as a ready resource, because the paralegals become more efficient, productive, and resourceful. Paralegals learn how to serve clients more personably and how to use checklists and other tools to interview and follow-up time. This results in an increase in paralegals' billable hours and helps them become more profitable to the firm. In addition, keeping paralegals challenged also prevents turnover because paralegals feel fulfilled when they are learning. Less turnover in the long run saves the attorney much money in training and related costs.

Paralegal students will reduce their on-the-job training time and will better prepared with *LESSONS* as a ready resource when they get their first job. Their confidence will soar with this tried and proven knowledge shared by successful experienced paralegal experts.

Paralegal educators will have a different resource to use to teach their students that goes beyond theory and procedures. The tips they find in *LESSONS* will be an addendum to their regular textbooks and a boon to their teaching.

LESSONS will help speed the learning process, improve efficiency and productivity, and avoid costly mistakes, extending beyond paralegal education, on-the-job training, and continuing paralegal education.

WHO SHOULD BUY *LESSONS?*

In addition to paralegals and paralegal students, *LESSONS* is helpful to anyone in the legal field. The paralegal experts share experiences that most have not heard about, and you learn from those and the wisdom they gleaned from their strategies.

Primary Market

Paralegals
Corporate paralegal staff
Paralegal supervisors and managers
Law office administrators and managers
Paralegal educators
Paralegal students
Paralegal schools
Law firm libraries
Paralegal school libraries
Corporate legal department libraries
Lawyers
Corporate counsel
Paralegal associations
Lawyers associations
ABA Standing Committee on Paralegals
Law office consultants
Law firm computer consultants
Legal personnel agencies
Legal secretaries
Legal secretary associations
Receptionists
Law students
Law schools
Law school libraries
Legal vendors and suppliers
City/county/state/federal court libraries
Court clerks

State Bar associations

Court reporting companies

High school career counselors and libraries

State Bar journals and other legal periodicals

Legal publishers

Secondary Market

College libraries

Print media (journals and periodicals)

TV shows about lawyers/paralegals

High school and college career counselors

Typists and temporary clerkss

Word processing document preparation department supervisors

Family and friends of the top paralegal experts

WHAT ARE THE LATEST TRENDS IN THIS MARKET?

The paralegal profession is growing so fast and schools are popping up everywhere. The American Association for Paralegal Education (AAfPE) presently has more than 450 members. AAfPE member schools currently enroll nearly 50,000 students and have nearly 200,000 graduates; 260 of them are ABA-approved. The public is becoming more knowledgeable about paralegals. Paralegals are rarely called legal assistants even though they may type on a computer. Seminars are being held by various institutes. Besides California's latest statute, Business & Professions Code, Section 6450, which has already been amended, many associations for legal adminstrators and paralegal managers have sprung up such as the National Federation of Paralegal Associations (NFPA), which was organized in the 1970s, the National Association of Legal Assistants (NALA), and the American Alliance for Paralegals.

As you will read in this book, technology is changing the face of the profession as paralegals learn new software programs and take charge of cases with a significant volume of documents. Now some paralegals are writing programs to meet their firm's needs.[2]

---

[2]See the section "Real Work Examples" in Chapter 14, Mathew D. Laskowski.

HIGHER EDUCATIONAL STANDARDS ARE NOW REQUIRED

With the State of California adopting legislation that defines the titles "paralegal" and "legal assistant" and setting educational criteria and continuing education requirements for paralegals, a new precedent has been set (and quite possibly other states may follow). Section 6450 defines "paralegal/legal assistant" as "a person who contracts with or is employed by an attorney, law firm, corporation, governmental agency or other entity and who performs substantial legal work under the direction and supervision of an active member of the State Bar of California...." The statute is intended to differentiate paralegals who work under the supervision of an attorney from persons who provide services directly to the public and are required under California law to be registered as legal document assistants.

The standards in the legal profession are high, and most law firms require some college background and formal paralegal education. Large firms usually require a bachelor's degree. Employers also require paralegals to have highly developed oral and written communication skills, plus organizational and computer skills.[3] However, there are many ways you may become a paralegal: (1) by obtaining a college degree and certification; (2) with a community college and associate's degree; (3) or through on-the-job training; and a bachelor's and master's degrees in paralegal studies. Other entrants have experience in a technical field that is useful to law firms, such as a background in tax preparation for tax and estate practices or in criminal justice, nursing, or health administration for personal injury practices.[4]

According to The United States Department of Labor, Bureau of Labor Statistics, *Occupational Outlook Handbook*,[5] paralegals and legal assistants held about 200,000 jobs in 2002 and 224,000 in 2004. Private law firms employed 7 out of 10 paralegals and legal assistants; most of the remainder worked for corporate legal departments and various levels of government.

Within the Federal Government, the United States Department of Justice is the largest employer, followed by the Social Security Administration and the United States Department of Treasury. A small number of paralegals own their own businesses and work as freelance

---

[3]California Business and Professions Code, Section 6450.

[4]Bureau of Labor Statistics, U.S. Department of Labor, Occupational Outlook Handbook, 2006-2007 Edition, Paralegals and Legal Assistants.

[5]Ibid.

legal assistants, contracting their services to attorneys or corporate legal departments.

TECHNOLOGY IS REINFORCING AND EXPANDING THE ROLE AND PROFESSIONAL NATURE OF THE PARALEGAL PROFESSION

"Paralegals are becoming more accessible to attorneys as the cost of new hardware decreases," says Gary Melhuish, former president of The International Paralegal Managers Association. With new software constantly being created and its use updated in almost every area of law, paralegals are able to perform their tasks with increased speed and accuracy. Law libraries in law firms are literally discarding their books in favor of online services for legal research. Paralegals who keep current with technology become invaluable to the firm, especially because they tend to stay with the firm, while associates and attorneys tend to rise up through the ranks or change firms. They become the institutional memory of the firm.[6]

WHY I WROTE LESSONS

While I was browsing through the books at the bookstore, I kept seeing leadership books, such as *The Top CEOs in Business*, and *Leading Women Executives Going to the Top*. As I perused these books, I realized the theme was learning from the leaders. I got the idea that paralegals could learn from their leaders and mentors. I researched the bookstores, libraries, and the Internet to determine whether similar books had been written for paralegals. To the best of my knowledge, there were no books for paralegals that were similar; the subject excited me.

LESSONS IS A QUASI-MENTORING BOOK

LESSONS will help paralegals and paralegals students, and many others mentioned previously, learn through the experience and wisdom of others. Personal mentoring is often difficult given the busy schedules of paralegals and attorneys.

What's more, *LESSONS* will also be a time-saver for novice paralegals and paralegal students. Law students will learn from it as well. Paralegal educators can supplement their teachings with secrets learned by experienced paralegals. Paralegal supervisors and managers

---

[6]Ibid.

can guide their paralegals with new ideas. Likewise, lawyers can learn from a paralegal in another firm and teach their paralegal. Associates will find *LESSONS* a boon to that first precarious year on the job.

Through this quasi-mentoring process, professional paralegals can capitalize on these secret techniques and tips these top paralegal minds have discovered. This innovative mentoring process helps growing paralegals avoid struggles that these paralegal experts had to suffer. I wanted to ask these paralegals to share their knowledge with everyone who reads *LESSONS*, but I wanted to give them credit for it.

During my 34 years of experience in law firms, I have seen how paralegals' knowledge and skills can become stagnant, even if they attend seminars, workshops, and CLE courses. They may become isolated and their contacts may not go beyond their firm and their paralegal associations. Paralegals may experience burnout unless they are challenged and continue to learn and increase their responsibilities. Many paralegals want to change fields, but they do not know how.

How Does *LESSONS* Respond to Market Needs and Emerging Trends?

LESSONS responds to market needs and emerging trends through the sharing of the latest techniques, methods, and shortcuts used by the top paralegal experts. These top 15 paralegal experts were selected according to specific criteria set by prestigious judges, all of whom are highly qualified and well known in the paralegal profession. The judges followed a carefully designed process as described in the introduction to this book.

Methods of Research

Again, I refer to the process of selecting and researching these top paralegal experts. They responded to two detailed questionnaires. Follow-up interviews of the candidates were conducted, along with their supervisors and coworkers.

Prerequisites/Basic Assumptions about Knowledge Needed Prior to Using This Text

Although readers of *LESSONS* need some basic knowledge of paralegal work, the information contained in this book are tips and techniques that will aid you when you get a job, and if you are an experienced paralegal, it will add to your knowledge and efficiency. Persons in the secondary market will find *LESSONS* a useful resource tool that you may use as needed.

ORGANIZATION OF THE TEXT

The primary purpose of *LESSONS* is to provide readers with advice and information from the top paralegal experts. Therefore, 15 detailed chapters will be devoted to these 15 paralegal experts. In addition, the Appendix contains interesting biographies on four judges, plus an informative Question and Answer series that includes pertinent answers to issues involving the paralegal profession through their perspective.

THE OVERALL SCHEME OF *LESSONS* AND THE RATIONALE BEHIND IT

The overall scheme of *LESSONS* is uncommon in a paralegal resource book because it contains the expertise of a first-class group of professional paralegals. I conducted an extensive nationwide search to find qualified candidates. Fifty candidates were nominated or submitted their application. All the candidates completed two detailed questionnaires. I chose 25 of the most qualified candidates out of the 50 submitted. I then prepared a summary report of these 25 candidates for the judges without their names or education indicated, along with the specific goals of the book. The education and other activities were not included so that the judges would concentrate on the goals of the book and not be prejudiced by these indicia. Again, the goals of *LESSONS* are to provide readers with the hidden secrets of the candidates from which the readers could learn.

The judges themselves selected the final 15 candidates. The judges include the following renowned professionals in the paralegal movement: Therese A. Cannon, Esq., who is the Associate Director of the Western Association of Schools and Colleges, one of the six regional accrediting agencies in the United States; William P. Statsky, attorney at law, paralegal educator, and author; James Wilber, principal, Altman Weil, law office management consultant and attorney; and Gary Melhuish, legal assistant administrator for the Philadelphia office of Ballard, Spahr, Andrews, & Ingersoll, LLP. He is the immediate past president of the International Paralegal Management Association (IPMA).[7] This prominent panel of judges has significantly contributed to the growth of the paralegal profession over many years.

---

[7]See the Appendix for more detailed biographies of the judges.

LEARNING TOOLS

The text contains the specific pedagogical features designed to help paralegals, paralegal students, and other legally related workers learn, comprehend, and apply the material. Each of the sections mentioned previously are included in the chapter about each expert, including the tips, techniques, and methods of these top paralegal experts from which readers may learn.

STEP-BY-STEP PROCEDURES

Wherever possible, systematic procedures are given, but in all instances, readers should check the local and state codes before beginning a task. Procedural rules become dated, and an astute paralegal will double-check to make sure that the particular procedure applied is still valid.

FORMS AND CHECKLISTS

This book contains many current forms and checklists provided by these top paralegal experts that paralegals could use today in their daily tasks. The following caveat is included:

The forms included in *LESSONS* serve as a guideline only and are not to be used verbatim. Likewise, the checklists supplied by the experts are guides and are not all-inclusive. The facts of the particular case or matter must always be taken into consideration when using these materials. If readers merely photocopy the forms and fill in the blanks, they are not only flirting with error, but it indicates a lazy attitude toward one's job. Use the forms creatively as a guide, and mold them to fit the facts of the case or matter on which you are working.

ETHICS

Lawyer and ethics author Therese A. Cannon[8] reviewed every page of *LESSONS* and inserted Ethics Caveats wherever she felt it was necessary to alert readers to remind them of the ethics involved in the task. The Appendices also contain the code of ethics for the National Federation of Paralegal Associations—a must-read for all paralegals. Paralegals must abide by the same code of ethics as lawyers. I recommend that all paralegals read at least one book on ethics.

---

[8]See the Appendix for Therese A. Cannon's biography.

How to Use the Text Elements for Best Benefits

Depending upon the area of law in which the student chooses to specialize, he could search the special index for information, tips, techniques, and methods about that area.

One key benefit of LESSONS is that students can read the chapters of the top paralegal experts in different areas of law and get a flavor of what that work entails to help them choose their career path. Paralegals wishing to change specialties or fields of law can read those chapters that interest them to get a look into what working in that area of law might be like.

ABOUT THE AUTHOR

Carole Bruno, a graduate of the two-year paralegal program at the University of West Los Angeles School of Law, is one of the pioneer paralegals of the 1970s, who helped to create and define a new profession in the legal field. Carole attended the University of Georgia for three years until she began working on her first book. Her career in the legal profession spans more than 30 years.

In 1979, Carole became the president of the Georgia Association of Legal Assistants and the representative for The National Federation of Paralegal Associations (NFPA). In 1980, she wrote the *Paralegal's Litigation Handbook* that was published by The Institute for Business Planning, a subsidiary of Prentice-Hall, Inc., which was followed by *The Standard Legal Secretary's Handbook* in 1986. In 1993, she wrote the second edition of the *Paralegal's Litigation Handbook* for West Publishing Company.

She has the honor of being in the 1994 edition of *Contemporary Authors of America.* In addition, she has written many articles for various legal publications, including *Legal Assistant Today, Legal Economics and Management, The American Lawyer, The National Law Journal, The Connecticut Bar Association Journal, The State Bar of Georgia, The Hawaii State Bar Journal, The Boston Association of Legal Administrators, The Pennsylvania Lawyer,* and many others listed on Carole's Web site (www.carolebruno.com). Carole also wrote a weekly column on law office management, paralegals, and related subjects for the *Fulton Daily Report* in Atlanta.

Carole's numerous affiliations and credentials include:

Paralegal's Litigation Handbook, Second Edition (St. Paul, MN: West Publishing Company, 1993);
Paralegal's Litigation Handbook, (Englewood Cliffs, NJ: Institute for Business Planning, Inc., 1980);

Legal Secretary's Standard Desk Book (Englewood Cliffs, NJ:
Prentice-Hall, Inc., 1987);
Contemporary Authors of America, 1994
Paralegal Certificate, University of West Los Angeles, 1973
President, Georgia Paralegal Association, 1979
Secondary Representative, National Federation of Paralegal
Associations,
Board of Directors, Hawaii Paralegal Association, 1995
Member, National Association of Law Firm Marketing
Administrators, 1986
Freelance Writer and Legal Marketing Consultant, present

ACKNOWLEDGMENTS

Writing *LESSONS* has been an incredible learning experience for me. Working with 15 paralegal experts and four prestigious judges has been such a privilege. I have always written in a vacuum, all by myself. This book has taught me the value of working as a team. As the book progressed and my vision evolved, I was excited and the paralegal experts were, too.

I accepted many of their ideas and incorporated them into the book. Each paralegal expert wrote his or her own chapter according to a specific design that I was aiming for. We did many rewrites, and I know there were many times that they did not want to answer the phone when I called. All this was in addition to their full-time jobs. For me, the process was new, and at times, I felt totally stressed. However, I knew a call from one of the paralegal experts would cheer me up. I am very proud of them. Not only are they extremely competent paralegals, but also they are terrific people.

I acknowledge the panel of judges Therese A. Cannon, Esq., Professor William P. Statsky, Esq., James S. Wilber Esq., and Gary Melhuish, who took time out of their busy schedules to select the 15 top paralegal experts. (See the Appendix to read about the judges, a Q & A session with them, and about the selection process.) In addition, I am sincerely grateful to Ms. Therese Cannon, Esq, who reviewed every page of the manuscript to discern what ethical caveats should be inserted in the text to ensure that readers are conscious of the important code of ethics that paralegals must follow, just as attorneys do.

Once I contacted the chosen paralegals experts, they were elated. The honor was rightly earned. Most of these experts have been practicing for more than 20 years, and they are actively involved in various paralegal associations. They were very responsive in supplying the information I needed. One expert said that every time I called, he knew that I probably needed something else, though I primarily contacted them by e-mail.

I thank all of the paralegal experts for their patience in working with me. I also sincerely thank them for being so responsive and cooperative. This is their book—and my legacy. It is my intention to give them the credit they so rightly deserve.

Hidden behind the publication of every book are some very important people. Behind the scenes were my colleagues who helped to make this book come to fruition: my editor; Robert L. Serenka, Jr., Esq., Managing Editor; Shelley Esposito, Acquisition Editor; Melissa Riveglia, Senior Product Manager; Gerard McAvey, Marketing Manager; and Melissa Zasa, Editorial Assistant.

If you have any questions or comments, please contact me at my e-mail address (carole.bruno@comcast.net) or leave me a message on my Web site (www.paralegalfocus.com). I hope you enjoy the book.

Carole "KiKi" Bruno
Santa Rosa, California
November 27, 2007

Part I

LITIGATION

CHAPTER 1

DWAYNE E. KRAGER

Senior Paralegal
FOLEY & LARDNER
Milwaukee, WI

DWAYNE E. KRAGER

"Last year Dwayne took on additional responsibility by providing a key role in the construction of an in-house high-tech courtroom and three jury deliberation rooms. This facility, known as the Trial Science Institute, LLC, is one way that our firm is breaking new ground in the legal community by providing a place where attorneys and paralegals can practice their roles and gain invaluable insights and experience. . . ."

Ralph A. Weber (former employer)
Attorney at Law
Reinhart, Boerner, Van Deuren, s.c.

EDUCATION/HONORS/CERTIFICATIONS:

- B.A., Southern Illinois University, Carbondale, IL, 1983
- Paralegal Certification, Roosevelt University, Chicago, IL, 1986
- *Legal Assistant Today's* Paralegal of the Year Award, 1995
- Certified Summation® Trainer

PROFESSIONAL ASSOCIATIONS/BUSINESS/PUBLIC SPEAKING:

- President of the Wisconsin Paralegal Association
- Dwayne Krager Consulting, LLC—I own a small consulting business that works with law firms on the implementation of technology as part of their litigation practice.
- Director of the Trial Science Institute, LLC
- Trained on the use of Trial Presentation Software (inData TrialDirector® & Verdict Systems Sanction™), imaging software by Imaging Capture Engineering, the makers of LAW Scanning software.
- Frequent speaker for the National Paralegal Institute and National Business Institute on litigation support topics.
- *Pro Bono*[1]—For the past 10 years, I have chaired the firm's Paralegal Food Drive. This effort raised over $14,000 and about 20,000 pounds of food for the local food pantry.

FIRM-AT-A-GLANCE:

FOLEY & LARDNER
777 Wisconsin Ave.
Milwaukee, WI

PRACTICE AREAS:

- Civil Litigation
- Business Law
- Government and Public Affairs
- Intellectual Property

---

[1] Without pay; donating time.

OVERVIEW OF JOB RESPONSIBILITIES

I. General Duties

    A. Maintain repository and/or database of current court rules. Review legal periodicals and material relevant to a specialty area of law and report or circulate pertinent facts to appropriate attorney(s). Track and report any pending legislation and/or case law that may affect clients.

    B. Maintain litigation docket, calendar, or tickler system, noting deadline dates for responsive pleadings/motions, court appearances, and other important deadlines. Remind attorneys and prepare for meetings, hearings, depositions, and trials.

II. Preliminary Investigation

    A. Attend initial interview with client; obtain background information. Obtain, review, organize, and analyze preliminary documentation and information supporting client's claim.

    B. Conduct research and determine appropriate jurisdiction. Review and summarize rules of procedure in court where action will be filed.

ETHICS CAVEAT:

Paralegals who interview clients must be careful not to offer legal advice about a course of action that the client should pursue and not to predict the outcome in the matter.

Therese A. Cannon, Attorney at Law and author of *Ethics and Professional Responsibility for Legal Assistants*

III. Initiation of Action

    A. Draft summons and service of process. Arrange for service of process. Work with attorney(s) to develop defenses, theory of case, and trial strategy. Draft answer to complaint and other defensive pleadings. Prepare motion to transfer venue, for special appearance, or special exceptions to the petition, if appropriate.

    B. Participate in alternate dispute resolution (ADR), mediation, or arbitration.

IV. Discovery

    A. Retain outside investigator, if necessary. Conduct or coordinate factual investigation, including interview of witnesses.

Draft interrogatories, requests for admissions, requests for production of documents, and requests for examination or inspection. Draft responses to discovery requests.

B. Supervise personnel, such as document clerks and junior paralegals assigned to specific projects for pending litigation; monitor progress of projects.

V. Document Production

A. Review and obtain all relevant documents in client's possession; work with attorney to determine documents to produce. Assist attorney in reviewing documents for privilege; draft log of privileged documents for production to opposing counsel in lieu of producing actual documents.

B. Perform, supervise, or coordinate objective/subjective coding of case documents. Consult in-house or outside sources to develop document databases for relevant case documents from document production.

VI. Depositions

A. Coordinate deposition schedule with client, attorneys, and opposing counsel. Draft notice of oral deposition and serve subpoenas.

B. If necessary, draft *duces tecum* language for inclusion in subpoena to acquire additional documents. Draft outline of questions for examining of witnesses at depositions. Review and assemble documents to be used in deposition. Index and summarize deposition testimony and exhibits.

VII. Briefing

A. Collect, organize, and maintain research reference file. Draft affidavits and assemble exhibits in support of briefs and petitions. Review briefs for accuracy of information, quotes, and citations to the record.

B. Check case history with *Sheppard's Citations*, which is a multivolume bound set of red books in the law library; it can also be accessed through the online computer citation service, organized by year. *Sheppard's Citations* allows you to search cases to check the "subsequent history" of any judicial decision on which your attorney relies on in her brief (analysis). With this service, you can determine whether the decision you are citing has been affirmed, overruled, followed, distinguished, questioned, or simply accepted or rejected for future appellate review. This process is referred to as "Sheppardizing." Secondarily, you can use such a citation services as you would a case digest to find other cases on point. The service will identify subsequent decisions that have cited the decision you are checking, and some of those subsequent decisions willl offer useful holdings or discussions. Review and assemble exhibits to be included in the appendix to brief.

VIII. Trial

A. Prepare and index key pleadings notebook, including cited authorities. Prepare trial notebooks. Work directly with experts, consultants, and witnesses concerning case. Coordinate arrangements with local vendors regarding technical courtroom equipment, space, and other requirements.

B. If the trial is in a distant city or state, set up "trial office." Coordinate design and preparation of graphic exhibits, video and/or computer presentations, and other demonstrative evidence materials for use at trial.

IX. Litigation Support

A. Train all paralegals and attorneys on the use of litigation, imaging, and trial support programs.

B. Operate and coordinate all activities associated with the Trial Science Institute, LLC.

C. Review and make recommendations on litigation support programs used in the department.

PRACTICAL TIPS, SHORTCUTS, AND TRICKS OF THE TRADE:

Organization and Time Management

1. Out of all the paralegal positions, organization and time management are two of the most critical skills for litigation paralegals. When you are involved in complex litigation cases, it is important that you keep track of tasks that each of the other trial team members are handling. Everyone has other duties, a heavy caseload and, on rare days, a private life outside of the office. There is no question that the most stressful times for a paralegal are pressing deadlines.

2. Although one methodology of keeping track of tasks is through a paper task list, Microsoft® Outlook® provides a more efficient task list function. The task list function of Outlook allows for the entry and assignment of tasks to each team member. Using name categories in Outlook, assign each case you are working on a specific name. Then when looking at your task list, the category field enables you to sort the tasks. Several other formats can allow viewing of tasks. One of the most useful categories to team members is listing the tasks by the individual who is responsible for completing the task.

3. There is no question that the well-organized paralegal and an effective time manager are great assets to their employer. No matter what area of law a paralegal works in, there are multiple tasks and deadlines to meet. While there are paper methodologies available to keep a paralegal's work flowing, today's technology provides many answers that allow more efficient ways to stay organized and on task.

Be a Techno-Savvy Paralegal

1. Today's litigation paralegal faces learning much more than procedure and how to organize a case. Because technology now offers the most efficient tools to utilize throughout the litigation process, it is imperative that litigation paralegals learn what these tools are and how to work with them. Paralegals that are not using a litigation support program are not working efficiently.

2. To be the most effective litigation paralegal, it is imperative that paralegals know how to use litigation support software, time management software, and trial presentation software, as well as have a thorough working knowledge of imaging and the electronic discovery process. Cases that have multitudinous documents require litigation support software that will create a document database and allow for the use of imaging/OCR technology.

3. The implementation of technology in the court system is changing quickly. Since 2003, the federal court system made a commitment to equip one-third of its district courtrooms with trial technology. State courts remodeling or building new courtrooms are including technology as part of their building plans. Because trial technology will no doubt add some complexity to preparing for trial, and the trial attorney will need to focus on what is happening in the courtroom, most trial teams are utilizing paralegals,

in-house technology managers, or outside trial technology counsel to handle the presentation of evidence in the courtroom. If you are a techno-savvy paralegal, your expertise in technology will be a definite benefit for your trial team and to your future career advancement.

4. Traditionally, most courts have accepted a printout of electronic data as a satisfactory method of complying with an electronic discovery request. Now, the electronic version of the document has additional information that is not available in the paper copy of document. For example, electronic e-mails may contain information that will provide links to other e-mails, e-mail attachments, calendar entries, erased files, and metadata. Metadata is electronic information automatically kept by a computer about the relevant electronic documents. An example of metadata from e-mail may include the date and time of the opening of the e-mail, the time it was sent, the sender's name, the receiver's name, to whom copies (or "blind" copies) were sent, if there was a reply, and if it was printed out. Law firms who are not making discovery requests for electronic versions of documents may be missing key information that can make a major difference in the representation of their client's case.

5. Assigning of categories in Outlook is a simple process. When entering a new task, simply click on the Categories button, and then click on the Master Category List. In the Master Category List, enter the client's name in the New Category box, and then you must manually check the box to apply the new category to it. From this point, when a task is scheduled, the client name should be checked under the Categories section. The tasks assigned to each case can be reviewed by clicking on View, Arrange By, Current View, and then by clicking on By Category. Microsoft Outlook 2007 is different, but simply go to the Help menu to obtain instructions.

6. Because communication among litigation team trial members is crucial, it is important to assign a paralegal to maintain and distribute the task list. When the task list has been updated, then an electronic copy of the tasks can be sent to each Outlook user. Team members understand their assignments, and, upon completing an assignment, it is easy to indicate the completion of a task on the electronic list.

■ Calendar the due dates for internal tasks upon assignment. Set court deadlines must be calendared. Microsoft's Outlook Calendar system is a good method for entering case deadlines. Just as in the Task feature of Outlook, each calendar entry can be assigned a case name using the same Categories section. You may enter appointments, deadlines, deposition dates, or other entries for the case name just as you did in assigning Categories.

■ To make it easier to manage time effectively, it is important to diary reminders so that an assignment deadline that may require weeks of work does not come up just days before it is due. Upon entering the deadline date, it is good practice to enter reminder dates 14 days, and then 30 days, before the actual due date.

ETHICS CAVEAT:

Missing a deadline such as a statute of limitations or appeal date can be fatal to a case and is a breach of an ethics duty. It is one of the most common basis for a legal malpractice case against a client, and if it happens often enough, it can subject a lawyer to discipline by the appropriate authority in the jurisdiction where the lawyer is licensed.

Therese A. Cannon, Attorney at Law and author of *Ethics and Professional Responsibility for Legal Assistants*

Assemble Contacts

Litigation cases also require a need to create a list of key people who are involved in the litigation. Typically, a litigation matter will identify key client and expert witnesses who will need to be contacted for interviews, deposition testimony, and appearances at trial. The Contacts section of Outlook is good way to keep track of people who are involved in the litigated case. The Contacts section allows for the entry of addresses, phone numbers, e-mail addresses, and you may add information on what relationship the person has to the case in the blank notes section. It is a good idea to cross-reference contacts. In addition, you may set up "groups" or "distribution lists" in contacts for mailing to specific people. When entering information into the Contacts section of Microsoft Outlook, it is important to assign a case name to each entry through the Categories section. Assigning a case name allows for viewing of contact information by each individual case.

TECHNOLOGY TECHNIQUES

- Ease the trial process with technology.

- What most attorneys do not realize is that using technology *does not change* how they present their case. In fact, technology can improve their trial presentation by enhancing the quality of organization and assisting the jury in focusing on the key pieces of evidence displayed. Your role is to help the attorney ease into the process as smoothly as possible.

- Traditional methods of trial presentation, like large blow-ups of documents and writing on an easel (referred to as demonstrative exhibits or visual aids), requires the same thought process as presenting a document electronically on a large screen or monitors. Microsoft® PowerPoint® is an extremly useful presentation tool that comes with the Microsoft Office program. It has many templates and graphic interfaces that assist the paralegal in making colorful and impressive illustrations for trial or negotiation meetings. This thought process includes the identification of main points and determines how the illustration will make things clearer to the jury.

Step 1—Planning For the Techno-Trial

- A firm should either choose someone from its staff or use an outside trial consultant when deciding to present evidence electronically at trial. If you are chosen to help present evidence electronically at trial, it is extremely important you know as much as possible about the case (i.e., type of lawsuit, number of plaintiffs and defendants, trial location, issues, evidence, and so forth) and the parties involved (attorneys, paralegals, and support staff). There must be a close working relationship between those on the trial team who assist in accessing materials to help avoid any miscommunication among team members. In addition, it is important to identify vendors who can easily help with any last-minute concerns that often occur at midnight before the trial begins. If the trial is taking place outside of your normal location, it is imperative to locate nearby vendors in advance to provide litigation support.

Step 2—Document Control

- All trials involve multiple boxes containing documents, depositions, demonstrative exhibits, and videotapes. Make sure that the materials given to the technology presenter are the actual exhibits needed during trial. The document collection should include opposing parties' documents as identified on the trial exhibit list. Knowing the volume of documents is extremely important when determining the time it will take to prepare for the trial.

■ Organization includes getting the documents imaged and numbered to match the trial exhibit list. Knowing the amount and type of documents will also determine what type of hardware will be needed to hold the imaged exhibits. Cases that contain only documents and photographs can be easily stored on a notebook computer that contains sufficient memory, a good processor, and a large hard drive. Small external backup drives serve not only as excellent backup in case of data loss, but also as additional storage devices. Remember that cases with a large amount of video require more memory intensive computers. So whatever you use, make sure that the laptop(s) used for trial are high-powered enough to run the trial presentation. Keep in mind that with the speed of technological advances, future computers, laptops, and other equipment may have the capacity you need. Today, lugging huge computers and other equipment into trial is no longer necessary. You must discuss the situation for each case with your technology consultant in advance. If you work for a small firm, you may have to work like you would have a decade ago due to cost considerations. Just be current on what is available; a good way to do this is to read computer magazines and to attend "Tech" shows—many of which are sponsored by the major paralegal associations like NFPA and NALA.

■ Along with identifying the trial exhibit collection and hardware, you should determine which trial presentation software to use. Two of the more popular software programs are TrialDirector (www.indatacorp.com) and Sanction (www.verdictsystems.com). Recently, both trial software programs have added more functionality and ease of use for the presenter. Both programs sell for at a minimal cost, and are wise investment for any size case you are handling. However, remember to do your research to make sure you have the latest and the best software for the case that your firm can afford. Remember, it changes faster with each day.

Step 3—Production Process

- The production process can be exceptionally difficult. Large trials with multiple plaintiffs and defendants may add up to hundreds of thousands of pages of exhibits and hundreds of hours of video. Know your limits if you are an in-house support person.

- It is typical for extremely large requests to come in at the last minute. Negotiate favorable rates with outside vendors who can assist with your project. Make it clear to the vendor in what format you need the final product. Competing presentation software programs have different features and requirements. Vendors you work with should be familiar with the trial presentation software you are going to use and what formats the programs can handle. Examples of formats are TIFF Images for documents, JPEG for photographs, and MPEG-1 for video.

Step 4—Coordination

- By this time, all of the trial exhibits should be on CDs or newer mini-storage devices. The exhibit CD should contain a load file for seamless integration into your trial presentation software package and named by its corresponding exhibit number. Video CDs should hold approximately two hours of video. All exhibits, including video should be loaded locally onto the hard drive of the computer you are going to use for presentation at trial. If an exhibit is not available on the computers' hard drive, the CDs can be a backup. After loading the exhibits, it is important to check the imaged copies of the documents with the original trial exhibits to ensure they are the same.

Step 5—Presentation at Trial

- While many courtrooms are equipped to display evidence electronically, additional expertise is required for those courtrooms not electronically equipped. When faced with setting up a courtroom to display evidence electronically, it is wise to hire an outside audio/video consultant. If you are using an outside technology trial consultant, it is reasonable to expect this individual to have the expertise needed to set up the courtroom.

The courtroom set up may include:

1. Large screen or monitors for the jurors to view the evidence.

2. If a screen is used, a 2000 Lumens or higher projector is necessary for the presentation of evidence.

3. Individual monitors for the judge, witness, and counsel tables.

4. Control switches that select which computer is showing evidence. The control switch should also provide the ability to see the evidence only at the counsel and judges table.

5. Speakers and an audio amplification system for playing videotaped deposition excerpts.

6. A CD to play video or other media.

7. Document camera—a document camera (a.k.a., "ELMO") is an overhead projector that uses a camera to show documents and photographs on a monitor or through a projector. The document camera display exhibits that were not imaged or as backup if the computer does not display the exhibit.

FOLLOW THE FIVE PS (PROPER PREPARATION PREVENTS POOR PERFORMANCE)

- If you are responsible for displaying the evidence, it is normal to be nervous from the pressures of trial. To ease the pressure I recommend you follow the Five Ps (Proper Preparation Prevents Poor Performance).

Proper Preparation

Each night before the trial day begins, do a quick run through of the witness outlines for the next day, and make sure you or your staff has loaded the necessary materials. You should also perform this same check each morning before trial begins. After arriving at the courtroom, check the displays and the sound in the courtroom. If for some reason the technology fails, make sure you have a backup system that includes a paper copy of the exhibit. You will need paper copies of the exhibits anyway for admission to the court.

Presentation of Evidence at Trial Requires the Attorney and Presenter to Be on the Same Page

Follow the attorney's lead as to when you should display an exhibit to the jury. Keep track of the exhibits shown, along with the ability to show a previously displayed exhibit on demand. If you and the attorney review what exhibits to use, while preparing a witness to testify at the trial, it will improve the coordination of exhibits.

ELECTRONIC DISCOVERY (E-DISCOVERY):

General Procedure—Requesting Electronic Documents

Depending upon the situation, before electronic discovery begins, the legal team must acquire a general knowledge of their clients or producing party's computer system. If you are producing the electronic documents, you can obtain information through an informal interview of a technical person or an employee familiar with the system. If you are seeking information from a producing party, it is wise to conduct a deposition when an informal interview situation is not possible. Some questions to ask during the interview or deposition are:

1. Identification of data files that exist and how to read them.

2. Identification of computers that contain the data you are seeking.

3. Identification of the people who have access to the computers.

4. Identification of the operating systems.

5. Identification of the company's back-up system and where back-ups are stored.

6. Identification of the company's e-mail system, including storage.

7. Review of sample data, including how to decipher the information.

8. To avoid chain-of-custody issues, it is usually wise to hire an outside computer forensics company to clone the produced electronic information. If an attorney or paralegal handles the original electronic information, there may be a potential claim of destroying data. In addition to cloning electronic information, computer forensic companies can assist in the electronic discovery process by identifying the potential universe of electronic documents, formulating a cost-effective electronic discovery plan, preserving evidence, and providing the information in a usable format for the requesting party.

9. After gathering the electronic information, the next challenge is how to effectively review and manage the potentially large amounts of data. Electronic data is typically on some form of storage media. Typical storage media types are DVD, CD-ROM,

tape, and hard drives. Depending on the storage medium, each source of information may contain multitudinous documents. For example, a DVD holds up to 100,000 pages of documents, and a CD-ROM can hold up to 20,000 pages.

10. Typically, when lawyers receive stacks of DVDs, CD-ROMs, or backup tapes produced as part of a discovery request, their first inclination is to request their firm's word processing departments to open each file and print them out manually. This approach is not practical once a law firm understands that there are many different computer data files, and that opening a file changes its metadata.

11. One approach to working with electronic data that is going to be produced, or has been received from a producing party, is to utilize the services of a digital discovery processing company. These companies take electronic data and convert it into a format that can be loaded into specific database programs like Summation, LexisNexis® Concordance™, and Microsoft® Access. The digital discovery process converts e-mail files, their attachments, and other electronic document files into a single or multi-page TIFF or PDF format. In addition, you may transfer the metadata (electronic information about the document) into set database fields. The final product is a self-populated database that typically contains the document's date, author, recipient, and subject line. You can use this database as an index to the typically converted TIFF file (image file) that allows the end user to see an exact copy of the document referenced on their computer.

12. When compared to scanning documents and manually entering information into a database, electronic documents may provide a distinct advantage. For example, you may convert an electronic production of e-mail into a database, including an image at a much lower cost per page. In addition to lower costs, quicker access to the information helps law firms because the electronic conversion process usually requires a lower manual processing time.

Working with Outside Vendors

Many companies are now taking an A-to-Z approach in offering services to the legal marketplace. Copy companies who previously elected not to offer technology services now realize that to remain competitive in today is legal industry, they must provide more than just copy services.

- With this A-to-Z approach to the legal marketplace, it has become imperative for paralegals who make technology vendor and software decisions to know what to ask. In addition, paralegals need the ability to decipher which company is going to offer the best and most accurate document management services.

- The comparison of imaging to photocopying is a relatively simple process. Once the copy button is pushed and a quality check done, the job is essentially complete. However, imaging requires technical specifications and up-front decisions that can affect how the images are stored and retrieved. A full-service litigation support vendor that has been providing imaging for many years knows the questions to ask and can make cost-effective suggestions for processing documents.

- When determining which company to use for document management services, you should consider several key criteria. These criteria are the company's stability, reliability, quality, expertise, security, and price. Part of determining stability involves finding out if the company has retained educated, experienced, and dedicated staff at all levels of the organization, from sales staff to the people production staff. Because it is important to trust vendors with whom you work, companies with a high volume of successful projects become valuable assets to the litigation process.

- Ideal vendors will provide timely project status reports. The company should also test all data deliveries in the target software application before releasing the data for law firm use. Another measure of reliability is how much capacity a company can handle, especially on complex projects that involve voluminous documents.

- The control measure quality in place for each project indicates the quality of a company's performance. Quality companies create and retain clear and accurate documentation of the project specifications and note any changes throughout the project. When a company completes the document management service on a project, quality companies develop and follow a comprehensive coding manual to produce a clear and consistent document database.

- The most important criterion you need to consider when selecting document management service is company expertise. The company's expertise must include project managers with a deep level of understanding of how the world of litigation operates and the importance of managing case documents, schedules, and deadlines. In addition, the company should have technical people with experience in the various database management applications available to the legal industry.

- Security is important because you are relying on an outside company to work with client documents without the direct supervision of an attorney or a member of your firm's staff. All documents must be stored securely and separately from other projects and handled by personnel who agree to follow strict confidentiality guidelines.

- In addition, after the completion of a project, security involves storing and backing up electronic data for future retrieval.

- Pricing for providing document management services can be determined by getting quotes from at least three separate vendors.

- Companies that succeed in offering complete A-to-Z document management services have the ability to educate paralegals on how to best utilize the technological tools that are available to meet their case needs.

- Image Capture Engineering Storm X[TM] allows you to extract and then distribute images.

- Both TrialDirector and Sanction are trial presentation software programs that give a trial team the ability to present evidence in either an imaged document or video format for use at court hearings or arbitrations.

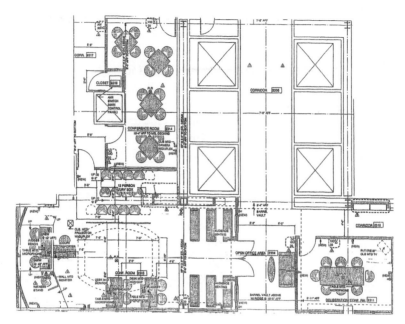

FIGURE 1-1 TRIAL SCIENCE INSTITUTE, LLC, FLOOR PLAN

- A company with an A-to-Z approach applies to when you want to present evidence at trial. Some law firms have the capability to work with trial presentation software without the assistance of an outside company. If nobody from your firm can commit to handling the trial presentation aspect of your case, then a trial consultant may be the answer. Because qualifications for people who represent themselves as trial consultants may vary, the trial team should look for a consultant with at least five years of courtroom experience. The consultant should also understand the litigation process, know both trial support hardware and software, and be able to provide advice to the trial team on what is the best methodology to present evidence. A good trial consultant will take over the technical aspects of the trial so that the trial team can focus directly on the case.

- Because the legal vendor and software market has taken an A-to-Z approach to offering services, it is important for you to have an understanding of document management services and the software programs that work the best with these applications. Plan a project all the way from selecting the proper vendor to the actual software programs that will produce an accurate result to reduce the risk of hiring the wrong document management vendor.

CHAPTER 2

NANCY B. HELLER, RP
Litigation Paralegal
VORYS, SATER, SEYMOUR, & PEASE, LLP
Columbus, OH

NANCY B.HELLER, RP

*"Nancy has a unique set of talents that makes her peers recognize her as a leader:
She is knowledgeable and makes a real effort to learn the field and to stay current;
she is good at including people in whatever she undertakes, and if she undertakes
a project, you can rely on her to get it done right."*

Sue Richards,
Chair, Litigation Practice Group
Vorys, Sater, Seymour, & Pease, LLP

EDUCATION/HONORS/CERTIFICATIONS:

- B.A., Forensic Studies, Indiana University, 1978
- Master's of Social Work (non-degreed),
  The Ohio State University, 1980

PROFESSIONAL ASSOCIATIONS:

AMERICAN BAR ASSOCIATION

- Commissioner, ABA Approval Commission, 1997–2003
- Legal Assistant Member, 1988–1991; 1997–1999

NATIONAL FEDERATION OF PARALEGAL ASSOCIATIONS

- *Pro Bono* Committee, 2000–2001
- Ethics Board, 1998–2002
- Education Committee Chair, 1997–2002
- ABA Approval Commission Representative, 1997–2003
- PACE Seminar Liaison, 1998–2000
- PACE Preparatory Program Liaison, 1996–1997
- Annual Convention Coordinator, 1994–1996
- Nominating Committee Chair, 1995
- Vice President of Development, 1992–1994
- Vice President of Administration, 1991–1992
- Outreach Coordinator, 1988–1990
- Committee Member, Legislative Committee, 1987–1988
- Committee Member, Professional Development
  Committee, 1985–1986
- Primary Representative, 1987–1988
- Secondary Representative, 1985–1987

PRACTICE AREAS:

- Toxic Tort litigation: asbestos, silicone breast implant, tire and rubber
  litigation matters
- Employment litigation: principally EEOC matters and wage and hour
  litigation

- Business and Commercial litigation (also includes mediation and arbitration work)
- Personal Injury/Medical Malpractice litigation, primarily defense, some plaintiffs' work
- Construction litigation (hospital addition)
- Consumer practice litigation
- Insurance litigation
- Compliance investigations of potential regulatory violations

YEARS EXPERIENCE:

29

FIRM-AT-A-GLANCE:

VORYS, SATER, SEYMOUR, & PEASE, LLP
Columbus, OH
Phone: 614.464.6469
Fax: 614.719.4758
Web site: www.vssp.com

FIRM SPECIALTIES:

- Commercial and Real Estate
- Corporate and Finance
- Energy and Utility
- Environmental
- Government and Lobbying
- Health Care
- Intellectual Property
- International
- Labor and Employment
- Litigation
- Probate and Estate Planning
- Tax
- Technology
- Toxic Tort

MANAGING PARTNER:
Russell M. Gertmenian

DIRECTOR OF PARALEGALS:
Donna F. Prehm

ATTORNEYS:
375

PARALEGALS:
70

OVERVIEW OF JOB RESPONSIBILITIES:

I. Development

    A. Creation and development of document review, coding, and productions

    B. Creation and development of litigation practice forms and reports to promote efficiency and consistency

    C. Creation and development of informational and document management databases for large complex litigation cases and development of document review and coding protocols

    D. Assistance in the training and development of litigation practices and procedures for new associate attorneys and entry-level paralegals

    E. Assistance in the training and development of continuing legal education programs for the firm's litigation and general paralegal groups

II. Supervisory and Coordination Responsibilities

    A. Coordination of all paralegal tasks in large complex litigation cases, such as class action lawsuits

B. Supervision of junior level paralegals, project assistants, and contract employees on a variety of large litigation matters, such as large document production, document review, and so on

III. Paralegal Task Responsibilities

   A. Review and analysis of documents, information, and preparation of summaries or analyses

   B. Interview clients, witnesses, and preparation of summaries, affidavits, and so on

   C. Drafti of pleadings, mediation statements, and a variety of other written documentation

   D. Preparation for and assistance at trial

   E. Coding, review, and analysis of documents in litigation databases, including e-discovery

   F. Preparation of document review and production protocols, supervision, and coordination of large document collections or productions

TYPICAL WORKWEEK:

In nearly 30 years working as a litigation paralegal, I don't think I've ever experienced a "typical workweek" or recognize what that might be. As I'm sure some of my colleagues have expressed, that is part of what makes being a paralegal ever challenging and demands always being on task. Flexibility is crucial, as you just never know what the day holds in store. Although each day I may have an idea early on of what I hope and need to accomplish, the majority of my job responsibilities involves putting out fires and attending to emergency matters, which may crop up at any time. Because the practice of law is a service profession, much like medicine or any other service profession, people's lives are at stake, and my job is to support the lawyers in helping to serve the firm's clients.

I am a huge list maker, and that is one of the biggest tools that keeps me and the attorneys with whom I work organized. As a civil litigation paralegal, most of the cases to which I am assigned tend to be larger and more complex litigation matters, so more often than not, I am working with a team of lawyers and other paralegals. In this regard, I am often responsible for the case administration matters. To supplement my to-do list, I often maintain task lists on these larger litigation matters to be sure that everyone is informed, updated, and coordinated on the case. Creating and maintaining electronic folders fosters and facilitates timely communication and efficiency on large litigation matters. Working in a large law firm, it is often inefficient and difficult to communicate personally with everyone about case information unless it is during a team meeting, so having electronic folders as well as e-mail, enhances the ability to communicate efficiently about important matters and allows all team members to access the information at their convenience.

On-line resources are major players on my team. Internet research has become a staple in my workday, whether it is used to conduct fact investigation, research, review court dockets, arrange for travel, a court reporter or process server, or perform other case–related tasks. What in the world did we ever do without the World Wide Web? In addition, on-line databases such as Microsoft® Access™ (information management) and Summation® (litigation document management), Lexis Nexis® Accurint®, and PACER among others, are additional staples in my workday. Most of the cases on which I work are in Access and/or Summation, and there are daily tasks to be performed in the databases, such as document coding, document searches, testimony searches and summaries, and other queries and reports. I am extremely fortunate to have the luxury of a litigation technology support group here in the firm, which is part of the law firm's IT department. This team of litigation support experts is invaluable in assisting with electronic discovery and trial preparation matters.

While each day is usually different than the previous one and cases vary, the resources and skills employed are much the same. Organization and attention to detail is particularly important when going through mail and e-mail to be sure I capture important dates and deadlines. Calendaring or some other form of docketing is very helpful in tracking case deadlines. Review and analytical skills are called upon when asked to prepare or respond to discovery, prepare for depositions, hearing, mediation, and trial. Lawyers are trained to evaluate the big picture and rely heavily upon paralegals to focus on the details. I find that I am in my element during trial preparation and trial. I thrive on the frenetic pace and find my organizational abilities are better when I work under pressure. Communication, flexibility, coordination and staying organized, utilizing checklists, focusing on details, and always having a Plan B in your back pocket help ensure a smooth and successful trial presentation.

I would be remiss if I didn't mention ongoing training as part of my job responsibilities, most of which I am able to get in-house. The firm's IT department has an education department that facilitates training classes on every type of application and software supported by the law firm. In addition, with the recent amendments to the Federal Rules of Civil Procedure with respect to electronic discovery, a 42-hour training program was put together by a team of in-house IT professionals, lawyers, and paralegals. And at the time of this writing, the first core training group has just completed this training, of which I was part.

TIPS, SHORTCUTS, AND TRICKS OF THE TRADE:

- Be flexible and learn to adapt to new situations. Things do not always go according to plan, so be prepared, and always have Plan B in your back pocket.
- No question is too "stupid" to ask.
- Be a team player.
- Organization and communication are key elements to success.
- Keep a road map and a compass of where you have been and where you are going.
- There is no wrong or right way to do many of the things paralegals do. Develop your own style and methods that work well for you.
- Take initiatives.
- Stay one step ahead of the game and try to anticipate.
- Always strive for competence, excellence, efficiency, and productivity.
- Never lose your sense of humor.
- Have fun.

ORGANIZATIONAL METHODS

- Develop an organizational method that works well for you.
- Keep yourself organized so that you are able to keep others organized.
- Utilize technology to maximize efficiency and accessibility.
- Maintain a work file on every case of each assignment so you will have a ready reference and be ready to respond to questions as they arise.
- Implement a tickler/docketing system so you are able to stay on top of deadlines.

TECHNOLOGY TECHNIQUES

- Take advantage of classes, demos, and on-line tutorials to learn all that you can.
- Be open to technological advances and investigate whatever techniques may make your job easier and more efficient.
- Be a teacher to those on the team who are less computer savvy than you are.
- (See Figure 2-1a for the for contract employees Heller supervises on a class action lawsuit.)

WRITING TIPS

- Gather the information you intend to communicate and put it on paper.
- Focus on organizing the information in a way that makes sense (e.g., chronologically, topically, and so forth)
- Learn how to create your document in an organized, concise, easily understood, and grammatically correct manner.
- Work efficiently by recycling previous work; however, take special precautions to redact (hide by using a black pen, Wite-Out or redaction tape to cover it) information previously used in another case. Create basic samples in electronic format with blanks for pertinent info and accompanying choices of alternative paragraphs.
- Write with a style that promotes an easy read and flow. Do not use legalese.
- "Just the facts, madam/sir."

DISCOVERY SHORTCUTS:

- Work efficiently by utilizing form interrogatories, requests for production of documents, and request for admission.
- If your case is in a database, investigate the possibilities of producing documents directly from that database and linking deposition transcripts and exhibits to that database (e.g., Summation).
- Always assign a Bates number to each page of every document you produce. This assures control over the document.

- Review the opposing party's responses to your written discovery and make follow–up lists of information and documents for discovery.

- Review your client's responses to the opposing party's discovery to follow up on anything to be supplemented.

INVESTIGATIVE/INTERNET TIPS

- Do not overlook obvious sources of information.

- Each piece of information obtained usually points leads to your next lead.

- Do not forget to document all findings along with the way you obtained them.

- Leave no stone unturned.

CLIENT INTERACTIONS AND INTERVIEWING

- Always keep in mind that the practice of law is a service profession.

- Communicate all interactions with the client to the supervising attorney.

- Help to ensure that the client understands your nonlawyer role and its limitations.

- When interviewing, prepare an outline in advance of what you want to cover.

- The best tool that I have used is the "Comprehensive Trial Preparation Timeline/Checklist" contained in the *Paralegal Trial Handbook* (3rd ed., Aspen Publications, 1995).

EXAMPLE 1: COMPLIANCE: CONDUCTING A DOCUMENT SWEEP ABROAD

Our Problem: Another paralegal and I were tasked with organizing a large document review abroad. Our client had several divisions throughout the United States as well as worldwide, so our charge was to develop a review protocol for the interviewing of relevant company employees, gather potentially responsive documents, analyze the information, and prepare a summary report. One of the locations we focused on was in Asia, which entailed organizing a team of paralegals or paralegal types abroad to assist us in conducting the interviews and gathering the documents, and most importantly, in helping with the language barrier.

My Strategy for Solving Our Problem: My colleague and I mapped out the various divisions of the company, brainstormed the most efficient ways of getting to the relevant departments within each division, and quickly educated ourselves on who's who. From there, we spent a lot of time meeting with the lawyers and the client to gain a solid understanding of what we needed to target and why. We developed an interview and document review protocol along with standard forms and explored various databases in which the information we gathered could be input and analyzed. We contacted a variety of third–party vendors in Asia to ascertain whether or not they could accomplish document imaging and meet other electronic needs and then compared them to our U.S. resources. We worked with a U.S. legal staffing agency that had a counterpart in Asia and they were able to provide us with a team of 10 paralegals to assist us in the interviews and document sweep. Extensive training was necessary with the team, and we continually fielded questions and concerns. Overcoming the language barrier and dietary differences was a challenge for both of us, but we maintained the "when in Rome, do as the Romans do" mantra.

What I Learned: There really is a universal language and a common ground on which we all meet. It can be a challenging journey, but eventually, you will get there! A review protocol and standard forms were critical for a large team undertaking document review and analysis. This shortcuts the margin for error and ensured that each team member was on the same page, so to speak. Organization and coordination were key at all stages. This encompassed frequent meetings and communications, continual confirmation, and planning for the next steps. Being flexible and comfortable halfway around the world worked to our advantage and reminded us that we were able to accomplish the very same things we could accomplish in Columbus, Ohio. As we cleared U.S. Customs in Chicago, we felt like Dorothy in *The Wizard of Oz*, because, "there's no place like home!"

EXAMPLE 2: LEGISLATIVE: COORDINATION OF A LARGE DOCUMENT REVIEW AND ANALYSIS

Our Problem: On a very short time frame, it was necessary to review hundreds of petitions state-wide that had been circulated on a particular issue proposed for a November ballot. My task was to conduct a preliminary review of the counties, organize the petitions and other information received from the Secretary of State's office, coordinate a team of 30 lawyers and paralegals to conduct the review, and produce a summary analysis of the results.

My Strategy for Solving Our Problem: After reviewing the preliminary information to gain a sense of how the information was produced, provided, and organized, I created an organizational protocol and supervised project assistants and other support staff who organized the documents prior to review by the team's lawyers and paralegals. I then drafted a document review protocol to ensure that the review and results being recorded were consistent among the 30+ members of the team. Training sessions were conducted to review the protocol, distribute standard forms and address questions, problems, and concerns. The next order of business was to ascertain the amount of time each team member could commit, as assignments were based upon priority and availability of reviewers. This often resulted in assigning a group of people to some of the larger counties, which had several thousand documents, as well as coordinating between three Ohio offices of the firm. Hourly status reports of the review were provided to the lawyers heading up the team as priorities or needs often changed and reassignments were necessary around the clock. Once the review was completed, I became involved in coordinating and working with our document services department who compiled the information and tallied the final results. This project was of critical importance, as well as extremely time-sensitive, and driven by deadlines outside of our control.

What I Learned: Again, protocols and standardization are critical whenever a large team undertakes document review and analysis. This shortcuts the margin for error and ensures that each team member is on the same page, so to speak. Organization and coordination are truly key components to being a successful paralegal. Communication and flexibility are equally important qualities that are necessary to be able to pull off such a large-scale in an expedited manner. Being a team player transcends all areas within the practice of law and every single member of our 30+ team contributed greatly to bringing the project in on time and producing a quality report for our client.

CHAPTER 3

MICHELE M. BOERDER, CP
Litigation Paralegal
HUGHES & LUCE, LLP
Dallas, TX

"Some fellow professionals add greatly to the satisfaction and pleasure of practicing law. Michele Boerder, who has supported the excellence of my trial group for 20 years, is such a person. I can sum up my experience of Michele in but a single sentence: in 47 years of trial practice, I have never met her peer as a paralegal. In addition, the general counsel of a Bell (telecom) operating company (now AT&T) confirmed my opinion with the following statement: "Bob, Michele is more valuable to me than several of your lawyers." To which I replied, "Just as she is to me."

Bob Davis
Trial Partner, Hughes & Luce, LLP
Former President
Dallas Bar Association

EDUCATION/HONORS/CERTIFICATIONS:

- University of North Texas, B.A., A.S., *magna cum laude*, 2003; El Centro College, A.A, 1979. (Outstanding Student Award for Applied Arts and Sciences, School of Community Service, University of North Texas.)
- Board Certified Paralegal, Civil Trial Law, Texas Board of Legal Specialization (first offering of such an exam for legal assistants, 1994)
- Certified Paralegal, National Association of Legal Assistants (NALA), May 1985.
- Completed Basic Mediation Training, and received certificate from the University of North Texas, Alternative Dispute Resolution Program, administered by the Institute of Applied Economics, August 2001. (Complies with Texas Alternative Dispute Resolution Act, § 154.052 of the Texas Civil Practice and Remedies Code to serve as a Mediator).
- Paralegal of the Year, 2005 (National Federation of Paralegal Associations).
- Paralegal of the Year, 1995 (Dallas Area Paralegal Association).
- Michele M. Boerder Lifetime Achievement Award, 2006 (Dallas Area Paralegal Association)

YEARS EXPERIENCE:

27

PROFESSIONAL ASSOCIATIONS:

- Dallas Area Paralegal Association, Paralegal Division, State Bar of Texas, National Federation of Paralegal Associations, International Paralegal Management Association
- Southeastern Paralegal Institute Advisory Board and guest lecturer (Introduction to the Profession course), 1988–97
- Southern Methodist University Legal Assistant Advisory Committee (Dr. Lennart Larsen, Chair 1988–90)
- El Centro College Advisory Board, 1989-90
- State Bar of Texas Paralegal Committee, 1990-present (Advisory group on paralegals to the State Bar of Texas)

FIRM AT-A-GLANCE:

HUGHES & LUCE, LLP
1717 Main Street, Suite 2800
Dallas, TX
Phone: 214.939.5500
Fax: 214.939.5849
Web site: www.hughesluce.com

FIRM PRACTICE AREAS:

- Civil Litigation
- General Business and Commercial Litigation
- Civil Tax Controversy
- Tax Litigation
- White Collar Criminal Defense
- Case Management and Case Organization
- Database Litigation Support

OTHER LOCATIONS:

Fort Worth, Austin

MANAGING PARTNER:

Ed Coultas

ATTORNEYS PERMANENT:

172

PARALEGALS PERMANENT:

12

TYPICAL WORKWEEK:

I count that after almost 27 years of experience, I have had over 1,400 workweeks! And, I do many paralegal tasks differently today than I did 1,400 weeks ago. However, many of the strategies are the same; they are just accomplished with more technology today (and, hopefully more wisdom on my part). Working in litigation means that the legal team is addressing controversy, conflict, and constantly on the search for information evidence that will help win the case for the client, or propel the parties to a settlement before a trial or arbitration. Therefore, a significant amount of my workweek may be the "same work, different case."

One of my responsibilities as a litigation paralegal is to gather documents and electronic information and to determine the best technological way to manage them, depending upon the scope and economics of the case. In almost every matter, this involves a database, and today with the cost-effectiveness of imaging, either imaging the material, or reviewing materials in native format, making decisions on what to collect, and then imaging.

The attorneys with whom I work expect me to give them recommendations on what formats should be used, what type of data should be captured in the database, as well as give them advice about what can and cannot be done with a database. I often consult our firm's litigation support manager for the technological requirements needed to support the formats I develop. The decisions made about initial database support will be important to case development, issues and themes determination, identifying evidence, and later in the litigation, in propounding and responding to discovery. Additionally, this database can become the resource for creating privilege logs during the discovery phase.

After documents and information are gathered, I review the material, and I may be in charge of directing a team of reviewers (usually other paralegals and associate attorneys). I may also work with the client to obtain these items. Because many of our clients are large corporations, I frequently work with inside counsel or company department managers. When doing so, it is important to document each stage of the documents requested, including what departments or employees were canvassed, the source of the materials provided to me, and a written confirmation sheet that is completed by the internal client or client's employee. This information could potentially be very important if there are discovery disputes that arise.

Another facet of information management that I do is to begin a chronology of facts, utilizing and documenting the source of each item. For example, some chronology entries may be based upon a fact that is not rebuttable, or is supported by evidence. Others may be opinions that would need other support to become admissible evidence. However, all of the facets of information that can be accumulated are useful to compile, index, and digest in a condensed form for the attorneys to review.

Ancillary information is often found through use of Internet searches. The research capabilities of Internet sites have created utilization for paralegals who have become adept at information gathering and skilled at honing in upon relevant information to the case. While I cannot claim to have attained expert status on Internet research, I have continued to learn and gather Web sites to help me be creative and productive with this information source. I also use the Internet to retrieve statutes and regulations research.

When the attorneys conduct interviews of the client, witnesses, experts, or others, I am frequently requested to attend and take notes, then draft an initial memorandum of the interview. Similarly, when the legal team meets to discuss the case and projects, I also attend to capture the to-do (Tasks and Assignments) and then draft a team assignments memo.

ETHICS CAVEAT:

Monitoring deadlines and due dates is an important role for many paralegals and is critical to the duty to perform competently. Sanctions and malpractice suits can be the result if deadlines are not met.

Therese A. Cannon, Attorney at Law and author of *Ethics and Professional Responsibility for Legal Assistants*

In summary, because most of the litigation in which I work involves large cases, a significant amount of my work involves obtaining, assembling, maintaining, and researching many forms of information. I have a visual analogy that, much like the surgical nurse knows what instrument to place in the hand of the surgeon, my role as a paralegal is to give the attorney the tools he or she needs to represent the client.

OVERVIEW OF JOB RESPONSIBILITIES:

I. Case Commencement

    A. Participate in the Initial Contact with Client-Client Interactions and Interviewing.

        When I participate in the initial meeting with the client, I am able to be of more assistance to the client, the case, and the attorney much more quickly.

    B. Case Materials

        1. Gather and Organize Documents and Background Information
          This process includes not only documents provided by the client, but also, the information that may be gathered from the Internet, databases, public media, and sometimes information that is already within the firm.

        2. Identify Parties and Players and Begin Chronology of Events

Identification of the persons, companies or corporations, other entities, lawyers, and paralegals involved in the new matter is the first learning curve. Some databases (e.g., Summation®), have a People segment for creating the list. And some software, such as CaseMap™, has built in People features. This is also useful later to compose a witness list. The chronology or timeline is also helpful to initiate begin early in the case to enable the team to see the progression of events, the illumination of facts and issues integral to the case and proof of the client's position. Begin a Contact Sheet to include the style of the case, attorneys involved parties, court, and others that are contacted often.

3. Begin Case Calendar and Docket
   Even a case that has not yet been filed as a lawsuit may benefit from a case calendar. This may show the initial meeting, memorandum of the meeting, the follow-up with the client, and later, will house the court dates and filing deadline dates and ticklers for those deadlines.

II. Discovery Shortcuts

A. Document gathering and review for interrogatories, requests for production, requests for admissions, depositions, and other discovery (review the rules requirements—either federal or state). While each state has its own discovery rules, many are similar to the Federal Rules of Civil Procedure.

B. Structuring and Management of Attendant Databases

Every case is distinct, even cases for the same client and subject matter. If database support is used, initial structure and construction is important to ensure the database captures the needed data from the beginning. Databases are only as useful as the information put into them, because that is only what they can retrieve. An initial analysis of what information is needed and the economics of the case/client, determine what type and to what extent litigation support is used.

III. Pretrial

A. Trial Planning

Many attorneys use an Order of Proof (or they may label it by another name), but essentially it identifies each allegation and defense in the litigation and ties specific proof (i.e., exhibits, testimony, etc.) to each as the case progresses to trial or mediation.

B. Exhibits

Typically, certain documents emerge as focus documents that influence the evidence. These always become exhibits—either in depositions, motions, or at trial. Databases can track usage of exhibits, and it is helpful to keep a full set of deposition exhibits (in addition to each individual deposition). Handle originals carefully.

C. Trial Notebooks and Materials

While many attorneys now use an electronic trial notebook, others continue to use a hard copy as a reference tool. A typical trial notebook might contain:

1. Contact Sheet (names, role, phone numbers, and addresses)
2. Important pleadings
3. Witness List
4. Experts and Expert reports
5. Exhibit List
6. Order of Proof

IV. Trial

A. Trial Logistics

I once worked on a case that went to trial in a smaller city 350 miles from my offices. I worked with the client to transport the files and materials and moved them in an 18-wheeler truck. An office was set up, which included metal racks for boxes, phones, copier, fax, and supplies. In another case in a different city, my team and I unpacked boxes in a small courtroom. With no room for the empty boxes, the client's paralegal came up with a solution—put the empty boxes underneath the seats.

B. Facilities and Courtroom

1. Is there an additional table available for your materials?
2. Will they need to stay in the boxes?
3. Where are the electric plugs in the room?
4. Are there computers or computer setups in the room?
5. Can you leave materials in the room overnight, or must they be removed daily?

C. Exhibits

Paralegals help the lawyers by ensuring that the exhibits have been properly marked, offered, and submitted.

D. Entry of Exhibits to Record

Paralegals keep track of when the exhibits are offered in the proceeding, whether there were objections and disposition by the Judge, either admitted or denied. A chart with "check-offs" is useful for this exercise (see Figure 3-1).

JONES V. ABC CORPORATION
Civil Action #123456
EXHIBITS

Exhibit #	Description	Offered	Objections	Admit	Deny
1	Contract	✓	None	✓	
2	Amendment to Contract	✓	None	✓	
3	Affidavit of Witness	✓	Yes		✓

FIGURE 3-1

E. Jury Selection

In large cases, it is likely that the lawyer will retain a jury consultant to work with the lawyers to prepare jury questionnaires, determine peremptory strikes, strikes for cause, and final jury selection. They may also oversee a mock trial project or shadow jury. In smaller cases, the paralegal may offer observations and input to the attorney during the jury selection process, noting potential jurors and their behaviors, reading materials, reactions during *voir dire,* and later during trial.

ETHICS CAVEAT:

Paralegals and others involved in the matter should not have any direct communications with the jury outside of court, even in hallways and restaurants, other than saying hello and goodbye.

Therese A. Cannon, Attorney at Law and author of *Ethics and Professional Responsibility for Legal Assistants*

F. Witnesses and Preparation

A paralegal may assist in witness preparation by drafting potential questions, setting up practice Q&A sessions, reviewing witnesses' prior testimony, showing a witness do's and don'ts of testifying, and arranging their appearance and testimony at deposition or trial. The paralegal also maintains the documents provided to the witnesses, both fact and expert witnesses. A paralegal may be asked to locate expert witnesses in various fields of expertise.

G. Document Management During Trial

Large complex cases may utilize paperless documents (i.e., using images on monitors or screens), and the paralegal may be involved in maintaining the database of those records. During trial, the paralegal must marshal many documents, papers, files, and other tangible materials. This involves returning the materials to the respective files at the close of the session and being able to retrieve items quickly, as the attorneys need them during trial, including anticipating their needs.

Over the past decades, the common challenge of large complex litigation has been management of the vast amount of documents and information. Technology has developed to provide database tools for such management and has become an area of expanded expertise for paralegals. However, technology itself must be managed—applying knowledge and administering the process is required to make the technology effective. I have seen attorneys rely on paralegals to provide this oversight, which has created new roles for paralegals.

COMMUNICATION TIP Just as attorneys fit their practice to particular clients, paralegals need to provide their support to attorneys on an individualized basis. This includes communication, such as some attorneys want bottom-line information in a short concise form. Others want more depth of understanding as to how you arrived at the answer. This applies to both written and oral communication. With some lawyers, I might chat briefly about something non–work related before discussing the case matter. (These attorneys are more people oriented.) Others prefer just to get down to business.

PRACTICAL TIPS, SHORTCUTS, AND TRICKS OF THE TRADE:

1. The Client is a "Customer," and the Lawyer is Your "Client."

There is a person or people behind that file folder—we call them "clients." We are in a service industry to serve people. As paralegals however, we have two customers: the client for whom the work is being done and the lawyer. Paralegals must market their services to both of these customers.

2. Confirm Everything You Do.

It may be an e-mail, a memo, a letter, a log, or a short handwritten note in the file, but always document what you did, when you did it, why you did it, and who instructed that it be done. This little hint may save you from making serious mistakes.

3. Communicate.

Ensure that you understand the task, the amount of time the attorney expects it to take, and the final product expected. Keep the attorney(s) informed with short progress reports (by e-mail, if possible, in order to retain a record of them).

4. Be Flexible and Multitask.

Accept the fact that rarely do we work on *one* project to completion before undertaking another; we must prioritize, but also realize that many days of the work we have planned to do never gets touched. We must be able to work on multiple projects for several lawyers.

5. The Paralegal's Job is to Support the Lawyer(s).

Paralegals possess legal knowledge and substantive skills, but the attorney makes the final legal decisions. We enhance the work lawyers can perform for clients, but we must take care not to cross the line of giving independent legal advice. A paralegal, who has demonstrated this ability to distinguish what *does* cross the line, will be given greater responsibility, because the lawyer can trust the paralegal's judgment.

ETHICS CAVEAT:

Experienced paralegals like Michele are alert to the difference between giving information to a client and giving them legal advice. A paralegal may, of course, pass on legal advice from the lawyer, so long as it is clear that the lawyer has generated the advice.

Therese A. Cannon, Attorney at Law and author of *Ethics and Professional Responsibility for Legal Assistants*

6. Form and Substance are Important.

A paralegal not only must possess technical skills (the substance), but also must be professional (the form). Professional form includes verbal communication (the words we use and tone-attitude), body language (eye contact and confident stance), and appearance (such as the clothing we wear). Appearance is our packaging that gives signals that are interpreted by others.

7. Understand and Appreciate the Economics of Legal Practice.

The premise of the paralegal profession when it was created in the 1970s was that paralegals would contribute to efficiency and affordability of legal services. However, we must also contribute to profitability. In a corporate environment, paralegals help save legal costs; in a law firm, paralegals leverage lawyers and contribute to profits.

ETHICS CAVEAT:

Paralegals can and do contribute the bottom line for law firms, and they also lower the cost of legal services to clients by performing work that would otherwise have to be performed by a lawyer at a higher rate.

Therese A. Cannon, Attorney at Law and author of *Ethics and Professional Responsibility for Legal Assistants*

8. Technology Skills are Our Products.

Possessing knowledge and information (and knowing how to use them) is what paralegals sell to lawyers and to ultimately to clients. The last decade of technological advances has provided opportunities for paralegals to become experts in Internet usage, database management, and computer skills. In some instances, paralegals are more skilled in these areas than the attorneys are.

9. Paralegals are Neither "Fish" Nor "Fowl."

For the first years of our profession, beginning in the mid-70s, no one knew what to do with us—we were neither the attorney nor the secretary of the legal environment. Were we professional staff or support staff? We have now created our own category as more clients and lawyers recognize the distinct services paralegals provide. It would benefit the lawyers with whom we work to introduce the paralegal to clients and communicate on how paralegals ultimately save fees for the client, as well as improve the efficiency of legal services.

10. Join and Participate in Paralegal Associations to Network.

Join a local, state, and national paralegal organization. Attend meetings if you can, and read the periodicals offered by these groups. The issues these associations address do affect you. Usually Continuing Legal Education (CLE) opportunities are offered through paralegal associations. You will find that interacting with paralegal colleagues is stimulating and encouraging to your career and professional development.

Writing Tips:

An outline can help focus the writing project. Learn various writing techniques (to inform, to persuade, to seek an action). I once had a college business communication class that taught me how to write and relay something negative in nonnegative ways, a technique I still use today.

In observing witnesses, I write both objective and subjective areas of information, but clarify what is factual and what is my observation and opinion. For example, I might describe the appearance of a witness by his or her clothing, hair, physical attributes, and I might describe his or her demeanor, adding what gave the impression of that demeanor.

For example, if a witness constantly shifts while seated in a chair, and taps his fingers, this could describe the demeanor of impatience. Always indicate the source(s) for the information you convey.

PROFESSIONAL TIP Although the profession of law is challenging in itself (with rules, regulations, and deadlines), a paralegal's challenge is not only learning to work for many different attorneys and provide them with quality paralegal support that meets their needs, but also, fitting in with individual work styles and preferences. Just as attorneys fit their practice to clients, paralegals need to provide support to attorneys on an individualized basis.

---

1. How to Survive as a Delegee and What to Remember as a Delegator

I believe it is important for paralegals to understand assignments, and to be able to communicate clear requests to others. This is integral to delegation. Delegation (and receiving delegated work) is part of the legal team concept and process to work more effectively and efficiently.

As a paralegal, your work will be assigned, or delegated, from an attorney, or possibly a senior paralegal. Additionally, you will most likely be making requests to paralegal interns, secretaries, other paralegals, administrative personnel, or others, such as vendors.

- We are all delegators and delegees on a daily basis.
- What is a successful pass-off of an assignment?
- Have you ever been frustrated by the feeling you have not been given enough information to complete an assignment? Have you ever spent hours on a project, only to miss entirely what the delegator had in mind?

2. Communicate the Specific Task as a Delegee

   Recap orally the task description and your understanding of the project, or preferably, via e-mail or some other type of written communication. Make it a brief synopsis to use as a confirmation tool.

   For example: "To confirm our discussion earlier today, you requested that I research all pending litigation against John Doe and Doe Corporation, and perform initial Internet research on this individual and corporation. I will do PACER checks (i.e., federal and county checks) and corporate status checks through the Secretary of State. Please inform me if I should search any other county information. If this project exceeds three hours, I will check back with you regarding the status. Otherwise, I will have a written report to you by (date)."

3. Communicate the Specific Task as a Delegator:

   Remember that you probably know much more than the delegee does. Explain or define acronyms. Be specific and explain what you are trying to accomplish with the task (the delegee may know a better way). Indicate if there are prior examples and explain where to find them. Inform the delegee the billing rate for the client for the work on the matter.

4. How the Task Fits in the Case and Matter

   As a Delegee: Ask if there are background materials (either facts or the law) that it would be helpful for you to read, or the delegator may give you a context for the task if prompted. Talk to another paralegal if the case has other team members. What is the viewpoint of the task?

   As a Delegator: Provide either this type of information or the source of them.

5. What is the Due Date for the Project Being Delegated and what is the Deadline for the Final Product?

As a Delegee: Include this date when confirming the task. Does the delegator desire to see a draft or partial completion *before* the actual due date?

As a Delegator: Be clear on due dates. Clarify whether you want updates on the progress, or whether you want to see a report on the project as it progresses.

6. How Long Should This Project Take?

Confirm the delegator's understanding of the time he thinks will be required for the project. If the delegator says, for example, five hours, and you are not half finished in four, then immediately inform the delegator of the status. You may have found additional information and reasoning that the delegator had not considered, or, you may be off track. As a delegator, be realistic about the time you believe the project will take.

5. What Expenses, if any, are Authorized?

Ask if LexisNexis®, WESTLAW® or on-line research be used. If so, is there a budget or is client authorization required? What about assistance from other paralegals or the librarian? Is it permissible to use these resources and incur these fees?

ETHICS CAVEAT:

The legal fee agreement is also governed by ethics rules. Ethics opinions have held that padding bills, or overcharging for expenses and the like, are ethical violations as well as breaches of the agreement with the client.

Therese A. Cannon, Attorney at Law and author of *Ethics and Professional Responsibility for Legal Assistants*

6. Always Ask Questions, If Unsure.

Ask other paralegals or return to the attorney with follow-up questions. You may want to try out your questions on paralegal colleagues before making inquiries of the lawyers.

7. Is There a Preferred Format for the End Work Product?

Remember that some lawyers have personal preferences, such as notebooks, folders, binders, or other formats. Ask her secretary to show you samples of how previous work has been done for them.

If you have a preference, remember to explain that in your instructions as delegator.

A leader (or good delegator) is someone who

- keeps a cool head and a warm heart.
- takes the time to make one feel important.
- knows when to ask what is wrong and when to say what is right.
- is the kind of leader people can respect and admire.
- makes the workplace a nicer place to be.

CHAPTER 4

PATRICIA G. GUSTIN, CP, CFEI
Freelance Associates
HARRISBURG, PA

PATRICIA G. GUSTIN, CP, CFEI
"Patricia can easily take a case from boxes of documents to ready for trial. She does not miss a thing–Very perceptive."

Carl J. Natale, President –
UBA Fire, Inc.
Harrisburg, PA; Fort Myers, FL

EDUCATION/HONORS/CERTIFICATIONS:

- B.S., Business Administration, Pennsylvania State University, 1987; Associate of Arts, Business, Harrisburg Area Community College, 1983
- Diploma, Private Investigation, 2002
- Additional college credit hours in Fire Science and Criminal Justice, Harrisburg Area Community College (1999-2002).
- Certificate of Appreciation, National Association of Legal Assistants, Inc. (NALA), 2004 (for services and contributions to the organization)
- Certificates of merit, recognition, and letters of commendation for work performed
- Conducted several presentations in various aspects of litigation at the local, regional, and national levels, along with authoring related documents for publication
- Three-year appointment on the NALA's Continuing Education Council
- Chair, CLA Study Guide and Mock Exam project team
- Past first VP for Education, former Keystone Legal Assistant Association (responsible for coordinating the 2003 conference that reaped the highest attendance and evaluations to date)
- Developed and presented an online CLE educational course for the National Association of Legal Assistants/Paralegals, Inc., NALA Campus Live

PROFESSIONAL ASSOCIATIONS:

- NALA, member since 1996
- NALA *Facts & Findings* Editorial Board
- National Fire Protection Association, member
- Keystone Legal Assistant Association

YEARS EXPERIENCE:

COMPANY-AT-A-GLANCE:

PATRICIA G. GUSTIN, CP, CFEI
Owner/President
Freelance Associates
Harrisburg, PA
Phone: 717.564.6012
Fax: 717.564.0119

PRACTICE AREAS:

- Products Liability
- Research/analysis
- Chain of custody of evidence
- Insurance litigation representing insurance companies in product liability and related litigation, autos, and accidents
- Criminal—arson, on a very limited basis and mostly on behalf of the defense Employment and Labor Law; to include labor/management relations, collective bargaining, background investigation, wrongful discharge, and employment discrimination
- Construction Law/Litigation - construction defects, code violations, and industry practice
- Administrative Law—agency enabling statutes, agency regulations, policy and procedure, legislative coordination, and regulatory review
- Nonprofit Law—write grant proposals when requested
- Ethics Law and Professional Conduct
- Investigation and litigation for insurance companies, law firms, and in support of expert testimony
- Social Security Law—has appeared as nonlawyer representative
- Expert witness testimony, related rules of evidence, and procedure governing same
- Trained and experienced community mediator

INTRODUCTION TO PRODUCTS LIABILITY

Products liability is one of the fastest growing and most economically significant branches of tort law. The more parties that are involved, the more significant the time element is involved in organizing and managing the case.

Products liability law refers to the liability of a manufacturer, distributor, or seller of products or goods, which because of a defect or lack of warnings, causes injury to the purchaser or a bystander. In essence, products liability involves the liability of any or all parties along the chain of manufacture of any product for damage or injury caused by the product. This includes the manufacturer of component parts, assembling manufacturer, wholesaler, reseller, and retail storeowner.

Product liability is a highly technical and complex field of law. It is a balancing act of documents, issues, allegations, changing courses, and effectively managing voluminous documents, along with time, energy, and resources. To represent the client properly, the firm must undertake a thorough investigation of the facts and circumstances that may result in many course corrections as the case unfolds.

The term "products" expands to include both tangible and intangible, writings, naturals, and real estate. The basis for claims includes negligence, strict liability, or breach of express and implied warranties of merchantability and of fitness, depending on the jurisdiction within which the claim arises. The assignment of culpability may include any or all parties involved in the chain of selling a product: designer, manufacturer, assembler, distributor, reseller, retailer, or individual, which product causes injury to a purchaser, end user, or a bystander. Only about four percent (4%) of consumers actually register their products with the manufacturer after purchase. Even fewer customers actually read the instructions or adhere to the warnings. A high percentage of consumers alter products—knowingly or otherwise. Today, many manufacturers are voiding warranty for alteration of a product.

OVERVIEW OF JOB RESPONSIBILITIES:

The product liability paralegal takes the case from start to finish and often guides client through the legal process. The paralegal carries the majority of the workload and becomes the "go to" person on staff. A product liability case can take the paralegal in many directions, such as into the corporate world of product design, manufacture, assembly, inspection, testing, and quality control measures prior to the product leaving the factory. Many paralegals work closely with the product's company, especially if the company is a defendant. A freelance paralegal works both independently (for nonattorney professionals), and as part of a team under the supervision of an attorney in products liability and tort-related proceedings.

There is no federal products liability law. At the federal level, the United States Department of Commerce has promulgated the Model Products Liability Act for voluntary use by the states. Most states have adopted their own statutes. Case law has also been instrumental in the application of products liability law to judicial decision. Article 2 of the Uniform Commercial Code (UCC) regulates the sale of goods. In addition, The Restatement of Torts, 3rd ed. and The Magnuson-Moss Warranty Act (15 U.S.C. Sections 2301 et seq.) addresses consumer product warranties.

The areas of knowledge that a product liability paralegal must know are (1) a command of the laws, treatises, and case law governing product liability and (2) a working knowledge of the rules of civil procedure and rules of evidence. In addition, in the highly technical nature of product liability litigation, the paralegal needs superior organizational, time, case, and project management skills.

When you meet with clients and other involved parties, make sure your role is clear to the client. Specifically, have the attorney tell the client you cannot give advice. In your work, you may handle personal injury, wrongful death, and code violations. State product liability law stipulates the plaintiff must establish proof based on the preponderance of evidence that:

1. The product caused the injury, loss, or accident.
2. The product was defective when it left the manufacturer or seller.
3. The product was unfit for its intended use, was inherently dangerous, or the defendant made the product unreasonably dangerous beyond what an ordinary customer would contemplate,

TYPICAL WORKWEEK:

Because products liability involves preparing an expert witness for testimony and trial, some tasks are predictable, but the casework can twist and turn on a moment's notice. Because of this, I usually organize my tasks by systematic methods and projects as opposed to days.

Every morning I check the calendar and double-check with client(s) regarding deadlines, needs, and calendar-related changes. If there are any changes, I enter them into the computer, and everyone will see them when they check the calendar that is firmwide. Everyone enters his or her own changes.

I conduct a fact-finding mission according to the client's request, prepare a summary report and fax it to the client, and then contact the retaining attorney's paralegal for further information. Next, I answer e-mails from client(s) requesting information. I perform research into codes and standards applicable to a particular product liability case being reviewed, then locate and summarize them for the record. Afterward, I discuss various product liability litigation, fire, and explosion matters with my attorney and the expert witness.

ETHICS CAVEAT:

Paralegals must be aware of the ethics rules on this, because clients with whom they work will often ask questions that would require them to give legal advice. The best thing to do in this situation is to refer them to the responsible attorney.

Therese A. Cannon, Attorney at Law and author of *Ethics and Professional Responsibility for Legal Assistants*

I return to my normal litigation review and deposition digesting for cases. Because my deadline is a few weeks away, I work two hours on the digesting. I receive a call from a client requesting an origin and cause investigation concerning a structural fire, and then I contact the insurance adjuster, homeowner, and fire officials for further information and access to the site, and then coordinate with other investigators. I prepare a new investigation file and computerize the information I have. After I complete the setup and organizational tasks, I send out a fee schedule and the expert's CV (circum vitae/resume). I perform cursory research into the events surrounding the investigation request. Lastly, I obtain directions from the Internet to save time.

I receive a call from client about a new fire/explosion case involving product liability and multiple fatalities. The client says that voluminous documents will be transmitted directly to my office, and the expert report will be needed within 20 days. I prepare a new case file. I develop a trial notebook for another case, a propane gas–related, product liability and personal injury (PL/PI) case for an upcoming expert deposition; complete abstracts of all documents, including pleadings, discovery, reports, insurance files, deposition transcripts, and key deposition exhibits; and then obtain a copy of expert report and expert's CV or resume for the trial notebook.

An investigator calls regarding the new case I received Tuesday, and he tells me the scene will only be available on Friday. I arrange to meet him at the scene, and ask permission to interview the homeowner(s) and others involved, if needed.

I consult with the expert witness about an upcoming deposition and preparation of the trial notebook to determine the date and location of the required delivery. I receive a new case as expected from a conversation with a client I had on Wednesday. I review the cover letter and note the deadlines, due dates, and follow up on the attorney's and my calendar. I alert the expert witness's office. I sort and organize case documents and materials, and prepare the document schedule. I determine which documents need to be reviewed according to the scope of expert testimony. I confirm determination of documents with the expert witness. I contact the retaining attorney's office, if necessary, for further information and follow-up request for documents not included. Next, I finalize the trial notebook for PL/PI case and deliver to the client. I confirm the scene investigation for Friday with the lead investigator, and prepare for the investigation.

I go to the fire scene to meet with the investigators and other official representatives, and then I conduct an on-the-scene investigation, including photo-documentation, measurements, interviews, and discussions. I identify and document physical evidence, and determine what physical evidence we need to retain. I note the information to establish the chain of custody of the evidence, and then I package and tag the physical evidence. After talking with the attorney, I contact the client with the results of the investigation. I obtain further instruction from my attorney, go back to the office, develop photographic documentation, and prepare the scene diagram.

TYPICAL WORK ASSIGNMENTS:

1. Create and maintain case management system for each case assigned.
2. Coordinate timeframes and deadlines. Maintain litigation docket, calendar, or tickler system, noting deadlines. Prepare necessary documentation and participate in meetings, hearings, depositions, and trials.
3. Review and obtain all relevant documents in client's possession.
4. Undertake a full factual review of cases referred to a nationally known expert witness, including a full review of photographs, diagrams, and other documentary evidence; complete case summary and other documents, as the case requires.
5. Prepare chronologies and timelines per deposition testimony, documents, and other factual records.

6. Index and summarize deposition testimony and exhibits.

7. Coordinate deposition and trial schedules with client.

8. Prepare trial notebooks of key documents and witness files.

9. Identify and analyze industry codes and standards, statutes, regulations, and ordinances.

10. Determine relationship of products to instances of fires and explosions.

11. Research product recalls, technical, and service bulletins.

12. Determine and monitor chain of custody of evidence.

13. Prepare documentation and complete review of documents in support of *Daubert*[i] challenges involving spoliation of evidence and admissibility of experts.

14. Research and apply rules of evidence and procedure.

15. Maintain reference library.

TIPS, SHORTCUTS, AND TRICKS OF THE TRADE:

I. LEADERSHIP

A. You can be the most outstanding paralegal in your work, but if you fail to get along with others, you will find your advancement hindered. Always maintain a professional demeanor. Stay focused on the task.

B. When you feel burned out, find new ways of handling the same tasks. You will be amazed at how you will be rejuvenated. A new style may even be contagious to others.

C. Your career is your responsibility. If you want something, go for it. He who hesitates is lost. Show your initiative, be inquisitive, and handle the problem directly. It is up to you to make things happen for yourself. Be willing to spend some of your own time and money on your career. In these economic times, law firms often do not have the resources to pay for extras.

D. Never lose your passion for your work. Even when it does not seem so, it is work worth doing.

E. Paralegals are, in many respects, investigators in their own right. While the investigation of cases will not turn you into an instant

---

[i] *Daubert v. Merrell Dow Pharmaceuticals* (92-102), 509 U.S. 579 (1993).

private investigator, it will embellish your existing skills to gather information critical to the success of the case.

F. You have to earn your place on a legal team. Merit goes a long way, but so does your ability to adapt, improvise, and overcome. Become a conduit for progress. Everyone is under stress, and no doubt some will handle it better than others will. Address the issue and offer a solution. The goal is to get the job done on time, accurately, and to the legal team's satisfaction.

G. Develop a file system that is simple to use and easy to retrieve, but also cross-references the needs and identification triggers of clients. When you freelance, you operate from a remote worksite, so it is important for you to be able to be identified by the client's established references, as well as have a system that can easily be accessed.

H. Establish checklists and use them wisely. I have a checklist I use that incorporates both the case management and billing information.

 I. Products liability litigation is a highly technical field. Handle your cases as if you were handling your life matters. Stay current in the field. The field has become very exact in its legal criteria, precedent, and requirements. If you want to excel as a product liability litigation paralegal, you must commit to continuing education—both formally, and on your own. Expand your skills by undertaking assignments in areas you have less experience, see them through, and feel the satisfaction of not only a job well done but the newfound arsenal of skills you have developed.

 J. Success in the product liability field is defined as follows: "Know your case, know your place, know your product, and know what you need to do to gain a favorable verdict and judgment for the client." Apply this rule to each case you work on. Go out into uncharted territory. You never know what you may find that could be critical to the case.

II. Legal Research Shortcuts

A. Research product recalls, service, and technical bulletins online.

B. Perform hard-copy and online research into industry codes, standards, and protocols.

C. Collect and analyze data; prepare preliminary report of findings.

D. Schedule meeting with client or counsel.

E. Assemble research documentation and prepare final report.

F. Consult with industry, governmental, educational, and professional association representatives.

G. Research applicable codes and standards, industry practices, manufacturer specifications, instructions, and warnings, which are incorporated into final opinions and conclusions.

H. Conduct research assignments as requested by attorneys (under direct supervision) and other nonattorney professionals (independently).

I. Research hard copy, Internet, and on-line services for applicable information.

J. Collect and analyze data, prepare preliminary reports, meet with client as needed.

K. Assemble research documentation and prepare final reports.

L. Check the firm's database before conducting research. You may not have to go any further than the database to find key information you would otherwise waste time researching. Perhaps, there is much information in the database related to the matter that will save valuable time and effort.

M. Establish a catalog of key information—such as the case name, type of case, summary of the case, and references (both hard-copy and on-line).

N. Cutting to the chase during an on-line search can be difficult, especially if you are in foreign legal territory. When conducting an initial search, start with very specific words relevant to your case and, if those searches do not yield results, move up the "ladder of abstraction" to more general terms. Visit some of the Web sites to see if they are useful. Keep the task at hand in mind. Be sure to bookmark Web sites that you find particularly useful for future searches.

O. Does this research project ring a familiar bell? Perhaps, someone else in the firm has already worked on such a matter. Check around the firm for information. In addition, check remote references, such as newspaper or journal articles that you recall might have addressed the issues.

P. Many research services such as WestLaw®, LexisNexis®, and Lois Law™ offer limited-time access to research materials. Especially if you are a freelancer or work for a smaller firm, the cost of maintaining on-line research services can be prohibitive. Give a call to these, and other, on-line research companies to see if you can strike a short-term or "as needed" access agreement.

Q. A law school or public law library can be of service. Call the librarian with a good description of needed information, and he or she will be happy to give you a hand. I believe librarians also like to see the researcher has formulated some ideas about basic issues, such as relevant, legal principles, and so forth. This shows the researcher is doing his own work. These librarians specialize in legal research and have access to a wealth of information that many of us do not. They are also very creative and innovative in their approach to researching a matter, often coming up with new information. When contacting a librarian, introduce yourself and briefly explain the nature of your call. Ask if they can help you, and then proceed with the request. Build a professional relationship with the librarian. Networking helps you get the job done.

R. If you need access to a law library's database for research purposes, see if either your supervising attorney or another attorney within the firm has an access code. Do not ask for the access code, but rather, ask them to get you on-line.

WRITING TIPS

A. Always write in conjunction with the audience and style required. The legal field has set ways of doing things, including how documents must be formatted and type of jargon to be included.

B. Follow the ABCs of reporting: Accurate, Brief (and to the point) and Clear. Whatever you do, be sure to fully address their inquiry, keep the focus of research and reporting back on that inquiry, and narrow down the facts, references, and other information. Put a notation at the end of the written work, stating to contact you if they need more information.

IV. Discovery Shortcuts

Evidentiary rules state that, with few exceptions everything an expert witness produces is discoverable. This includes anything from a written report to a telephone message. The supervising attorney should clearly define, explain, and monitor the paralegal's role in working with an expert witness. In addition, products liability litigation will involve the application of industry codes and standards, industry and/ or government testing, and approval processes. The product liability paralegal is not expected to have a command of such specialized information. The expert witness will have the responsibility of defining, applying, and defending codes and standards, and the testing and approval processes, as part of their overall scope of expert testimony.

Discovery can generate a voluminous array of documents that sometimes are simply dumped at your doorstep for you to organize, sort, index, and file. The duration of a case is often unpredictable— a case can lay dormant for years, and then become top priority.

Product liability litigation is especially challenging when it comes to completing work for expert witnesses. Expert discovery is usually at the end of the discovery phase. Expert witnesses are busy professionals who need ample time to prepare their opinions.

ETHICS CAVEATS:

1. *When paralegals interview witnesses and other underrepresented persons, they must be certain the persons understand the law firm is not representing them.*

2. *Interpreting the law for a client is considered one of the main functions of practicing law; therefore, a paralegal conducting legal research must be sure he or she is supervised by a lawyer when relaying the lawyer's advice to a client about rights, responsibilities, or a course of action under the law.*

3. *The ethics rules relating to competence may now require research be updated electronically as electronic resources are often the most current; however, beware not all information on the Internet is reliable or valid.*

Therese A. Cannon, Attorney at Law and author of *Ethics and Professional Responsibility for Legal Assistants*

V. DOCUMENT PREPARATION

A. Conduct full fact-finding analysis, from the date of occurrence, up to the date of trial, including timelines, cross-analysis documentation, digesting, and indexing.

B. Research laws, regulations, industry codes and standards, as well as industry procedures.

C. Interact with clients to coordinate information, complete requirements, and provide status reports.

D. Complete reports and related informational documents.

E. Initiate, coordinate, prepare, and update trial notebooks.

F. Prepare the fact investigation portion of expert reports upon request.

G. Assist in the preparation of discovery and testimonial questions for fact and expert witnesses.

H. Manage litigation files of all types and complexity, along with associated deadlines.

I. Maintain current knowledge of court rules of procedure and evidence.

J. Assist in preparing expert for *Daubert* hearings.

K. Provide other related assistance as requested.

VI. INVESTIGATIVE TIPS

A. Be the Lead Fact Investigator.

Many paralegals discount the fact that they are, in a true sense, the lead fact investigator of the case. Although there may be a private investigator employed by the office, it is the paralegal who sets out to find the needle in the haystack.

B. Follow Your Instincts.

Do you have a hunch about something? Follow your instincts, but do not spend much time on it if you do not have the time to spare. See what preliminary information you can find, and then bring it to the attention of your supervisor. You may, at first, get a puzzled look, but if you feel you are on to something, explain what it is and why. Sometimes, it is the most obscure or unusual fact or circumstance that can actually make or break a case. Always seek the hidden meaning.

C. Develop a Sixth Sense for Fact-Finding.

You do not actually have to be formally trained in investigation. Through education and experience, paralegals usually develop a sixth sense for fact-finding. Creativity, ingenuity, hard-core facts, and circumstances already at your fingertips will be your guide.

D. Conduct a Background Investigation.

When conducting a background investigation, determine what information a client or witness has provided. Then check the file to determine if these statements or allegations are supported by written documentation (be it a writing itself, a photograph, or even a hand-drawn diagram). From there, determine what you need or should have, and then search for that information. Once ample information is gathered, pull together a report, with a summary sheet attached to the front, and transmit it to the requesting attorney. In addition, prepare a brief presentation of your findings in the event that you are asked to provide further information or clarify information that is contained in the report.

E. Keep Focused.

Take a fact-seeking approach to conducting investigations. Although you could uncover some very interesting information, it may not be germane to the case at hand. Keep your focus on the specific nature of the investigation, but at the same time, do not create a tunnel vision that will narrow your options in finding information.

F. Check First.

If you are seeking information as part of an investigation effort, be sure to check whether there are any statutes, regulations, or policies before requesting the information. For example, most state police agencies will not provide an investigation report unless a request is a subpoena.

G. Conduct independent origin and cause investigation upon request of insurance companies and on behalf of an expert witness. Specialize in residential structures, warnings and instructions, and product liability, with potential or actual subrogation issues. Investigations are conducted pursuant to NFPA 921-Standard for Fire Investigation.

H. Obtain assignments, conduct background research, and prepare for on-the-scene investigation; develop case file.

I. Conduct scene inspections/investigations, including photographic documentation and scene diagrams.

J. Interview witnesses and victims, and prepare interview transcriptions.

K. Prepare investigation reports for clients.

L. Secure and take into custody physical evidence, log the evidence in detail, and create chain of custody.

M. Attend/participate in physical evidence/artifact inspection and testing.

N. Maintain investigation files in both hard-copy and electronic format.

O. Establish and maintain chain of custody of evidence.

CASE MANAGEMENT:

1) Interact with clients to coordinate receipt or transmittal of information.

2) Provide status reports.

3) Maintain case files of all types and complexity.

4) Monitor and meet deadlines.

5) Retain files both electronically and in hard-copy formats.

6) Develop and maintain case management retrieval system.

7) Complete and preserve documentary evidence as requested.

The paralegal should ask specific questions to assist effectively in the development of a comprehensive case file, such as the following:

What Happened?

■ Circumstances surrounding the incident

■ Loss or accident

■ Injury

■ Death

Who was Involved?

■ Injured party(ies)

■ Eyewitnesses

■ Public agency representatives

■ Private agency representatives

■ Government and private investigators

■ Supervising party(ies)

■ Sponsor(s)

Where Did it Happen?

■ Location

■ Home

- Industrial or commercial setting
- Recreational activity

When Did it Happen?

- Date
- Time

How Did it Happen?

- Events surrounding the incident
- Injury
- Loss

Why Did it Happen?
Who/What is to Blame?

PHYSICAL EVIDENCE BECOMES "EVERYTHING"

The paralegal will often interact with fact witnesses and expert witnesses during the course of litigation. Fact witnesses help to establish the facts and circumstances surrounding a case, while the expert witness brings a specialized knowledge, beyond that of a layperson, through investigation, testing, knowledge, education, experience, and, in accordance with principles surrounding the expert's profession, in reaching formal opinions and conclusions with respect to the product at issue. Particularly over the past decade, the use of the expert witness in a products liability case has dramatically increased. The precedent-setting decision by the United States Supreme Court in *Daubert* sets forth both the judge's role as the gatekeeper of expert testimony and four-part criteria for the admissibility of expert testimony at trial.

It is important the paralegal understand and appreciate the chain of custody of evidence. In most cases, the combination of physical evidence and sound expert witness testimony makes or breaks a case. The playing field is set—and there is no deviation in the requirement the plaintiff must meet his or her burden of proof in a product liability case in order to obtain a favorable verdict and judgment. The product liability paralegal must understand and appreciate the importance of the chain of custody of evidence, and have familiarity with the rules of evidence. The best defense in support of maintaining chain of custody of evidence is to leave it to the experts.

Spoliation of evidence is the intentional or otherwise untimely and unnecessary destruction of evidence, creating prejudice to a party (or parties) that would not otherwise exist had the remains of such physical evidence and component parts not been altercated or destroyed by the custodial party.

ETHICS CAVEAT

Remember that a lawyer must review all documents that you draft, like interrogatories and requests for productions.

Therese A. Cannon, Attorney at Law and author of *Ethics and Professional Responsibility for Legal Assistants*

CLIENT INTERVIEWING:

Paralegal work is a service-related field. Consider the client as a customer and provide stellar customer service always. Remember that the client will be counting on you and will need you to guide them through the litigation process. Set the boundaries, but also assure the client that you are acting in behalf of their best interest.

ETHICS CAVEAT:

Be sure to let the clients know that the lawyer supervises you.

Therese A. Cannon, Attorney at Law and author of *Ethics and Professional Responsibility for Legal Assistants*

I. Always treat the client with respect and dignity.
   The overwhelming majority of clients are feeling anger, loss, or other emotions that can cloud their judgment and alter their behavior. However, do not let a client unreasonably harass or insult you. When this happens, be assertive about how you feel, and help the client understand that you are trying to do the best job possible for them.

II. When you are asked to interview a witness, consider the entire person.
   Was this person directly involved in some way? Is this the victim? Is this an eyewitness? You have to adapt to the person and not expect them to adapt to you. For instance, if you are interviewing

a child, be sure that the parents are present or approve of you talking to the child alone. Approach the child with comfort and care, and ask questions at their level. Allow a few minutes for them to chat so they can become more comfortable with you, and then steer the interview to the questions you need to ask. You will be amazed at what information you will gather.

ETHICS CAVEAT:

Remind a witness that you or your firms do not represent him.

Therese A. Cannon, Attorney at Law and author of *Ethics and Professional Responsibility for Legal Assistants*

III. *Practice active listening and communication techniques.*

When interviewing clients, or others, maintain good eye contact, be interested in what they have to say, paraphrase answers if you do not understand them to clarify information.

IV. *Keep a professional but empathic demeanor.*

One thing you should not do is buy into comments or innuendos that a client shares with you. This will appear that you are getting personal with the client, and they will then expect more of you than you can ethically and professionally provide. It is hard not to feel empathy for a victim of circumstances or someone who feels they should not be involved in a lawsuit, but keep a professional but empathic demeanor at all times.

V. *Each party has their own perspective.*

When conducting an interview, be it with a client, witness, or other party, always remember that there are two sides to every story, and then there is the truth, which is usually somewhere in-between. This is a realistic way to remember that each party has their own perspective, which is reality to that party. It is your job to report the facts as they are relayed to you, and not judge the person's character or integrity. Keep this in mind when you are conducting an interview.

VI. *Be aware of body language.*

Spoken words are one thing—but body language can also tell you a story that could be much more profound than any words will portray. Make it a point to watch non-verbal cues when conducting a client interview or interviewing any party. Learn some of the primary cues of non-verbal language, such as eye contact, posture, and seating position.

VII. *Be patient with each client.*
These are very emotional times for clients. Most are not knowledgeable about the legal field, have preconceived notions that are often misguided, and most importantly, they are either going through a traumatic experience or are on the receiving end of a lawsuit.

COMMUNICATIONS:

I. *Be assertive, but make your point.*
If you are feeling emotional or angry about a matter or at a person, step back for a few minutes and think about it. Go for a short walk, have a cup of coffee, relax to calm yourself down. Then approach the person or matter. Those few moments away will clear your head and no doubt help you avoid negative results.

II. *Address problems as soon as you can.*
Personality clashes, competition, and differences in style prevail in any workplace. Keep focused on what you are doing and how well you are doing it. If these things begin to interfere with the job, address them now rather than later. Precious time cannot be wasted.

III. *Nip conflict in the bud.*
Little things build up. Try to resolve the matter yourself first. If you are not successful, and the matter or person continues to interfere with the performance of your job, take the matter to your supervisor. Keep a level head when outlining the problem, and have possible solutions in mind. Do not play "victim."

IV. *Use e-mail wisely and professionally.*
The last thing you want to do is fire off an angry or emotional e-mail to anyone, regardless of how they addressed you. Once written and transmitted, it cannot be retracted. Your professionalism is at stake. If you need to have a discussion with this person, call them and either arrange to meet or talk by phone. A good rule to remember is to put good news and business information in e-mails, but deliver bad news either in person or by phone.

V. *A paralegal's work is very stressful.*
You are often under the gun of impossible deadlines, eleventh-hour requests, and larger-than-life assignments. When you start to feel overstressed, step away from the stressful situation (that is, if it's possible to do so), take a few moments to think it out and calm down, and then return to the task at hand. If that is not possible, then inconspicuously count to 10, and then move on. If counting to 10 does not work, take it to 20! You have a job to do, and self-destructing is not going to get that assignment completed.

TRIAL POINTERS:

I. Establish a plan to prepare for trial as soon as possible.
For instance, what exhibits do you need to prepare? What types of exhibits need to be produced and/or enlarged (exploded view, PowerPoint, or slides)? Coordinate your needs with both internal staff and external contractors. Put them on alert by providing advance notice that things could possibly change, additional work may be needed, and other things.

II. Get familiar with the courtroom technology.
Ensure the law firm technological equipment is compatible. Be sure judge and jury and see all of the trial exhibits, whether presented on poster board, via laptop and projector, or by other means. This will be a very important step of "support" for effective client representation.

III. Visualize the courtroom, as it would be filled during the trial.
Think of seating arrangements, vantage point for counsel, witness stand, judge's view, and the like. Place yourself in counsel's shoes. Can you see/hear them? If not, then perhaps no one else will either.

COMMON CHALLENGES IN THE PRODUCT LIABILITY LITIGATION FIELD:

I. Timely receipt of information and documents.
The single biggest challenge in working a product liability case is when your attorney asks you to make a full review of boxes of documents at the eleventh hour. It is even more annoying when the documents were available in a timely fashion but were not

transmitted or exchanged. Last-minute review can be dangerous because of existing multiple priorities that need to be completed, resulting in a lack of time to conduct a comprehensive review of the latest stack of documents. Key information, or important information that has yet to be uncovered, could be missed. That is why it is so important that the product liability paralegal, regardless of what party he or she is working for, follow sound organizational, case management, and professional courtesy protocol.

II. Preservation of evidence and evidence spoliation issues.

The single most important artifact in any product liability case is the actual product itself. When physical evidence is altered by either accidental or deliberate means, has been otherwise prematurely disassembled, removed from its incident-related posture, is stored improperly, or left unprotected from the elements, it becomes most difficult, if not impossible, for all parties to have a full opportunity to fully inspect the artifact. Even photographic evidence cannot take the place of actually viewing the artifact in question.

The mishandling or destruction of physical evidence by a party also leads to spoliation of evidence issues, which can be quite time-consuming and difficult for the paralegal. Most importantly, the mishandling or destruction of physical evidence can alter a client's chances of prevailing at trial, especially if it is the fault of the firm's hired expert witness.

III. Managing multiple cases simultaneously.

When under tremendous pressure, it is sometimes hard to decide what priority should be completed first, especially when cases are simultaneously being prepared for trial. If you find yourself in a whirlwind of documents, deadlines, and demands, remain calm and stay focused. Establishing priorities through discussions with lead counsel is one way that you may accomplish this. Ensure that all cases are well organized and managed, both in hard copy and electronically. This will enhance easy location and retrieval of documents, exhibits, and other information vital to successful representation.

REAL WORK EXAMPLES:

EXAMPLE NO. 1: FATAL FIRE

Over the past ten years, I have been involved in over 370 product liability cases. The overwhelming majority of cases were very interesting. However, there are certain cases that have made an indelible mark on my career. The first was a fatal fire that occurred in an apartment building in the New England area. The tragedy behind this fire was the fact that three children under the age of six lost their lives because of carbon monoxide poisoning. The custodial parent was not home at the time of the fire.

The state police fire marshal's office investigated and determined that the fire originated in the electrical panel on the opposite side of the apartment bathroom on the lower level of the building. It was also determined that multiple code violations occurred with the construction, maintenance, and repair of the building and its electrical, and possibly, mechanical systems. Over a dozen parties were put on notice. I worked as part of the team representing one of the potential defendants. A daylong investigation was conducted. The scene had been altered by the fact that the electrical panel in question had been removed prior to the parties having an opportunity to view the artifact in its immediate post-fire state. The manufacturer that the firm was defending was exonerated from the case. To this day, I wonder what actually happened to take the lives of three innocent children. Some cases you just cannot shake off.

Example No. 2: An Office Product is Alleged to be The Cause of a Fire

The second case was a multi-million dollar loss involving a large office building in a mid-Atlantic state in which an office product was blamed as the origin and cause, but the evidence overwhelmingly pointed to a deliberately set fire. The litigation spanned a five-year period. Although there was only one plaintiff and one defendant, the case involved a wide range of legal issues. I was part of the legal team representing the defendant. Two schools of thought reigned: (1) the office product was the origin and cause of the fire, and (2) the product could not have caused the fire because independent investigation disclosed that the actual origin of the fire was approximately 50 feet from the location of the product. The debate escalated as the case progressed and throughout the expert discovery phase.

The product in question actually contained only a few combustible components; the rest of the product's components were incapable of sustaining a fire based upon their fire retardant qualities. Documented and verified engineering design and testing clearly supported these findings. The physical evidence regarding an incendiary fire mounted, with new information uncovering the fact that a police/fire task force had been established, focusing primarily on an employee in the building as the major person of interest.

The firm retained behavioral specialists from the FBI and investigators from the ATF, together with a host of prominent origin and cause and engineering experts. Over 50 witnesses were deposed.

Unfortunately, arson fires are hard to prove because the perpetrator often acts alone and at a time when there are no witnesses in the immediate area. The identification of the exact ignition source was not possible. An asbestos-related issue surfaced when crews began their cleanup. The building had to be imploded, and a new building was constructed in its place. A weeklong trial was held in district court. At that point, many of the expert witnesses did not testify, which was a very interesting twist in the case, considering the number of expert opinions that were proffered during the investigation and discovery processes. The jury returned a verdict in favor of the defendant. The cost of litigation alone surpassed two million dollars.

CHAPTER 5

SUSAN G. IPPOLITI

Litigation Paralegal, President, and CEO
Solutions in Litigation, LLC
Rochester, NY

SUSAN G. IPPOLITI

"Sometimes you have to take the leap and build your wings on the way down."

Kobi Yamada

SOLUTIONS IN LITIGATION, LLC

Solutions In Litigation, LLC is a litigation support company that offers a solution to all litigation needs. We travel any distance at any time to meet whatever your case management requirements may be. Such services include case management, compliance with Federal Rules and procedures, court filings, courtroom and office technology and support, drafting of pleadings, motions and discovery, document coordination, analysis and management, and many more.

In addition, Solutions In Litigation, LLC is a practice management support company offering consultation services law firms and corporate legal departments. These services include practice management, project management, staff training, record keeping analyses, and database support. These types of services can be extremely beneficial to remaining on the cutting edges of technology, document management standards, and practice management.

The mission of Solutions In Litigation, LLC is to provide quality legal support services to attorneys and law firms who need assistance in the area of litigation. Solutions In Litigation, LLC adheres to the highest ethical standards set forth in the National Federation of Paralegal Associations, Inc.'s Model Code of Ethics and Professional Responsibility. Solutions In Litigation, LLC also abides by the ethical standards set forth by the American Bar Association's Standing Committee on Paralegals. Solutions In Litigation, LLC will not give legal advice to clients and will only perform legal tasks under the strict and constant supervision of attorneys.

EDUCATION/HONORS/CERTIFICATIONS:

- B.A., St. John Fisher College, Rochester, New York, 1997

PROFESSIONAL ASSOCIATIONS:

National Federation of Paralegal Associations

- Chair, Strategic Planning Committee, May 2006–present
- Marketing Committee, July 2004–May 2006
- Vice President and Director of Membership, Board of Directors; April 4, 2004–present
- Award of Distinction for Superior Achievements and Excellence of Performance as NFPA's 2003–2004 Regulation Review Coordinator
- Regulation Review Coordinator; May 2003–May 2004

- Special Research Coordinator; May 2002–September 2002
- Convention Host Coordinator, Rochester, New York, Fall 2001

Paralegal Association of Rochester

- Vice President of Professional Development, Board of Directors, June 2000–May 2001
- NFPA Primary, May 2003–May 2004
- President-Elect, May 2003–May 2004
- NFPA Secondary, May 2001–May 2003

Italian American Community Center

- Second Vice President, Board of Directors. November 1998–July 2000

New York State Bar Association Law Practice Management Committee

- Member, January 2004–May 2004

Empire State Alliance of Paralegal Associations

- Chair, April 2002–Present

Generazione Next

- Chair, Young Adult Organization of the Italian - American Community Center, August 1997–December 1999

PRACTICE AREAS:

- Toxic tort - asbestos
- Product and premises liability
- Employment litigation (wage and hour, discrimination, EEOC)
- Patent litigation (trademark and patent infringement, both domestic and international)
- Research and compliance regarding Hague convention
- Translation and service
- Construction litigation (architectural and design)
- Malpractice defense, product liability defense related to medical devices
- Personal injury defense work (minimal)

OVERVIEW OF JOB RESPONSIBILITIES:

I. Pre-suit and Case Investigations
   A. Investigation of claim
      1. Participate in interviews with client
      2. Review client files; gather and organize factual data
   B. Conduct or supervise fact investigation
      1. Conduct corporate searches through LexisNexis®, WestLaw®, Dun & Bradstreet®, and other electronic and Internet sources
      2. Examine premises, locations, and objects; take notes and/or photographs; gather records
      3. Arrange for outside investigator
      4. Obtain and examine public records, including police, accident, and other municipal reports
      5. Obtain, review, and analyze medical and employment records
   C. Organize investigation documents
      1. Locate, interview, and obtain witness statements
      2. Maintain personal injury plaintiff file, including contact with carrier, client, health care providers, and employer
      3. Compile records of patent of product, history, and information regarding similar products
   D. Draft necessary documents
      1. Draft demand letters
      2. Draft petition and obtain appointment of limited administrator

ETHICS CAVEAT:

Paralegals have to tell the witnesses they interview that they are paralegals and not lawyers and are not representing the witness.

Therese A. Cannon, Attorney at Law and author of *Ethics and Professional Responsibility for Legal Assistants*

II. Research
   A. Legal research
   B. Product research (products liability cases)
   C. Site medical

D. Expert interviews, retention, and contact

E. Familiarity with sources of expert witness

F. Investigation of potential expert's credentials and prior testimony

G. Contact and interview potential experts

H. Retention letter; provide case background and information for expert

I. Investigation of opponents experts' credentials and prior testimony

---

ETHICS CAVEAT:

When contacting and interviewing prospective witnesses, be sure not to tell them anything about the case until you are sure that there is no conflict of interest

Therese A. Cannon, Attorney at Law and author of *Ethics and Professional Responsibility for Legal Assistants*

III. Document Drafting and Other Related Tasks

A. Pleadings

1. Notice of Claim, Summons, Notice of Appearance, Complaint, Answer

2. With defenses, demand for bill of particulars

3. Federal Civil Docket filing sheets, index number applications, and proofs of service

4. Motions

5. Notice of motion, affidavits, Request for Judicial Intervention (RJIs), and select exhibits for affidavits

6. Interview witnesses

7. Obtain facts for affidavits

8. Cite checking (checking the citations using the *Bluebook* and Sheppardizing the citations—see Chapter 9, Legal Research and Writing, Celia C. Elwell), fact checking, quotes for accuracy

9. Orders

B. Discovery

    1. Obtain and examine public records

    2. Omnibus demands

    3. Interrogatories

    4. Answers to discovery demands and interrogatories

    5. Notice to produce

IV. Document Coordination Analysis and Management/Electronic Discovery

    A. Consult with attorney and/or client regarding effective means of managing documents

    B. Organize and track documents from clients and opposing parties, including coding of documents

    C. Be familiar with and utilize litigation support systems for management of documents

V. Case Management

    A. Maintain deadlines and response dates and alert attorneys

    B. Assure client is continuously updated and aware of current case status

ETHICS CAVEAT:

However, do not answer questions that amount to legal advice, like, "How good is my case?" or "How much will I get?"

Therese A. Cannon, Attorney at Law and author of *Ethics and Professional Responsibility for Legal Assistants*

   C. Management of file, all documents, and medical records

   D. Attend inspections; research product history and information

   E. Prepare summaries of medical records; perform basic medical research

   F. Locate, interview, and obtain statements from witnesses

ETHICS CAVEAT:

Be sure not to tell witnesses how to testify if they ask you what they should say.

Therese A. Cannon, Attorney at Law and author of *Ethics and Professional Responsibility for Legal Assistants*

VI. Trial Preparation

   A. Locate witness

   B. Subpoena, judicial/*duces tecum* with fees

   C. Review affidavits of service

   D. Schedule for order of appearance

   E. Thank you letters to notify of settlement

   F. File preparation

   G. Prepare demonstrative exhibits

   H. Prepare and obtain certificates of authentication

   I. Assist at trial (e.g., with witness coordination, exhibits, note taking, jury monitoring, and other organizational tasks)

   J. Prepare, file, and serve judgments and bill of costs

ETHICS CAVEAT:

With proper lawyer review and signature, of course.

Therese A. Cannon, Attorney at Law and author of *Ethics and Professional Responsibility for Legal Assistants*

K. Review, index, gather, and summarize documents produced by opposing and third parties

L. Work directly with experts, consultants, and witnesses regarding case and preparing them for trial

M. Prepare and serve *subpoenas duces tecum*

N. Attend, supervise, or monitor product, accident, or vehicle inspection

O. Check cites and/or Sheppardize and proofread briefs

P. Coordinate arrangements with local vendors regarding equipment, space, and supply requirements

Q. Coordinate witnesses and experts, especially in out-of-town trials

R. Prepare trial notebooks and witness files

S. Draft list of documents and testimony to use in impeaching opposition witnesses

T. Draft pretrial statements and settlement conference memoranda

U. Obtain jury list and biographical information on jurors

V. Draft jury instructions and *voir dire*

W. Develop dossiers on adverse experts

X. Coordinate witness attendance at trial

Y. Prepare charts, graphs, and demonstrative exhibits for use at trial

Z. Attend trial taking notes on testimony

ZZ. Maintain list of exhibits as mentioned, offered, admitted, or objected to

ETHICS CAVEAT:

See above regarding preparing witnesses. Do not tell them how to testify. Over-coaching can be seen as suborning perjury.

Therese A. Cannon, Attorney at Law and author of *Ethics and Professional Responsibility for Legal Assistants*

TYPICAL WORKWEEK:

A typical workweek is such a difficult thing to assess. However, I am able to describe how I go about my week. On Monday, upon arrival into the office, I try to assess what the week may bring. I review my on-line and paper calendar and all of my attorneys' electronic calendars to the extent that they are available. I make notes of pressing deadlines and assignments I know will have a drop-dead due date that week or at least that I need to start to be able to meet a future deadline. Then I return or place any phone calls that have carried over from the previous week. I will also try to spend a few minutes with each of my attorneys to review what they may have on their plate or discuss any "foreseeable emergencies," as I like to call them.

The remainder of my workdays may include scheduling depositions, answering a complaint, drafting discovery responses, preparing for trial, reviewing documents, indexing and summarizing documents, or medical records in my databases. Duties include a myriad of tasks, such as client contact, case investigations, research, and expert retention and contact, document drafting of pleadings, motions and discovery, document analysis and management, and trial preparation. Working in the world of litigation, a paralegal's life can be somewhat unpredictable.

In Upstate New York, you have to be prepared to drive long distances at the drop of a hat to file papers. So, wherever possible, I make certain that I go to work with a full tank of gas, bottled water, and snacks in my car. I have made trips in a snowstorm to file complaints, motions, or pleadings in a clerk's office that was more than three hours away. One thing I have learned is that attorneys have little or no concept of time or procedure and truly have no idea what it takes to get papers filed and the amount of stress you exert to get it done. The heart-racing, blood-pumping, and adrenaline-flowing situations usually occur at least once a week. It is what keeps me on my toes.

On Fridays, I will review the workweek, complete that week's timesheets, and try to assess the coming week. In addition, I usually make a determination on whether I need to work in the office over the weekend or take work home. It does not happen very often, but it does happen. When you are preparing for trial, remember that your time is not your own. You belong to the trial team, and if they need you to be in the office at 7:00 A.M., stay until 11:00 P.M. and still come in over the weekend, then you do it. It is just the nature of litigation. I choose the path. Do I love it? Yes!

PRACTICAL TIPS, SHORTCUTS, AND TRICKS OF THE TRADE:

- Calendaring is a major proponent of any successful career. It is a way to keep track of any major deadlines. Most firms now will require it as part of their loss-prevention guidelines.

ETHICS CAVEAT:

Missing a deadline may cause you to lose a case and open your firm up to sanctions or a malpractice suit.

Therese A. Cannon, Attorney at Law and author of *Ethics and Professional Responsibility for Legal Assistants*

- Create or find charts to keep track of medical records, financial records, timelines, and so forth.

- Use Bates numbering and document control. For large document cases, scanning and placing into a database is the way to go.

- Whether you are on a document production or getting ready for trial, it is important that you bring extra everything along with you: staplers, hole punches, paper clips, pens, folders, anything you can think of, including medications like Advil, Tylenol, aspirin, and Band-Aids. Some paralegals use large fishing tackle boxes to keep supplies like pens, paper clips, sticky notes, and so on. Do not count on the fact that you will be able to buy it when you get there. If my trial is out of town, I will usually create my shopping list, add to it daily and then pre-order everything well in advance of my necessary date. This way, if I have forgotten anything, there is still time. Those boxes of supplies are sent in advance to my site.

- Try to get to know everyone you will be working with, from the deputy to the judge's law clerk and secretary. Building these relationships will prove to be beneficial to you during your trial.

GENERAL ADVICE:

- *Know what you do not know.* You cannot be afraid to ask questions. If you take on a task, assuming you know how to do it, and then find out that you completely misunderstood what was desired, it can have disastrous results.

- *It is always about the client.* You have to remember this when the day begins and the day ends. Ask yourself this question: Did you act in the best interest of your client?

- *Do not be afraid to think outside the box.* When attorneys ask for your suggestions or advice, tell them what you think. They really want to know.

- *Find a mentor.* That person will be your guardian angel. Every paralegal needs one or probably had one at some point in their career. That mentor is the person that will help you be the best paralegal you can be.

- *Be sure that you have enough information.* Attorneys often do not tell you the whole story. Once you receive your task, assess your information and decide if you need more. You cannot be afraid to ask for more information. The last thing you want is to do your project incorrectly because you were too afraid to ask for more information.

- *Calendaring.* Use a calendaring system, both electronic and paper. During the past few decades, Day-Timer, a paper-driven desk and pocket calendar was the popular calendar system in the legal industry; the company later developed its own software. However, with today's technology, there are many different methods to maintain an efficient calendar, ticklers, and reminder system.

  Many smalller firms find that Microsoft Outlook® works well as an electronic and paper calendar/reminder/tickler system. In the calendar mode, you and schedule appointments, court dates, assignments, and other important events. These events will appear on your attorney's and the firm's main calendar if the firm's computers are networked (linked to a server on a special in-house network, called and "Intranet"). In addition, Outlook serves as a reminder system that will pop up to remind you of the scheduled event, according to the time you set for your reminders—e.g., one week before the event, two days, or a certain number of hours or minutes before. You can print out the calendar in advance by the month, week, or day for you and your attorney's convenience. At the end of the day, make sure all of your paper appointments have made it to the electronic calendar. Take a copy with you everywhere you go, including home.

For firms that want to give their on-the-go paralegal professionals a mobile system to access information unique to the legal industry, then a BlackBerry device or Palm Pilot [also known as a Personal Digital Assistance (PDA)], is useful. A PDA gives paralegals the tools needed to stay connected and make the most out of their day. In addition, your PDA syncs with your computer and after a full day's work, you may download notes and information directly to your hard drive.

■ *Put things in perspective.* Challenge yourself to see the big picture. Look beyond the paper in the file and do not concentrate on the details. Creativity is the key to any good method of case management.

■ *Welcome a new attorney.* In your own personal way, you may want to welcome a new afforney by introducing yourself, and saying "It is my job to make you look good." Assist them in any way to make them feel confortable. Be their sounding board and only offer constructive criticism. Be kind and be available. This will make the attorneys trust you and will forge a strong working relationship. It helps to make you a better person too.

■ *Docketing.* Use a universal firm docketing system. You can calendar up to four date reminders of the same project. It is very useful; I use it for all the attorneys that I work for. Attorneys are visual, so for them to see it on paper is often the best method for reminders.

■ *Databases.* Typically, I use databases to store information. Large document projects go into a summary database, as well as an image database. I can look at the summary of the document and have a photo of it at the same time. The photo feature, which is different for all databases, has redaction tools, and other features needed for document productions. This is an extremely efficient way of managing (and eliminating) paper.

■ *Bookmark important information.* In New York State, we have several "rule books." We have the Civil Practice Law and Rules, the Federal Rules of Civil Procedure, and many more handbooks. When I research something, I typically flag that statute and label it so that it is easy access in the future. I use these books daily, and often I will check the same rule over again to make sure I am following proper procedure. It makes it easier and more efficient to have those pages flagged.

■ *Use spell-check.* Often it is a writer's best friend and yet so few people actually use it. Have a dictionary, thesaurus, and a grammar guide with you all the time. An excellent thesaurus is *The Synonym Finder* by J.I. Rodale (Warner Books, 1986).

■ *Anticipate discovery.* Try to anticipate what types of discovery you may be receiving. Do not wait for discovery demands to cross your desk. If it is possible, get to your client's office and review documents that may be related to your case. Claim those early, and if you deal with corporate clients, make sure your client has a preservation policy in place. Try to also anticipate if you are going to have a huge amount of discovery or very little. If you think you will have voluminous documents, it is best to find an efficient electronic way of managing the paper.

■ *Bates number all your documents.* The Bates numbering system is simply a mechanical stamp that numbers documents as you stamp them in consecutive order. This will help you know how to reference them. If both sides exchange documents, you need an identifier to indicate which documents came from your office. If the opposing counsel does not label their documents, then you should label them when you receive them. Those labels should be entirely different from the labels placed on the documents you provided to opposing counsel.

■ *Respect the clients' financial needs.* Think outside the box, but before you make any phone calls or set up assignments for any outside investigator, talk with your attorney about your ideas. Remember, the client is spending the money, not you.

■ *Make the client feel as though they are the only client you have.* Be courteous and polite. Do not get frustrated with clients. They want you to help them, and you have to convince them that you are doing everything you can to assist their needs.

■ *Use e-mail appropriately.* It is the communication superhighway, but it can also be dangerous because you cannot determine the tone of the person using the e-mail. Be certain to word your e-mails in a professional and informative tone. E-mail is also efficient because it is a quick way to send updates without interrupting an attorney. He can read it later. Memos and written updates to the attorneys you work for are very important. I try to update my attorneys as often as possible on the projects that I am working on for them. Then at least they are aware that they are on my radar.

FIGURE 5-1
JURY CHART

J5	J6	Alt.	
J1	J2	J3	J4

■ *Jury charts are important.* You should keep track of jurors' emotions and reactions to certain testimony. This will help the legal team determine which direction the jury may be going. One of the ways you can be helpful at trial is to record the various ways the jurors respond to certain witnesses' testimony, exhibits that are introduced into evidence, and the presentation of the lawyers. If you study their body language and facial expressions, you may be able to get a good idea of how they may vote on the verdict. You may make a chart illustrated above by adjusting the sizes of the columns:

■ *Know where everything is during trial.* Be prepared to hand your attorney a folder, exhibit, or whatever they need during the trial. If you are not needed at trial, then be sure that your attorneys can find everything easily and quickly so that they do not waste time fiddling around in court.

■ *Be creative.* It is what makes a paralegal good at his or her job. We have the ability to act independently and use independent judgment on so many occasions. Always find new ways to develop your skills and improve them.

TECHNOLOGY TECHNIQUES:

Databases are convenient for keeping track of large document cases. I can catalog all of my documents, make notes as to relevance of each one, and create privilege logs. I try to stay on the cutting edge by finding efficient ways to manage documents. Databases are a great way to facilitate this. It is important to do your research, get training courses, and stay current regarding changes in modern technology.

Explore all of your resources. There are many services out there, and you have to find the one that best suits your needs. Electronic research is efficient, faster, and more accurate than books.

REAL WORK EXAMPLES:

EXAMPLE 1: INTELLECTUAL PROPERTY LITIGATION—TRADE SECRET MISAPPROPRIATION/CRIMINAL CHARGES

Our Problem: Our client was a world-leading manufacturer of a product. One of the creators of the product was let go. Upon leaving, he took all of the specifications for that product with him and sold it to a major competitor overseas. Our client used a local company to assist in the manufacturing because this assisting company offered a unique product unavailable anywhere else. The competing company, decided to come to the United States to utilize this same service. The assisting company recognized the specifications to be that of our client and contacted our client immediately.

My Strategy for Solving our Problem: This case was extremely technical. Upon receiving the assignment, I did as much research as possible to familiarize myself with this product. I learned immediately that because this was such a major industry that this case would be highly confidential.

In addition, the party that was about to become the defendant in a highly publicized civil trial would be the subject of a major federal investigation. Because there was such a huge appearance of trade secret misappropriation, the Federal Bureau of Investigation (FBI) would be involved and likely press criminal charges on the former employee of our client. Because this case dealt with overseas defendants, I had to do research on the Hague Convention, and the Federal Rules of Civil Procedure (FRCP) statute that governs filing and service on foreign defendants. This procedure complicates matters. Not only does it require translating documents to the appropriate language, but also it required a special standard of service, a "central authority," or liaison, that assists in serving foreign and overseas corporations.

This case had a tight filing deadline and required highly specialized procedures. It would not only be filed in the Western District of New York, but also it would be filed under seal to protect it's confidentiality of scientific information provided within the complaint. A protective order and grant would be needed by the assigned judge. It also required a preliminary injunction and temporary restraining order to halt any future production by the alleged guilty parties. The preliminary injunction would advance the case immediately to discovery so that collection of documents, information gathering, and depositions could take place.

In addition, the documents would need translation, and then they must be served upon the overseas defendants. After documents were filed, translated, and served, the case began. With very technical and highly confidential information in my hands, I had zero margin for error. It was very important that I track every document that came in and out of our office.

I had two separate databases and hard files of client documents. One database contained pristine, clean documents and the other, redacted filed documents. Because information was confidential, the parties could not exchange any drawings or specifications between each other without a confidentiality agreement and protective order in place. Although all matters filed in the courts are public, this highly confidential case was not. Only the parties and the judge would receive unmarked, unredacted documents. This was an agreement that both sides entered into to preserve our respective trade secrets.

What I Learned: While this case ended up settling almost three years after it begin, I learned a lot from it because it was like nothing I have ever done before. I was able to expand my knowledge and resources, through research and the challenge of something new. I became familiar with foreign laws and gained a bit of scientific knowledge due to the extensive information involved.

EXAMPLE 2: CONTRACT LITIGATION SET FOR ARBITRATION

Another case was more recent. It was a contract litigation set for arbitration right around December 2005. Arbitrations are similar to trials, except that the American Arbitration Association (AAA) governs them. An independent panel of arbitrators is hand picked by the AAA to preside over the trial or arbitration. Unfortunately, this case was handed off from attorney to attorney until it landed with my team. By the time it reached us, however, it had virtually no paralegal supervision.

My Strategy for Solving our Problem: We had to prepare for arbitration. In litigation time, that is about two days. Discovery was not complete without any depositions taken. Because neither party was anxious to move this along and was willing to just let it sit as long as possible, due to the possibility of bad publicity on all parts, the AAA had to be the one to force both hands and get the ball rolling.

This matter was a contract negotiation gone bad. It involved a major corporation and the negative public relations did not help our client. However, this was exciting because it gave me a chance to work in a different area of litigation. My role was to be the case manager. I had to get us ready for trial quickly and efficiently. I spent many long days and nights at the office, preparing the case under tight deadlines. As depositions were completed and expedited transcripts arrived, they needed to be summarized. It took many people to complete 30 transcripts at about 200 pages each. In addition, we needed to prepare witness binders, review documents, and prepare them as exhibits. A vendor had to be located that could be on call for copying, printing, preparing exhibits, and so forth.

I had to determine what supplies were necessary so we could work in the evenings in our hotel rooms. We were feverishly working around the clock to prepare. Four lawyers and I spent countless hours preparing for this arbitration. We were forced to push other assignments aside. We sent other requests for work elsewhere. To make matters worse, it was the holidays. Because it was out of town, we needed computer equipment, portable printers, wireless Internet access—all those luxuries you have in the office, or at least locally if your case is at trial in your own hometown.

Clearly, I could not afford to sweat the small stuff. The paralegals and the attorney were under tremendous stress. If anyone unleashed some of their frustration, it was going to come down on me, not because it was my fault, but because I was the case manager—the most accessible.

What I Learned: As a case manager, I had to take care of my people. I took great pride in getting this case ready and being the one, they all came to when they needed something. I knew this file inside and out. I made myself indispensable. A smart paralegal always does.

A conscientious paralegal always understands that the entire team is under significant pressure from their clients. Things will go wrong and you have to expect it. However, this case too settled one week before we were set to leave for New York City.

Just know that if the attorneys get angry, it is not personal. Paralegals must adhere to the same standards as attorneys, and you have to take a certain amount of responsibility for getting the job done.

ETHICS CAVEAT:

I am happy that Susan made this important point. If a paralegal does not act competently and ethically, the client suffers just the same as if a lawyer made the error. The lawyer will be sanctioned as though the lawyer had made the error.

Therese A. Cannon, Attorney at Law and author of *Ethics and Professional Responsibility for Legal Assistants*

Part II

∎

INTELLECTUAL PROPERTY

CHAPTER 6

D. GRACE CARTER, CP

Intellectual Property Litigation Paralegal
North Carolina Certified Paralegal and NALA Certified Paralegal
SYNGENTA BIOTECHNOLOGY, INC.
Research Triangle Park, NC

EDUCATION/HONORS/CERTIFICATIONS:

- B.S., Florida State University, Tallahassee, Florida, 1986
- Adjunct Instructor, Meredith College Paralegal Program, Raleigh, NC (course planner and speaker on topics ranging from professionalism to general litigation and electronic legal research)

PROFESSIONAL ASSOCIATIONS:

- Certified Legal Assistant, National Association of Legal Assistants
- Chair, North Carolina Bar Association Legal Assistants Division, 2003–2004
- Board Member, Board of Paralegal Regulation, North Carolina State Bar
- Parliamentarian, North Carolina Paralegal Association, 2004–2005
- *Pro Bono* Co-Chair, North Carolina Paralegal Association
- Vice Chair, North Carolina Bar Association Legal Assistants Division, 2002–2003
- Council Member, North Carolina Bar Association Legal Assistants Division, 1998–2001
- Chair, *Pro Bono* Committee, North Carolina Bar Association Legal Assistants Division, 2004–2005
- Co-Chair, CLE Committee, North Carolina Bar Association, Legal Assistants Division
- LAD Section, Liaison to the Intellectual Property Section of the North Carolina Bar Association
- LAD Delegate to the Alliance for Paralegal Professional Standards, North Carolina Bar Association

COMPANY-AT-A-GLANCE:

Syngenta Biotechnology, Inc.
Research Triangle Park, NC
Phone: 919.765.5200
Fax: 919.765.5132
Web Site: www.syngenta.com

Syngenta is a world-leading agribusiness committed to sustainable agriculture through innovative research and technology. The company is a leader in crop protection and ranks third in the high-value commercial seeds market. Syngenta employs some 20,000 people in over 90 countries.

GENERAL COUNSEL:

Christopher Mäder, Head of Legal, and Taxes

OVERVIEW OF JOB RESPONSIBILITIES:

CIVIL LITIGATION

I. General Duties

   A. Ability to review and understand current state and federal court rules

   B. Maintain forms and checklists

   C. Review articles relevant to current cases and circulate to staff and attorneys

   D. Review docket with attorneys and assist in preparing for meetings, hearings, depositions, and trials

   E. Review and verify information provided by client and opposing counsel

   F. Conduct case law research and research relating to corporate, experts, and other entities (electronic and traditional)

II. Case Initiation and Discovery Duties

   A. Draft summons and cover sheet; arrange for service of process.

   B. Coordinate with client, and opposing parties, the review of client files; organize and summarize materials collected

   C. Obtain public records

   D. Conduct research on the location and retention of expert witnesses

   E. Review and summarize documents and physical evidence

   F. Summarize factual information

   G. Review deposition testimony, documents, and other factual records and prepare chronology of same

H. Correspond with client and with in-house, outside, or common counsel as directed

I. Review PACER and other public databases for hearing notices and/or proceedings

J. Monitor case assignments for project assistants and other legal staff

K. Review and obtain relevant client documents; facilitate and assist attorney review of documents to determine what should be produced. Maintain schedule of document productions and materials received by client and opposing party.

L. Coordinate coding of case documents and assist in the development of document databases

M. Assist attorney in review of opposing party's production of documents. Index, analyze, and summarize documents produced by parties.

N. Review responses to discovery requests, track outstanding discovery requests by opposing party and update discovery responses as information is obtained.

ETHICS CAVEAT:

One of the important ethics rules you need to know for document productions is what to do if a privileged document is inadvertently produced to you. You should stop reading it as soon as you realize that it is privileged and give it to the supervising attorney. He should alert the opposing counsel, who will want it returned.

Therese A. Cannon, Attorney at Law and author of *Ethics and Professional Responsibility for Legal Assistants*

III. Depositions

A. Coordinate and calendar depositions with client, attorneys, and opposing counsel

B. Draft notice of deposition and subpoena; and request court subpoena for out-of-state depositions

C. Gather and organize exhibits for deposition

D. Contact reporting service and videographer as necessary

E. Attend and assist attorney during deposition

F. Index and summarize deposition exhibits

G. Perform research on witness or expert; obtaining copies of prior testimony and publications

---

ETHICS CAVEAT:

One ethics controversy is whether paralegals can attend depositions without the lawyer present to observe. Paralegals should, of course, not attend with a client whose deposition is being taken without the lawyer present, but may, with agreement of opposing counsel, attend to observe when someone other than the client is being deposed.

Therese A. Cannon, Attorney at Law and author of *Ethics and Professional Responsibility for Legal Assistants*

IV. Briefing

   A. Assist in preparing motions

   B. Research procedural requirements and case law

   C. Assist in preparing discovery, pretrial, and trial motions or responses to same

   D. Draft affidavits and assemble exhibits in support of briefs

   E. Confer with court and opposing counsel regarding hearing dates, filings, and so forth.

ETHICS CAVEAT:

When communicating with opposing counsel and the courts, be sure to identify yourself as the paralegal so that you are not mistaken for a lawyer.

Therese A. Cannon, Attorney at Law and author of *Ethics and Professional Responsibility for Legal Assistants*

   F. Review briefs for accuracy

   G. Sheppardize case law to ensure citations are valid

   H. Proofread filings

V. Trial

   A. Draft pretrial statement and gather accompanying materials

   B. Attend pretrial conference

   C. Prepare trial notebooks (primary documents and witness materials)

   D. Work with experts, consultants, and witnesses and assist in preparing them for trial

E. Coordinate with vendors to arrange for courtroom technical equipment, space, and other requirements. Set up "trial office" if venue is outside home city/state.

F. Coordinate witnesses' attendance at trial and draft subpoenas

G. Review and identify potential exhibits with attorney

H. Organize, mark, and index trial exhibits

I. Consult with attorney and vendor regarding the design and preparation of demonstrative exhibits for use at trial

J. Coordinate exchange of trial exhibits with attorneys and opposing counsel

K. Manage physical and demonstrative exhibits during trial

L. Attend jury selection and summarize information

M. Prepare chart of information gathered during jury selection process for each juror

N. Attend and assist attorney at trial

ETHICS CAVEAT:

Again, be sure to identify yourself as a paralegal when you accompany the lawyer to court.

Therese A. Cannon, Attorney at Law and author of *Ethics and Professional Responsibility for Legal Assistants*

O. Maintain list of exhibits (identified, offered, admitted, or objected to)

P. Compile and coordinate daily transcripts from trial proceedings

Q. Order, index, and summarize transcripts

VI. Post-Trial

A. Assist attorney in drafting post-trial motions and notice of appeal (if appropriate)

B. Prepare draft of bill of costs

VII. Corporate Records Manager Duties

A. Ensure for the implementation of, and compliance with, the Record Retention Policy and Procedures throughout the company.

B. Provide procedures and/or guidelines for the program that includes, but is not limited to, vital records, in-active records, litigation management, retention schedules, record compliance audits, laboratory notebooks, and so forth.

C. Provide instruction/training on all elements of the Syngenta Records Management Program.

D. Provide consultation and direction for records management practices, methods, and processes for managing records with the record coordinators, tax, legal, regulatory, and all functional areas.

E. Assist with the investigation of new technological solutions for records management compliance.

F. Support legal and regulatory agencies during litigation and governmental/regulatory audits/actions.

G. Monitor retention compliance on all media through regular clean-out activities and audits.

H. Assist with the suspension and reinstatement of retention schedules due to tax and legal holds.

I. Provide input into regulations and retention periods and apply to company records.

J. Ensure retention is met on electronic records by working with IT.

K. Ensure that all company records required for regulatory purposes and litigation are complete, well indexed, secured, and available to authorized persons as necessary.

L. Create, operate, and maintain the databases that support records management and Good Laboratory Practice (GLP) archives, which include laboratory notebooks, GLP and non-GLP studies, inactive records, and so on.

M. Manage laboratory notebooks sufficiently in order to provide safety, integrity, protection, and access.

N. Provide support and training as needed for all electronic document management systems. Support document collection for the archives and off-site record center.

TYPICAL WORKWEEK:

Like many patent litigation paralegals, I rarely have a typical workweek. Being in contact with my team (attorneys and staff) is always number one on my To-Do list each day. You never know what might have happened after you left the office last night or before you got in that morning. A review of the docket and a discussion of the week/ month's calendar is an important part of this conversation. If there are upcoming depositions, I call to reconfirm the court reporter and videographer. I never assume the reporter/videographer will show up and always reconfirm at least a day or two before. In addition to my personal docket, for any federal matters, I check PACER for new filings, as there are cases that I may not work on every day but want to keep up with what is going on. I always try to make my way through my e-mail and incoming mail. Making a decision whether to act, file, or trash items as quickly as possible is important. In addition, I always try to leave the office with all of my e-mail responded to and physical mail docketed (if necessary), filed, and distributed.

I am always overextended in discovery, and a review of ongoing projects with the IT department and/or third party vendor is always valuable. Another instance of never assuming everything is okay! A case meeting with everyone involved is the best way to communicate changes in the case and keep everyone on track. Of course, no morning is complete without a visit to the Internet. The USPTO Web site is invaluable and I check regularly for rule changes, training, and so forth.

Conferring with any local co-counsel is important and I regularly call or e-mail to make sure lines of communication remain open. This is also important for patent and technical experts; make sure they have everything they need for reports and depositions. Cataloging items sent to experts can be as easy as outlining the items in a cover letter. Drafting pleadings and responding to discovery requests is usually part of my daily routine. Reviewing and preparing documents for production takes up the bulk of the day, as I need upload each document to the database and code it.

Deposition preparation is probably the most stressful part of my job. Conducting searches on the litigation database to determine what documents should be reviewed is only scratching the surface of this task. I have to review pleadings, deposition transcripts, and physical exhibits. In addition, I will make sure multiple copies are available for review during the deposition and segregate the documents by witness. There is one task that is imminent—keep track of your time on each case that you work. Also remember to describe clearly, what you have done on the case—"Document review" is not an acceptable entry.

GENERAL ADVICE:

Communication and shared experience are two of the greatest gifts a paralegal can offer. Maintaining good communication is not always easy in a legal environment. Stress, intimidation, and job concerns can color your speech. Without revealing confidential client information, openly discussing and sharing information will benefit everyone, encourage more discussion, and ease the flow of established guidelines.

Sharing "war stories" with experienced and inexperienced paralegals allows everyone the benefit of learning from others' mistakes and feeling human. Often people look at experienced paralegals as near perfect in their work product. Not only is this almost impossible to live up to, but also, it places knowledgeable paralegals on an untouchable pedestal. Paralegals who connect with each other add value to the profession. Paralegals should not follow their protocol obsessively. When this happens, our attorneys and clients cannot receive the benefits of the discovery process. Surrendering our views and ideas to each other can provide something far better that what can be accomplished alone.

TIPS, SHORTCUTS, AND TRICKS OF THE TRADE:

Top 13 Ways To Enhance Your Professional Value

1. Remove obstacles—never let an outside influence interfere with your work. Those co-workers with a negative attitude will try to take you down with them. Keep your head high and your outlook positive.

2. Know in your heart that you can do the job ahead of you—you can figure out the details as you work with others to complete the task.

3. Always look for the best—everyone has strengths. Look for the strengths in others to complement your abilities and make your team strong.

4. Know your limitations and ask for assistance in areas that you are not familiar. Acknowledge your weaknesses and learn from others.

5. Demonstrate your willingness to do whatever it takes to complete the task.

6. Be responsible for your project. Although you may have to ask for help from others, be aware of their own schedules and keep up with their progress as well as yours. Be flexible!

7. If you make a mistake—admit responsibility for your actions and commit to fixing the problem. Do not drop the ball and then leave the game. You learn too much from your mistakes to abandon them.

8. Keep your home life at home and your work life at work. Communicate day-to-day stress involved with family members and ask them to respect your work time.

9. Along those same lines, communicate with co-workers the importance of having downtime away from the office and the effect it has on everyone's productivity.

10. Sometimes to lead you have to follow. Realize that someone else may have a better way to accomplish a goal.

11. Most important—even the most mundane of tasks is important. Everything you do makes an impact on a case.

12. Keep your own calendar that blends all of your responsibilities (home and work).

13. Set aside a time of day (I usually do this in the morning) to file, go through your Inbox, and so on. If you have an assigned time to do this, you will accomplish much more.

TECHNOLOGY TECHNIQUES

■ Keep up with the latest information on the Internet via blogs and e-mail news updates.

■ Know how to do more than the basics on Corel®, WordPerfect®, Microsoft Word®, Excel®, PowerPoint®, and Access™. Understand databases. Take a class, ask questions, and build your own. Soon you will find you are ready to tackle more practice-specific programs. Summation®, Lexis Nexis®, and Concordance™ are a few examples of litigation support databases.

■ Use the Internet to its fullest advantage.

SYSTEMATIC PROCEDURES

■ Utilize checklists—even routine tasks must never be taken for granted. Usually the tasks you do regularly are the easiest to make mistakes on.

- Understand what systems are in place at your firm/company and utilize them. Do not try to reinvent the wheel if you do not have to. If you know someone at your firm/company has knowledge in a certain area, pick their brain, and ask them how best to accomplish the project.

- Get training from your Westlaw® or LexisNexis representative. Utilize the 800 number on the back of your account info card. Do not be too proud to ask for help.

WRITING TIPS

1. Know your audience.

2. Write with clarity and show you have researched your topic.

3. Have someone read your work.

DISCOVERY SHORTCUTS

- Utilize production indices.

- Catalog everything.

- Introduce yourself to the opposing parties' paralegal.

- Scan production materials, and keep your originals safe and away from attorneys.

- Make sure everyone on your team understands procedures (whether you are in the office or not). Most mistakes happen when you have not communicated with your team how to handle incoming or outgoing production in your absence.

- Know your client, opposing counsel, and third parties. Familiarize yourself with all the details. Read the patent, contract, or other materials that form the basis for the litigation. In other words, try to know as much as your attorney (if not more).

DOCUMENT PREPARATION

- Find out where your documents came from and index them accordingly.

- Make sure you know what type of confidentiality is appropriate.

- Communicate with your attorney and review the discovery requests associated with the production.

- Review the documents with fresh eyes—looking for privileged or non-responsive materials.

> ### ETHICS CAVEAT:
>
> *This is critical as if you are not especially careful, you may be responsible for inadvertently producing a privileged document to the opposing counsel.*
>
> Therese A. Cannon, Attorney at Law and author of *Ethics and Professional Responsibility for Legal Assistants*

INVESTIGATIONS

Have a knowledgeable vendor you trust to assist you, but also investigate on your own. You need to know what may be available without cost to your client and utilize this information to inform your vendor.

CLIENT INTERACTIONS AND INTERVIEWING

- Keep interactions professional—never become too familiar with the client. Realize that revealing personal information to a client could cause them to question your competency or dedication to the litigation.
- Make sure you are always available to the client—take their phone calls (even when your attorney will not).
- Do not give them legal advice—remind them of your position.

OFFICE COMMUNICATIONS

- Try not to become involved in office politics—this will be difficult (and sometimes impossible).
- Do participate in office activities (whenever possible). Show you are a valuable member of the office and not a hermit.
- Keep your outlook positive! You will be surprised how negative people will avoid you if you are always putting a positive outlook on the job.

SOFTWARE HINTS

- Know your firm/company's policies on software purchases and/or downloads.

Trial Pointers

1) Look at trial as the reward for a long hard discovery process!

2) Get excited to go forward and participate as much as possible in the process.

3) Make sure you have got great contacts at the clerk's office—make friends, be the person they smile at when you walk in the door. However, be professional at all times.

4) Know your opposition and be prepared to watch those persons your attorneys cannot while they are presenting their argument(s) (i.e., counsel, jury, judge, judge's law clerk, and even the marshal, or other guards). Today, as we all have seen, anything can happen; courtrooms are becoming quite volatile.

REAL WORK EXAMPLES:

EXAMPLE 1: LITIGATION PRACTICE—A HOME AWAY FROM HOME

Our Problem: Building a Functional Satellite Office.

Working in patent litigation, it is rare to have a case in your own backyard. Sometimes this is a blessing (no family to worry about) or a curse (you are worried about your family).

My Strategy: In any case, the best way to handle a traveling trial office is to work very closely with your attorney and your client. Discuss with your attorney the particulars of a satellite office during trial and how much communication you should have with the client regarding logistics before the trial date. If you are instructed to work closely with the client, make sure the client is aware of the differences between the costs associated with hotel stays for three attorneys, two paralegals, and a word processor over an eight-week period versus the cost of possibly renting corporate apartments for the same amount of time. Give the client options, and let them feel a part of the process.

This advice comes from my experience in planning for a trial hundreds of miles away from North Carolina. We rented corporate apartments, leased temporary office space, and rented copy machines. I worked very closely with the client whose headquarters were located in the trial venue. After weeks of telephone calls and face-to-face meetings, vendors I confirmed, and had all contracts and billing sent to the corporate offices. The client felt this would give them control over expenses associated with setting up and maintaining a trial office.

The client went so far as to arrange for supplies from their corporate vendor, and their staff planned and executed the lunchtime meals.

A trucking company was contacted, and finally the day came when we loaded up the semi-tracker trailer with thousands of boxes, computers, laptops, and eight weeks of clothing for attorneys and staff, and various items for each person.

Once all of our materials were unloaded and arranged into a manageable chaos, the attorneys began their work, and the rest of us set up a network for the computers, printers, and various electronic devices. Over a weekend, we established our home base and were ready for trial.

EXAMPLE 2: LITIGATION PRACTICE—WHAT TO DO WHEN A CASE IS CONTINUED

Our Problem: Effectively shutting down and archiving documents from a satellite office.

My Strategy: Surprise, Surprise! Monday morning arrived and, during our first hearing, the Judge decides the trial would not go forward. This resulted in a mass exodus by the attorneys and most of the staff, leaving me to work with the client to shut down the office and work with the corporate apartment leasing office to cancel our short-term lease. It was painful, but without the client having been included on every contract negotiation, it would have been a disaster. We sent the documents back to our home office, placed into storage and carefully inventoried.

Like a phoenix rising from the ashes, the case finally went to trial almost 10 years later. We learned from our first experience and, again, included the client in all our research and negotiations. The litigation databases everyone had worked so hard on the first time around did not last, but the paper lived on. Alas, technology does have a shelf life! The trial went on for almost six weeks, and everything we learned from our first experience made our second that much easier.

ETHICS CAVEAT:

It is important to document your time daily as this paralegal does and to do it as accurately as possible.

Therese A. Cannon, Attorney at Law and author of *Ethics and Professional Responsibility for Legal Assistants*

CHAPTER 7

VICTORIALEI "NOHEA" NAKA'AHIKI, RP

Senior Paralegal, PACE Registered Paralegal
Intellectual Property Litigation, General Business Litigation
Commercial and Complex Litigation, Maritime/Admiralty Litigation
CARLSMITH BALL LLP
Kailua-Kona, HI

"The joy of working with Nohea was that every project was important to her, no matter how small or seemingly insignificant, and that the job could be handed to her with the confidence of knowing that when it came back, it would be exactly what was hoped for. If there is one person I have worked with that lives up to the saying, 'give a person a job and let them do it,' it is Nohea."

David Ledger, Partner
Carlsmith Ball LLP
Guam, U.S.A.

EDUCATION/HONORS/CERTIFICATIONS:

- *Legal Assistant Today* Paralegal of the Year, 2000
- Five Star Paralegal of the Year, 1999
- Certification of Recognition, Mayor of the City and County of Honolulu for being the first paralegal from Hawaii to be nationally recognized for paralegal achievements, 1999
- Career Achievement Award (presented by the Hawaii Paralegal Association), 1998
- President's Certificate of Recognition (presented by the Hawaii Paralegal Association), 1998
- Outstanding Professional Achievement Award (presented by the law firm of Carlsmith Ball, LLP), 1997
- Paralegal Advanced Competency Registered Paralegal (PACE Examination, National Federation of Paralegal Associations), 1997
- Paralegal of the Year (presented by the Hawaii Paralegal Association), 1996–1997
- First-year law student, Monterey College of Law (elected first-year Class Representative), 1993
- Associates of Science Paralegal Studies, University of Hawaii, Kapiolani Community College (ABA approved program), 1993
- Behavioral/Social Science, Brigham Young University, Hawaii, 1981–1984
- Diploma, ICS Legal Assistant Studies (distance learning), 1988

PROFESSIONAL ASSOCIATIONS:

- Hawaii Paralegal Association, 1989–present. I have served in many capacities over the years, including president, secondary representative, newsletter editor, and member of various association committees.
- Santa Clara County Paralegal Association, 2000–2007
- National Federation of Paralegal Associations, 1989–present. I have served in many capacities over the years including vice president/director of membership and international relations coordinator.
- National Association of Legal Assistants, 2000–present
- California Association of Paralegal Associations, 2000–2007
- Federal Bar Association
- Native Hawaiian Bar Association

- Brigham Young University, Hawaii Alumni Association, San Francisco Bay Area
- International Paralegal Management Association, 2007
- Campaign Manager for Local City Council Candidate (now Mayor), 2004–2007

SEMINARS AND PUBLICATIONS:

- Frequent Paralegal Seminar Lecturer/Panelist: Litigation, Discovery, Document Production and Organization, and Ethics.
- Co-Author: "Admiralty Law—the Law of the Sea: An Overview from 800 B.C. to 200 A.D." by Barbara Lawley and Victorialei "Nohea" Naka'ahiki, *The National Paralegal Reporter* 25, No. 6 (June/July 2001).

YEARS EXPERIENCE:

17

FIRM AT-A-GLANCE:

Carlsmith Ball LLP
Kailua-Kona, HI
Phone: 808.329.6464
Fax: 808.329.9450
Website: www.carlsmith.com

MANAGING PARTNER:

Robert D. Triantos

ATTORNEYS (PERMANENT):

5

PARALEGALS (PERMANENT):

1

FIRM PRACTICE AREAS:

- ■ Intellectual Property Litigation
- ■ General Business Litigation
- ■ Commercial and Complex Litigation
- ■ Maritime/Admiralty Litigation

OVERVIEW OF JOB RESPONSIBILITIES:

I. Case Management

A. Review and Analyze Complaint

1. Note factual and legal issues
2. Note patent, claim language, and related data
3. Begin inputting data into working issues chart for attorneys

B. Compile Cast of Characters

1. Identify client witnesses and custodians
2. Create and compile data on to witness directory
3. Identify opposing party custodians and witnesses and add information to witness directory
4. Identify third-party witnesses and add them to third-party list

C. Compile Timeline of Events

1. Review all relevant data, including initial pleadings, initial disclosures, and other materials to determine chain of events and begin to compile a timeline of events using Microsoft® Excel® or Word tables. (Note: I have used CaseMap™ in the past, which is an excellent tool for creating timelines. Other tools can be used to create timelines, so utilize what is available at your firm, what works best for you, or if you are aware of a tool that is out on the market that may benefit your firm and your client, set up a demonstration with the vendor.)
2. Compile relevant, supporting data corresponding with timeline of events

D. Compile Preservation/Legal Hold Notice Table

1. Obtain list of all client employees who will receive or have received preservation/legal hold notices
2. Compile preservation/legal hold notices tracking chart and keep updated, as legal hold notices are re-generated.

II. Document Management Organization

A. Create and Compile Case Binder

1. Create a working case binder that will serve as a quick-reference guide for historical and current "key" information.
2. Ensure that all key documents are in the binder, which includes initial pleadings, discovery orders, stipulations, protective orders, discovery logs, witness logs, deposition and exhibit logs, key motions and orders, and other key documents.
3. Create subject binders as requested by attorneys. This may include separate prior art binders for each category of document, expert binders for each expert, or separate files for cited references and prosecution files.

B. Organize, Identify, and Segregate Relevant Client Documents

1. Track and log all documents collected from client
2. Segregate by custodian, noting details of the documents received
3. Scan the documents for electronic database, load files on to a designated server, separated by custodian and date of collection
4. Return original documents to client
5. Keep a working set (whether in hard-copy form or electronically)

C. Compile, Organize, and Identify Patents at Issue and Related Materials

1. Retrieve all patents at issue
2. Convert patents into PDF format and load into prior art database
3. Order file wrappers and prosecution history
4. Create index and organize patent and prosecution history as requested by attorney (binder, velobound, or converted to PDF and loaded into a database)
5. Compile cited references and prior art and convert to PDF and load into prior art database
6. Ensure that data entry reflects accurate information for all prior art materials to include title, date of publication, authors, Bates or control numbers, and any important notations by attorneys, such as importance of any given cited reference

III. Factual Research and Investigation

A. Internet Research

1. Conduct research via the Internet using various search engines to track down information on experts, opposing counsel, publications, articles, and other information as requested by attorney (i.e., conduct Google searches, peruse Web sites of opposing counsel, expert Web sites, library archives, government Web sites, and so on).

B. PACER, Court Web sites, USPTO (United States Patent and Trademark Office), SEC (Securities Exchange Commission through EDGAR)

1. Use PACER to retrieve federal court dockets, linked case documents, and filings

2. Conduct search on individual state court Web sites to retrieve state court dockets, linked case documents, and filings

3. Go to USPTO Web site to obtain information on patents, patent applications, patent assignments, and related information

4. Use EDGAR (Electronic Data Gathering, Analysis, and Retrieval System) to obtain information relating to SEC filings

5. Go to Secretary of State Web sites (e.g., California Secretary of State, California Business Portal) to obtain corporate and related information on businesses

6. Go to eHawaii.gov (website of Hawaii Department of Commerce and Consumer Affairs) to obtain corporate and related information on businesses

C. Westlaw®, Delphion™, and MicroPatent®

1. Use Delphion to retrieve, download, and save certain patents and patent applications in PDF format

2. Use MicroPatent to retrieve and download certain patents

D. CiteSeer™ and Other Publication Sources

1. Conduct on-line research via CiteSeer (Scientific Literature Digital Library) for full-text or abstract publications as noted in cited references and prior art

2. Conduct on-line research via IEEE Electronic Library™ (Institute of Electrical and Electronics Engineers) for full-text or

abstract publications, articles, or conference proceedings as noted in cited references

3. Search for and review conference proceedings as noted in cited references

IV. Discovery Management

A. Discovery Requests and Responses

1. Assist with drafting discovery requests and responses
2. Compile summary of discovery requests received from opposing counsel, noting the categories of documents being requested
3. Compile objection and response chart from discovery responses received from opposing counsel to determine patterns in objections and responses
4. Assist in compiling exhibits to responses to interrogatories

V. Document Collection, Tracking, Review, and Production

A. Collection

1. Schedule date and time to interview client custodians and collect documents
2. Prepare outline of collection interview questions (See Figure 7-1.)
3. Prepare outline of collection categories
4. Draft collection procedures memo to client employees (outlining how the collection interview and collection process will work)
5. Draft internal collection procedures memo for collection team (outlining how the collection process will work with segregation of documents and files, use of collection source sheets, marking of banker boxes, processing of documents, vendor pickup, and so on)
6. Compile final collection interview schedule and provide to attorneys (See Figure 7-2.)
7. Prepare collection supply box to ensure all collection supplies are available (include external hard drives, collection tracking sheets, collection source sheets, Redweld expanding files, rubber bands, paper clips, extra banker boxes, and so on).
8. Segregate and organize all documents collected by custodian, ensuring that tracking sheets are used.
9. Prepare original documents and e-data for processing by vendor.

10. Quality-check all documents returned by vendor to ensure completeness of documents

11. Draft collection return letter to custodian and return all original materials collected to custodian

Fig. 7-1— Document Collection Interview Outline

Case Name

Client/Matter No.

DOCUMENT COLLECTION INTERVIEW OUTLINE

Month, Year

- Confidentiality/Attorney-Client Privilege
- Overview/update regarding litigation
- Employee's background
- Positions, responsibilities, supervisor/direct reports
- Former position
- Current position

OVERVIEW OF DOCUMENT COLLECTION PROCESS

WHAT?

Collect every potentially relevant document from client and client (s) employees and independent contractors involved in the matter.

HOW?

Walk through collection memo; employee indentifies, collects, and provides appropriate documents for copying. The attorney will review all documents and determine what is relevant and what must be produced.

WHEN?

Conduct a timely detailed dicussion of potentially relevant documents.

WHERE?

Where do you keep documents now? (onsite/offsite files, server space, local machines, hard drives, laptops, backup drives, storage data equipment, home, other offices, or storage facilities.)

OTHER ISSUES:

(List other case specific issues, questions, and categories here.)

FIGURE 7-2
SAMPLE INTERVIEW SCHEDULE
XXXX-YYYY
SAMPLE INTERVIEW SCHEDULE
2007

	MONDAY 10/20/2007 SINGAPORE—ABC CONFERENCE ROOM		TUESDAY 10/21/2007 SINGAPORE—ABC CONFERENCE ROOM		WEDNESDAY 10/22/2007 SINGAPORE—ABC CONFERENCE ROOM
9:00-10:00 am	Legal Team Presentation	9:00-10:00 am		9:00-10:00 am	
10:00-11:00 am		10:00-11:00 am		10:00-11:00 am	
11:00-12:00 pm		11:00-12:00 pm		11:00-12:00 pm	
12:00-1:00 pm		12:00-1:00 pm		12:00-1:00 pm	
1:00-2:00 pm		1:00-2:00 pm		1:00-5:00 pm	Coordinate visit to warehouse to identify and retrieve documents.
2:00-3:00 pm		2:00-3:00 pm			
3:00-4:00 pm		3:00-4:00 pm			
4:00-5:00 pm		3:00-5:00 pm			

	THURSDAY 10/23/2007	FRIDAY 10/24/2007	SATURDAY 10/25/2007
9:00-10:00 am	SINGAPORE—ABC CONFERENCE ROOM	SINGAPORE	Singapore Admin. Contact Jane Doe, Division, Phone # /Ext.
10:00-11:00 am			
11:00-12:00 pm		TRAVEL DAY—LEAVE FOR TOKYO, JAPAN	
12:00-1:00 pm			
1:00-2:00 pm			
2:00-3:00 pm			
3:00-4:00 pm			
4:00-5:00 pm			

B. Tracking

1. Assemble custodian list by location and volume of e-data
2. Order detailed collection log of all documents (hard-copy and electronic data) collected
3. Prepare Collection Progress Tracking Table/Chart
4. Compile transmission log to vendors to track all documents sent for processing into review or production database
5. Load copy of e-data on designated server in file with subfolders for each custodian
6. File and store custodian data contained on CDs or external hard drives, making sure to label them properly

ETHICS CAVEAT:

In the kind of work that Nohea is doing, one of the most important tasks of the paralegal is to ensure that privileged documents are handled carefully and that no documents are inadvertently released to other parties involved in a matter. Note how she identifies and segregates the privileged documents. This advice is so important to the paralegal's ethical duty to perform competently.

Therese A. Cannon, Attorney at Law and author of *Ethics and Professional Responsibility for Legal Assistants*

C. Review

1. Review all documents for responsiveness, non-responsiveness, and privileged documents
2. Cull out and segregate documents into categories identified above
3. Second review to be conducted by attorney to confirm responsiveness, non-responsiveness, and privileged status
4. Compile responsive/production log
5. Compile non-responsive and privilege log
6. Compile redaction log

D. Production

1. Prepare all responsive documents for production (either on hard copy or electronically).
2. Brand production documents (Bates numbers).
3. Review final production set (quality-check) to ensure documents are all responsive and set for production.

4. Attorney review of final production set (double-check) to ensure documents are set for production.

ETHICS CAVEAT:

A lawyer should oversee the document production process to ensure that privileged documents are not inadvertently revealed. If they are, a court may decide that the privilege is waived.

Therese A. Cannon, Attorney at Law and author of *Ethics and Professional Responsibility for Legal Assistants*

---

5. If documents are being produced electronically, triple-check by checking the data contained on the CD, ensuring that the data is accessible and branded correctly; ensure that the CD label correctly identifies the documents contained on the CD.
6. Identify and log documents produced by opposing counsel.
7. Review and analyze documents produced by opposing counsel (search for "Hot Docs").
8. Note any discrepancies in production set from opposing counsel; inform attorney and follow up as instructed (advising opposing counsel of discrepancy or missing production data).

E. Post-Production

1. If this is a rolling production, keep track of productions by noting date of production, data produced, how produced (CD and label), amount produced (Bates range), and so on.
2. Follow Up.

VI. Deposition Preparation and Support

A. Coordinate Deposition Preparation Meetings with Client

1. Coordinate deposition preparation meeting logistics with client witnesses and attorneys; obtain availability of client witnesses.
2. Create and compile deposition preparation meeting schedule, noting dates, times, and locations of meeting proposals.
3. Prepare and compile deposition preparation binders to include key witness documents for review by attorney and witvness during preparation meeting.
4. Advise witnesses on materials to bring to deposition preparation meeting.

> ### ETHICS CAVEAT
>
> *Preparing witnesses for depositions is an important paralegal function. Paralegals must be careful not to advise witnesses how to testify.*
>
> Therese A. Cannon, Attorney at Law and author of *Ethics and Professional Responsibility for Legal Assistants*

5. When preparing for offensive depositions (depositions taken by your attorney), identify, compile, log, and organize potential deposition exhibits; prepare final deposition exhibit folders/sets to be used at any such deposition (remembering to make a set for the witness, the court reporter, opposing counsel, your attorney); prepare name list for the court reporter and coordinate with reporter regarding preferred format for receiving deposition transcripts and electronic rough drafts/final transcripts, as well as any requests by your attorney for a live-feed (e.g., LiveNote).

B. Coordinate Deposition Schedule with Client and Opposing Counsel

1. Coordinate deposition schedule logistics with client, client witnesses, attorneys, and opposing counsel
2. Create and compile deposition calendar and provide to attorneys and client deponents

C. Tracking Deposition Transcripts and Exhibits

1. Upon receipt of deposition transcripts, log the transcripts and all exhibits on deposition transcript tracking chart
2. Organize deposition transcripts in deposition files segregated by deponent
3. Load deposition transcripts into firm's preferred electronic format (e.g., LiveNote, Summation, or similar)
4. Provide copy of deposition transcript, signature, and correction pages to client witness with instructions to review, correct, and sign and return relevant pages
5. Return relevant pages to court reporter
6. Prepare deposition summary or coordinate outsourcing deposition summary with outside vendor such as Concise Deposition Summary Service

VII. Third-Party Subpoenas
   A. Receipt of *Subpoena Duces Tecum*
     1. Review *subpoena duces tecum*
     2. Note details of subpoena on subpoena tracking chart
     3. Meet with attorney to discuss scope of subpoena and follow up
     4. Draft written responses and objections
   B. Collecting and Identifying Responsive Documents
     1. Identify and collect responsive documents
     2. Log all documents collected, noting responsiveness, non-responsiveness, proprietary designations, and privileged communications
     3. Segregate documents according to responsive categories
   C. Privilege Log
     1. Identify and log all privileged documents
     2. Keep privilege documents together with privilege log, but separate and keep apart from responsive documents to eliminate any commingling of documents (or mix-ups)

ETHICS CAVEAT:

See comments one and two regarding the privilege. A critical paralegal task in litigation is to protect the privileges, which requires paralegals to have a keen awareness of the kinds of documents that might be privileged.

Therese A. Cannon, Attorney at Law and author of *Ethics and Professional Responsibility for Legal Assistants*

VIII. Trial, Mediation, and Arbitration—Preparation and Support
   A. Preparation and Support
     1. Assist in compiling trial, mediation, or arbitration binders
     2. Assist with drafting or preparing pretrial or settlement conference statements
     3. Organize, log, and mark trial exhibits (to include demonstratives)
     4. Coordinate courtroom logistics with courtroom clerks, IT support staff, and other support staff regarding the transport and storage of banker boxes in the courtroom, use of demonstrative

evidence, laser pens, judges' preference in exhibit binders, designation of depositions (e.g., highlighting, flagging, and so on)
5. Compile trial supply box
6. Coordinate arrangements with vendors regarding use of electronic equipment in the courtroom (to include trial presenter and trial graphics vendor)
7. Coordinate the attendance of witnesses and experts
8. Prepare and serve trial subpoenas
9. Assist attorney with witness preparation work (this includes participating in witness prep meetings with your attorney and client witness, helping the attorney identify, compile, organize, and log all exhibits identified in his/her examination brief and organizing them in the proper order for presentation, and making sure that the trial presenter has the latest order of exhibits before each examination)
10. Provide overall trial support as needed (to include taking notes during trial, tracking exhibits admitted and marked into evidence, tracking objections, keeping time of witness examinations, pulling exhibits for your attorney(s), and so forth)

ETHICS CAVEAT:

Many lawyers have paralegals present at trial so that they can take notes, find exhibits, and handle last-minute matters as they arise. Lawyers should introduce paralegals to the court and opposing counsel so that everyone knows who is a lawyer and who is a paralegal.

Therese A. Cannon, Attorney at Law and author of *Ethics and Professional Responsibility for Legal Assistants*

IX. Case Closure—Storage and Disposal of Case DocumentsUpon receipt of final judgment or settlement documentation, and pursuant to retention policies, terms set forth in settlement agreements or protective orders; arrange for storage or disposal of case documents.

A. Advocating Adherence to California Business & Professions (B&P) Code, Section 6450

B. Keeping Attorneys Informed about California B&P Code, Section 6450

1. Remind attorneys about the provisions of B&P Section 6450 and MCLE requirements relating to MCLE
2. Request for in-house MCLE approved training

C. Keeping Paralegals Informed about California B&P Code, Section 6450

1. Upon permission from firm, paralegal manager, or managing partner, present training/presentation to paralegals regarding provisions of B&P Section 6450
2. Provide attorneys with materials relating to B&P Section 6450, including FAQs, copy of the code, and MCLE tracking forms
3. Serve as a source of information for paralegals with regard to questions they may have relating to B&P Section 6450, paralegal ethics, and professional responsibility (e.g., provide them with copy of B&P Section 6450, FAQs, and related materials, as well as materials from NALA and NFPA that relate to ethical considerations and professional responsibility).

TYPICAL WORKWEEK:

My work varies depending on the phase of a case (i.e., initial case investigation, discovery phase beginning with document planning, collection, review and production, responding to discovery requests, and depositions; motion filings, pretrial workup, trial, and post-trial). The sample week below is from a typical document collection and invalidity workups. Each attorney member is responsible for a specific area of a case: one will handle the collection, review, and production tasks; another will handle drafting discovery responses, objections and requests; another will handle the invalidity claims (reviewing and analyzing patents, claim language), and another will handle the damages aspect. I, of course, assist all attorney team members in all areas.

Typically, I begin each day by checking my voicemail and e-mail. I respond to urgent messages first, and then prioritize my work for the day. I meet with my assistant to determine the status on any pending projects, determine his workload, and reprioritize work assignments, if necessary.

I assist the attorneys with the patent review and an analysis, and then create a patent chart. I identify and retrieve prior art reference materials from the patent art database (LexisNexis® Concordance™ software) for the attorneys. **Prior art** is defined as being an "existing body of technological information against which an invention is judged to determine if it is patentable as being novel and unobvious. It must be early enough in time to be cited against the [patent] application" [*source:* "Understanding 'Patentese'—A Patent Glossary," by Arnold B. Silverman and George K. Stacey, *JOM* 48, no. 9 (1996)]. I search the Internet for prior art reference materials, and then I perform research using the United States Patent & Trademark office Web site and company Web sites for company "X" patents, patent applications, and patent assignments. I research through the company Web site for company "X" mergers and acquisitions, press releases, and other relevant data.

I revise and edit the witness directory. I update the custodian list and sort by location. Next, I update the collection progress table to reflect recently collected documents, and then I update the vendor transmission log to reflect a new batch of hard-copy documents and electronic media ready for pickup, scanning, and processing for the review database.

I update the detailed document collection log and work with in-house legal contact regarding scheduling custodian collection interviews. I prepare prior art materials for transmission to the vendor for scanning and processing for our prior art database. I prepare original hard-copy documents and electronic data collected from custodian for transmission to the vendor. I update the preservation memo/legal hold notice tracking chart. I compile latest collection data and provide it to the attorney for incorporation into the case dashboard. (A **dashboard** is a central document used to update the entire team on statistics and logistics relating to document collection and review and production efforts.)

I attend and participate in a weekly case/team meeting. I follow up on pending matters as a result of the meeting and delegate work to my assistant regarding the data entry of prior art references into the prior art database (Concordance). I delegate work to my assistant regarding conducting a quality-check/cross-check of prior art references received from co-party with our list of requested references to ensure we received everything we requested. I identify, log, and prepare one hundred prior art reference materials from the patent art database requested by the co-party for shipping. I also cross-check documents with a list provided by co-party (quality-check) to ensure all requested materials have been pulled, and I draft a letter to the counsel transmitting the documents.

Using Westlaw, LexisNexis, or Delphion I do a patent search to identify and retrieve patents requested by the attorney for review and analysis. I also add patent information from all patents retrieved into a patent analysis chart, and I update and organize patent binders with newly retrieved patents.

I accompany the attorney to the client's facility; assist with client interviews and collection of e-discovery media (via external hard drives) and hard copy documents. I then identify, log, segregate, and box all documents and media collected. I return to the office and draft a status memo to team recollection efforts, interviews, and documents collected. I draft a collection interview memo. (*Note: we prepare an introductory memo that we give to the custodians before our scheduled appointment and review again in detail with them during the interview meeting. The memo informs the custodian of the pending litigation, indicates the importance of collecting and producing documents [required in litigation, assists attorneys prepare case]. We then list all documents mentioned in the requests for production.*)

I update the collection progress table to reflect documents collected from custodians and update the document collection log with detailed descriptions of documents collected. I check data collected on all external hard drives; copy data over from external hard drives to the designated case server into proper categories, folders, and sub-folders (by custodian and collection date). I update the transmission log to the vendor, prepare all documents and media files, and segregate and identify all documents and media by the custodian for pick-up by the vendor for scanning and processing into our review database. I follow up with the vendor regarding return of original hard copy documents and ensure scanning process is complete. In other words, I ensure that all custodian original documents are turned over to us for scanning and that we receive the CD/volume containing the scanned images.

I participate in several teleconferences with the vendor regarding document coding the manual and e-data review database and instruct the vendor to load custodian data into a sample/test Concordance database with metadata, extracted text, and native file links. I follow up with in-house counsel regarding electronic media (CD) accessibility issues (encryption and password-protected problems). I meet with the client to discuss organizational chart issues. I attend a face-to-face meeting with the vendor regarding review and production databases and meet with the client regarding collection of financial documents. I draft a document return letter to the custodian, and then prepare the original documents for hand-delivery.

I perform a complete troubleshooting of certain electronic media collected from the custodians; load files into designated case server files, and prepare media for pick-up by the vendor. I handle the research for issued and pending U.S. patents and patent applications for company "Y," and then I compile search results into summary; draft research status memorandum; and provide these materials to the attorneys.

I conduct a federal docket search using Public Access to Court Electronic Records (PACER) for any infringement related cases of companies X, Y, and Z, then pull court dockets and relevant documents, including complaints, answers, cross-claims, and motions for summary judgment. After organizing search results and documents, I draft a status memorandum for my attorneys. Next, I conduct research regarding company Z third-party license agreements. When I complete my research and information collected from available public records relating to XXX from company Z and companies recently acquired by company Z, I prepare a status report of my findings for my attorneys.

TIPS, SHORTCUTS, AND TRICKS OF THE TRADE:

The following is a compilation I like to call "Sure Shot Tips for the Career Paralegal":

- *Never Assume.* Never assume that someone else has done what he or she was supposed to do when he or she was supposed to do it. In other words, confirm completion of tasks. When your case has a filing deadline, do not assume that your attorney has remembered it. Double-check the calendar, remind your attorney that a filing deadline is looming, and then ask if there is anything you can do to help meet the deadline.

- *Inquisitive Minds Want to Know: Ask.* When an attorney gives you an assignment, before you walk out of his or her office, ensure that you understand the scope of the assignment. Turn the instructions into a question format to make sure you understand them. Start out by saying, "Just to make sure I understand, you would like me to... [proceed with instructions]." When you delegate work out and the project comes back to you completed, verify that the project is in fact complete. Ask for systematic processes used to complete the project, ask whether the data has already been quality-checked for accuracy, and ask if all the proper references were utilized. Make it a habit to ask questions in all that you do to ensure completeness, accuracy, and to avoid additional time, effort, and expense in the end.

■ *The Organized Paralegal Is the Efficient Paralegal.* A paralegal must be organized in order to be efficient. One of the skills paralegals pride themselves in is the ability to organize case files and keep their attorneys organized. Using checklists, document logs, tracking charts, color-coded files, subject binders, and databases to organize case materials and documents are just a few tools one can use to sort through the data. However, the data must also be organized in a manner in which it can be quickly identified, accessed, and retrieved by the attorney. Whether you organize the data in manila folders, redwelds, binders, or in electronic databases, the key objective is to access the data quickly and efficiently.

When an attorney comes to you at 5:30 P.M. and asks you to locate a certain document and bring it over to him, if you have an organizational system in place, you will know exactly where the document should be located or housed, allowing for a quick retrieval and turn-around. If the document is in hard-copy form, housed in a binder or folder of some sort, then your organizational system should point you to it. If the document is in electronic format, housed in a database, again, your organizational system should point you to that document. Being organized helps you be efficient. It saves time and money, which in turns benefits the firm and the client.

■ *Document Management Will Save the Day.* Example: I keep tracking charts for everything. When there were staffing changes at our outside counsel's office, they were pretty embarrassed to tell us that they could not locate certain documents that we had collected and provided to them over the last six months of the case. I had kept a detailed log, indicating the date, location, custodian, a detailed description of the documents collected, and a detailed transmission log showing the date transmitted to our outside counsel, the attorney's name, and a brief description of documents transmitted that I had provided to counsel whenever transmitting documents to them. Therefore, I was able to ensure counsel of the documents they had in their files. By using my detailed collection log, they were able to sort through all their materials and re-create their files. I was later told by the outside counsel's lead attorney that I had "saved the day." Thus, keep track of your documents—it *will* save the day.

- *Embrace Technology; it is here to stay.* In today's litigation practice, the normal course of discovery includes requesting electronic data. Therefore, it is important during the collection phase to identify all electronic data housed by your client and client employees. A checklist now incorporates searches of, to name a few areas, personal computers, memory cards, network servers, external hard drives, CDs, and DVDs. Information technology people or employees familiar with a client's system are tapped for information to include electronic retention policies and archive files.

  When all data are collected, using databases to organize it (e.g., Summation, Concordance, Microsoft Access, and other electronic management systems) is crucial. More and more productions are being exchanged through CDs and DVDs, with confidentiality markings and Bates brandings imaged on the documents. We must embrace and keep up with technology if we wish to remain marketable in today's profession and if we wish to remain a valuable asset to our employer. Take a continuing education class in electronic discovery management, look into the various e-discovery management vendors out there and take them up on their free demo software. Read up on the changes in e-discovery and technology and tap into experienced paralegals to mentor you in this area.

ETHICS CAVEAT:

Be sure that documents that are given electronically to others are scrubbed of metadata, such as, previous versions and comments.

Therese A. Cannon, Attorney at Law and author of *Ethics and Professional Responsibility for Legal Assistants*

■ *Be Prepared for the Unexpected.* Be aware that unexpected situations are common in the legal field. If you are one-step ahead, you will never be completely caught off guard. Some examples of unexpected situations require that you be prepared for notice on Monday that you need to travel to another state on Tuesday to attend a last minute meeting with client representatives. (Note: *prepare your family ahead of time—let them know to expect last-minute travel notices or that you may have to work late in the coming week.*) Be prepared when your attorney tells you at 2:00 P.M. that you need to go over to the client's office now to pick up documents or to extract data onto an external hard drive. Be prepared at 4:00 P.M. to help on a fellow paralegal's case for a rush filing. The list goes on. Be prepared. (Note: *have extra hard drives, CDs, DVDs, and banker boxes on hand, just in case*).

■ *Never Give your Attorney Original Documents.* It is usually disastrous when you give an original document to an attorney. With all the documents and files they work on throughout the day—the originals are bound to get lost in the shuffle. Always keep the originals and give your attorney a copy of whatever he or she asks for. Keep a back up working copy for yourself in case they have dismantled the set you gave to them and tell you that they have scattered the documents about and cannot find a specific document or set of documents. Do not give in to their pleas for original documents or their promises that they will guard them with their life. You will sleep better at night knowing that the original documents are safely stored away, and that your attorney is shuffling through copies that, if lost, can be easily and quickly reproduced.

■ *And that is All I Have to Say About that…Speak Up…Voice your Opinions.* You are part of a team, and together work toward a common goal of successfully resolving a client's case. When you attend team meetings, speak up, and voice your opinion. If you have ideas about case management, organization, electronic databases, certain aspects of procedures and processes for a case, then speak up. Your attorneys will appreciate your input and may even consider implementation of your ideas. Your ideas will not be used if you do not speak up. If you have suggestions, offer them.

■ *Knowledge, Experience, and Skills Equal Power: Take Control of your Paralegal Career.* You are the master of your career. You decide where you want to go and how you are going to get there. If you want to develop a career as a paralegal and set yourself up for advancement, then you need to expand your knowledge, skills, and experience. Enroll in an ABA-approved paralegal program. If you already have a certificate or degree from a paralegal program, take continuing legal education courses in areas that interest you or in areas you wish to develop your skills in (e.g., electronic discovery).

Join a local, state, and/or national paralegal organization to expand your networking circle in order to receive the many benefits offered by associations, workshops, seminars, study groups, and interesting publications and reading materials, such as NALA's *Facts and Findings* or NFPA's *The National Paralegal Reporter*. Subscribe to professional magazines such as *Legal Assistant Today*. At the end of the day, you are ultimately responsible for your career. Take charge and make it happen.

■ *In the words of Yoda, the Great Jedi Master, "There is No Try, Only Do." Be Proactive.* Do not wait for the work to come to you or for the attorney to ask you to work on a certain project. Be assertive, observant, and proactive. When you see discovery requests come in, ask your attorney if you can take the first stab at drafting responses or better yet, go ahead and prepare a summary of the requests and circulate it to the team as a roadmap to responding to the requests; prepare an objection/response chart for your attorneys to work with.

If you observe madness and chaotic rushing going on in another case because of a last minute filing or production, approach the lead paralegal on the other case and ask what you can do to help. If you see secretaries and other support staff collating an inordinate amount of exhibits to a filing that has to get out the door, step in and help them. As you gain experience, you will learn to anticipate the needs and know what you can do before being asked to do it.

■ *Get your Hands Dirty: the Life of a Paralegal is not all Glamour.* If anyone has ever told you that the *only* responsibilities that fall under a paralegal job description are to conduct research, draft documents, meet with clients, and assist their attorneys at trial, they were clearly wrong. As paralegals, we work in the trenches (i.e., we work the entire case), doing whatever it takes to get the job done. For example, we will dress in grubbies, go to ware-houses, review, and collect thousands of documents that have been drenched in water that seeped through cracks in the roof of the building. We will pull out old, stinky, moldy files from boxes with bugs crawling about. We will cart boxes of docu-ments to and from collection sites, court hearings, and trials. In addition, we will get in there and stand at the copy machine all day long to help support staff collate pleadings and exhibits for a rush filing. We will accompany experts on site inspections and climb through attic spaces looking at drywall and construction defects; we will attend site inspections wearing hard hats and safety glasses on highway bridge construction defect cases. The list goes on—our job description is endless. The bottom line is this: we will do whatever is necessary to get the job done.

■ *Take Heed to the Three "Cs":*
    QC—Quality-Check
    DC—Double-Check
    TC—Triple-Check
Always check your work, the work of your assistants or sup-port staff, the work of the vendor, your attorney, or anyone else when it comes to documents that will be exchanged with other parties, filed in court, and sent to the client, third-parties, experts, witnesses, the judge, and others. Check data entry in databases, charts, logs and other document management tools; check for proper citations, grammar, and spelling.

    Moreover, when you are done checking these items, you should check again. Have someone double-check your work, or make sure you double-check the work of others. Then right before the documents go out and the labels have been prepared, check the contents of the box, package, envelope, or e-mail one last time before transmission.

ETHICS CAVEAT:

This advice is so important to the paralegal's ethical duty to perform competently.

Therese A. Cannon, Attorney at Law and author of *Ethics and Professional Responsibility for Legal Assistants*

■ *"Thank You" Goes a Long Way.* Everyone plays a role on a case. When there is a rush filing, attorneys, paralegals, support staff, copyroom support staff, and messengers are all involved. In addition, during all the madness, stressful and tension-filled moments, and running around, it is important to remember that the combined efforts of everyone involved resulted in a successful filing or one that just made it to the court's office with minutes to spare. Each person should be acknowledged for his or her assistance. Appreciation goes a long way, especially when future rush projects creep up and you and your attorney need the cooperation and support of all support staff once again.

When paralegals or support staff under your direction have gone the extra mile on a project, have worked long hours to complete a project, or have otherwise helped you or your team complete a project, thank them, tell them how much you appreciated their work and their assistance. Pick up lunch for them when they are working through their lunch hour on a project or grab them a cup of coffee. It does not matter how you express your appreciation, just as long as you remember to thank them.

■ *Be a Jedi Master…Serve as a Mentor.* Share your knowledge, your experience (trials and errors), and your insight with junior paralegals. By serving as a mentor, you play a significant role in the development of young rising paralegals—ensuring that our profession continues to strive for excellence. When you delegate work to a junior paralegal, be sure to take the time to explain how you want the project done and when you would like the project completed. Some junior paralegals are college graduates, with little hands-on experience, so it is important to take the time to explain systematic processes, the whys, and the hows. Review the completed project with the junior paralegal by offering praise and constructive criticism for future similar projects.

Develop process manuals or trial binders for junior paralegals to use as training guides in such areas as discovery. Provide in-house brown bag seminars or workshops on specific topics. Incorporate training sessions for all incoming junior paralegals to cover all the areas they will be expected to learn and job responsibilities they will be expected to perform. If you have time, serve as an instructor or team-teach a course in a local paralegal program. Be creative and choose your own method of serving as a mentor.

TIPS FOR PARALEGAL STUDENTS EMBARKING ON INTERNSHIPS

I also have a few tips for paralegal students embarking on internships with law firms. The following is a sample of the tips I provide to a paralegal student about to begin his or her internship with a major entertainment law firm:

1. *Do not be afraid to ask questions.*

   I know that sometimes we feel that if we ask questions, the attorney may feel we are incompetent, but realistically, it means is that you care enough to get the information straight the first time around so there is no mistake about what your assignment is.

   The worse thing you want to do is assume you know what is being asked of you, and then spend hours on a project only to find out that it really isn't what the attorney asked or intended you to do. So, ask questions, even if you have to repeat the question. For example, the attorney says, "Marge, I'd like to you put a timeline together in this case." (Ah...okay...a little ambiguous, there are many questions here.) My response would be something like, "Okay, will do. Would you like me to put a timeline together in this case based on the facts outlined in the complaint and the documents received? Is there something else I should refer to when compiling the timeline?" The key is to get the proper instructions for your project.

2. *Be Proactive.*

   Some law firms will put the interns to work; others may not. If you are not being utilized enough, ask if there is anything else you can do. Look at the daily calendar print out (most firms have these) and see what is coming down the pike. If you notice a hearing or arbitration on the calendar, ask if you can help with any preparation work in anticipation of that hearing or arbitration (i.e., putting hearing or arbitration binders together, marking exhibits, or logging documents).

3. *Learn the Trade/Specific Area of the Law.*

   Learn more about the specific industry or area of law you will be working in. Do your homework and read about entertainment law. The attorneys will be impressed with your drive to learn. If they see you are interested, they will be more apt to give you more work. Learn what it is your attorneys do as entertainment law attorneys, and learn how you can help them in this area. Visit the firm's library on your downtime and see what books they have on entertainment law. Check out the firm's trade magazines or journals relating to entertainment law. Observe what books are in your attorney's office so you know what they refer to, and check it out when you can. Learn as much as you can.

4. *Go the Extra Mile with Your Time.*

Be willing to put in the extra work, or put in the extra hours. Make sure that they know that you are flexible and can come in early or stay late if they need your help for a rush project (such as getting ready for a hearing or trial). Do not be a clock-watcher or worry if you haven't had time to take a break when you are supposed to or if you're not able to take your lunch on time. Do take a break, and do take your lunch, but don't worry about it if it doesn't happen when it is supposed to happen. There will be times when you are working on a filing deadline that will have you and the rest of the crew scrambling to get documents out the door.

REAL WORK WORLD EXAMPLES:

Example 1: Toxic Tort Multiple Party Case

Our Problem: Before the age of electronic discovery, one of my first document intensive cases involved over one hundred plaintiffs who claimed personal injury, property devaluation, and other claims against our corporate client due to geothermal emissions from a geothermal project in proximity to a residential area. The magnitude of this case involved the management and tracking of thousands of documents. Whenever there was a document production looming or documents received in response to a document request, boxes were lined outside my office. Because my office was located in a corner, with the door leading to the building's stairs and fire exit—I would often get in trouble for blocking the fire exit. Because the case involved many parties, experts, and claims, the need for document management was vital. The question then was, "How do we organize this stuff?"

My Strategy for Solving Our Problem: We handled the paper documents manually and we organized them by inserting them into binders that we indexed and tabbed by hand. We had extra shelves specifically built into my office for housing the current and often referred to case materials, which amounted to hundreds of files and binders. I also had large drawers and bookcases added to my office.

There were many categories of documents to organize, analyze, and summarize—all needing the right tracking and logging tools. We prepared and tracked medical summaries, deposition summaries, photographic journals, devaluation claims charts, and various document tracking charts for just about everything you could imagine. Although I was the lead paralegal on the case, I worked closely with Barbara Ritchey, a well-known, highly respected veteran paralegal who was not only my mentor, but also a close friend. She was freelancing at the time and helped us with this case on a part-time basis and offered valuable insight and maintained excellent document management tools that kept us organized and on top of current claims. She introduced me to the value of using Microsoft Excel spreadsheets for logging and identifying documents and for calculating damages (devaluation claims).

What I Learned: I learned the importance of diligence and organization. In addition, I learned the value of teamwork, persistence, and keeping track of what we had done so we could pick up where we left off the next day. I also learned that the tracking tools and system we set in place provided us with the ability to quickly identify, retrieve, and provide key documents to our attorneys. Keeping the case materials as organized as we did helped the attorneys remain focused on the issues of the case. The senior partner told me that the management of these documents was key to the success of our case, which settled favorably for all parties involved.

EXAMPLE 2: MARITIME CASE ENDING IN TRIAL

The Case: Another interesting case, with fewer documents than the one described earlier, was a maritime case that I worked on from its inception to its conclusion (trial). Although all the maritime cases I worked on were interesting, this one was special because of the various aspects of the case. The case involved numerous parties, including crewmembers, the captain's wife, the owner of the vessel, ship builders, ship repairers, and insurance companies. It was a case almost out of a suspense novel or movie. The fishing vessel had recently been repaired, set sail in the dead of night with a full crew, suffered a leak in the boiler room, and sank. Although the crewmembers were able to get off the vessel in time and ultimately saved, the captain was not so fortunate.

Our Problem: Whenever a case has multiple parties, document management is imperative. As the only paralegal working on the case, I needed to keep the attorney focused and organized.

My Strategy for Solving Our Problem: The case files were organized by party, with color-coding to identify the different categories of files or subject binders. We used tracking charts for depositions, witness files, medical files, medical summaries, third-party records obtained through subpoenas, research files, Coast Guard files, reports, records, and production logs.

I began compiling the trial binder, which I called my "case binder" at the onset of the case and constantly updated it with documents and information as the case progressed. As we got closer to trial, exhibit lists, designation of depositions, witness lists, and motions in limine[1] were easily incorporated into the trial binder. Exhibit and witness lists were easily converted to the court's trial forms because we had started compiling the data early on in the case via Word tables.

What I Learned: When trial was imminent, we were completely prepared and organized. The case was successfully tried. I felt satisfied to see how far we came in this case and to see how all of the case and document tools came together in the end for a smooth presentation of evidence.

EXAMPLE 3: PRODUCT LIABILITY—DEFECTIVE WATER HEATER

The Case: Unlike the other case mentioned above, this particular case was not a huge case, but it did involve an insurance company, a construction company, a water heater manufacturer, and a heating element manufacturer. The document management for the case of the defective water heater was similar to the other case. There were

---

[1] *Motion in limine:* (lim-in-nay) n. Latin for "threshold," a motion made at the start of a trial requesting that the judge rule that certain evidence may not be introduced in trial. This is most common in criminal trials where evidence is subject to constitutional limitations, such as statements made without the Miranda warnings (reading the suspect his/her rights).
See also: *in limine, Miranda, warning motion*

many parties and third-party records, expert files, blueprints, and related documents to organize.

Our Problem: Our problem was not in document organization or case management, but rather filling in for my attorney at a joint site inspection of the defective water heater with all parties and experts. The supervising attorney for this case was preparing for an upcoming arbitration in another matter and needed someone to fly to an outer-island to attend this site inspection, take photographs, notes, and pretty much be his eyes and ears during this meeting. The problem was, there were no attorneys available to assist him with this one-day outer-island site inspection.

MY STRATEGIES FOR DEALING WITH OUR PROBLEM: I volunteered for the assignment, convincing my attorney that I could provide him with support he needed for this particular project. He was more than happy to assign this project to me, and I was more than eager to show him I could represent him, the firm, and our client effectively, while being cost-efficient.

I caught the first flight out in the morning to the outer island, attended, and participated in the site inspection by doing all the tasks asked by my attorney, including taking photos at each stage of the heater's dismantling, taking notes, listening to the experts discuss their findings and theories, and taking more notes. Upon my return to work late that afternoon, I prepared a detailed and comprehensive status report for my attorney, attached my photos (this was before the age of digital cameras, but the 1-Hour Photo Labs worked just as good back in the day), and presented my report package to my attorney. He was so impressed by my work that he had me put a similar package together to send to our client. He also used these materials at follow-up meetings with the parties in this case.

What I Learned: Taking initiative and being proactive will provide you with opportunities to show your attorney what you are made of and convince him or her of the value you can bring not only to the firm, but also to the client. Your attitude, willingness, and professionalism will be appreciated, while you will feel a sense of pride for coming through for your attorney.

EXAMPLE 4: TRADEMARK INFRINGEMENT CASE

The Case: Another interesting case was a short-lived trademark infringement case. The work-up of the case was minimal as our role, initially, was to investigate the local counsel hired to look into possible infringement of a certain product being offered to consumers by a certain retailer. Initially, my job was to pose as a customer at this certain retail place, identify the infringed product, purchase a few samples, and return them to my attorney.

My Strategy for Solving Our Problem: It was actually an exciting assignment and out of the ordinary course of my paralegal duties. Therefore, one weekend my seven-year-old son and I took a trip to the retail establishment. I browsed around, looked at different products, and then located the alleged infringing product. I made the purchase, brought the samples back to the office, and prepared my accompanying report for my attorney.

What I Learned: The investigative work that I did, posing as a consumer, confirmed the infringement. With the findings, noted in my report to our attorney and our client, we were able to proceed with the case, seizing all infringing products, and settling the case in favor of our client.

COMMON CHALLENGE—INCREASED USE OF TECHNOLOGY

The common challenge in this area of law is the increased use of technology to manage documents and information, and to produce and make this information available through technology-based approaches. It is amazing how quickly electronic discovery and electronic management has emerged over the years. I share stories of how we "old-timers" used to manually stamp documents with the old Bates® machine and tell war stories about the days when we used to sit locked up in a conference room or "war room" with hundreds of banker boxes and documents segregated in piles (taken from those boxes) for review.

Today, Bates numbers are branded on documents electronically (even Avery labels are being outdated), and workrooms now consist of laptop computers with document reviewers who use an electronic system to review and categorize documents as responsive, non-responsive, and privileged. Today, instead of shipping boxes to the opposing party, we send CDs filled with our production documents. We label the CDs with the production range, production date, and other data. The data contained on the CDs have responsive documents that we brand with Bates numbers and confidential markings.

Today, law firms seek vendors that offer comprehensive technology and process solutions to include image capturing/scanning, digital production capabilities, computer forensics, database services, coding and indexing, e-discovery services, and web repository services. Because of all of the electronic discovery (e-discovery) needs and requirements, paralegals are now leading the way in choosing vendors that have the comprehensive technology and process solutions.

Paralegals are leading the way in training attorneys, other paralegals, and document reviewers on electronic systems for electronic document review and production processes. Paralegals who develop a niche in this area often see themselves expanding their role or specializing in the area of electronic discovery and may be charged with the sole responsibility of handling the entire firm's (working all cases) e-discovery needs. They will serve as the contact and negotiator with the vendors and will play a significant role in the design and structure of electronic databases and processes. These paralegals will implement e-discovery processes and procedures and train users. This is just one of the challenges facing paralegals in this area today. Challenges such as this will become exciting and fruitful new ventures.

CHAPTER 8

DEBORAH A. HAMPTON
Intellectual Property Manager
LIMITED BRANDS INC.
Columbus, OH

"Deborah's technical abilities, professionalism, and dedication, as well as her sense of humor, have made her a key player on our team. Beyond that, she tirelessly demonstrates her commitment by performing services that support the trademark community."

Carol M. Matorin
Senior Vice President, Senior Counsel
Limited Brands Inc.
New York, NY

EDUCATION/HONORS/CERTIFICATIONS:

- Bachelor of Arts, Political Science, University of Cincinnati, Cincinnati, OH, 1981
- Paralegal Certificate, Adelphia University Lawyer's Assistant Program, New York, NY, 1983

PROFESSIONAL ASSOCIATIONS:

- Board of Directors, International Trademark Association (INTA) 2007–2009
- Member, National Association of Legal Assistants
- Project Team member, INTA's In-House Counsel Forum, 2007
- President, National Federation of Paralegal Association's (NFPA) Foundation for the Advancement of the Paralegal Profession
- Co-Chair, INTA Trademark Administrators conference, 2004
- Speaker and Intellectual Property Track Team, National Association of Legal Assistants, 2003 convention
- Contributing author, "Electronic filing (E-filing)," NALA's *Facts & Findings,* November 2003.
- One of the first paralegals to serve on INTA Trademark Administrator's Committee created in the early 1990s to address the needs of nonlawyers.
- Participant, NFPA Writing Workshop, PACE exam revision 2001.
- Leader, Trademark Administration Group, INTA 2006 Annual Meeting Planning Committee.
- Project team member, INTA's Administrators Conference Planning Committee, 2002.
- Revision Committee for the trademark module for NALA's on-line campus.
- Contributing author, NALA's *Facts & Findings; Legal Assistant Today Magazine;* and INTA *Trademark Bulletin.*
- Co-Inventor, Cellular Device Data Transfer to Mobile Telephone Device (patent pending).

YEARS EXPERIENCE:

COMPANY AT-A-GLANCE:

Limited Brands Inc.
Columbus, OH 43062
Phone: 614.577.6948
Fax: 917.522.7158
Website: http://www.limitedbrands.com

CEO:

Les Wexner

GENERAL COUNSEL:

Doug L. Williams

ATTORNEYS (PERMANENT):

10

PARALEGALS (PERMANENT):

10

OVERVIEW OF JOB RESPONSIBILITIES:

I am currently an intellectual property (IP) manager for Limited Brands Inc., a corporation whose labels include the well-known Victoria's Secret®, The Limited®, and Henri Bendel®.

As a manager with expertise in managing all phases of prosecution, I assist counsel with domestic and international searching, clearing, prosecuting, maintaining, and enforcing our IP portfolio and conflict resolution. I am a subject matter expert with thorough knowledge of domestic and international statutes, policies, and practices required to successfully protect and maintain IP. In my previous position, I was responsible for managing a yearly trademark budget in excess of $100,000.

A trademark is a corporation's greatest asset. If maintained properly, it can last forever. Some of the most well-known trademarks are over 100 years old.

In the past I have been a member of a three-person team that consisted of Patent Attorney and Reverse Engineering with expertise in managing all phases of negotiating and collecting license royalties from third parties that infringe on company patents. My other responsibilities have included domain name registrations and maintaining domain name portfolios. I am responsible for the international trademark portfolio, managing worldwide trademark registration programs, and overseeing international opposition and cancellation proceedings.

In addition, I work with outside counsel to conduct internal educational seminars on the proper use of trademarks, copyrights, and trade-dress issues.

Working with in-house and outside counsel, I review various agreements, such as letters of consent, licenses, and coexistence agreements to protect the proprietary rights of the company and to comply with regulatory and statutory requirements. I also work with counsel to review intellectual property clauses of supply and distribution agreements to ensure they comply with licensing, regulatory, and contractual compliance issues. I work with the senior vice president and senior counsel to implement policy and procedures concerning enforcement and policing of trademarks, patents, copyrights, and trade dress.

My other duties include ensuring that proprietary rights are protected by monitoring media sources and materials. I review and approve marketing materials and other collateral for trademark accuracy and legal requirements.

IP paralegals typically work or specialize in one of three areas, patents, domestic, or international prosecution and maintenance. Rarely do they specialize in all three. However, it does happen. In my particular case, my specialty is the global protection and maintenance of trademarks. I do work on copyrights and patents, and, in my current position, I manage all three, but my first love is and always will be trademarks. The main function of a trademark paralegal is to work with business groups from the birth of a trademark to registration. As a trademark paralegal, you can specialize in domestic protection only or work on both domestic and international trademarks. Most specialize in global protection.

I have specialized in the global protection and maintenance of IP since I began my career. The main purpose of a trademark paralegal is to assist attorneys with the three main steps involved in allowing a business to use a trademark as a source identifier. Those steps involve the searching, clearance, and registration of trademarks. I am involved in all aspects of protecting IP and am involved from beginning to end. IP paralegals can also specialize and become an expert in any of these areas. This is often the case with companies with large portfolios. For example, the IP paralegal may be a prosecution expert, working on all aspects of prosecuting the application to registration.

I love what I do, and I would do it free. To be in this field, you have to love it. It is an extremely stressful occupation and the time constraints and demands of the client can be overwhelming. We serve two masters: the attorney and the client. Both can be demanding. If you love it, then it will be the tool that gets you through those days when it seems you can please no one. If you do not love it, eventually you will burn out. You have to love it!

TYPICAL WORKWEEK:

Like most paralegals in my field, there is no such thing as a typical workweek. I handle many files, and each file is in a different stage of work in progress. I may review a patent disclosure statement for catalog division and work with the outside counsel and the client to determine if preparations should begin for filing a patent application. Our interactions are different, depending upon where we are in the process.

For example, it may be determined that a letter of consent from a third party is needed to use and register the trademark. I would work with my attorney and outside counsel to secure the letter of consent.

For example, when I worked on the "Beauty Holiday" naming project for the beauty division I preliminarily screened 20 proposed trademarks and reported the results to the client. The client requested comprehensive searches for 15 of the proposed marks. I contacted outside counsel and requested that they order searches for the 15 marks. Once the comprehensive search results were completed and reviewed by counsel, the client selected a trademark from those successfully cleared, and then I filed an application with the USPTO. We file our trademark applications and renewals electronically with the USPTO.

I reviewed graphics for the fall sleepwear collection for the catalog division and met with clients to review the upcoming schedule for spring, summer, and fall rollouts of product lines for beauty and lingerie.

A big part of my regular responsibilities is conducting factual and Internet searches on potentially infringing trademarks. I send samples of potentially infringing packaging to the client for review to determine if the packaging is infringing our IP. After I finish my research, I discuss the information with my supervising attorney and a determination is made on whether to take further action or to close the file on the matter. If it is decided to proceed further, a cease and desist letter will be sent to the infringing party. I work with counsel for any action that may arise thereafter. I send out frequent reports to the beauty, catalog, and store divisions on due dates for trademark registrations due for renewal and prosecution activities due to maintain the applications.

The client may contact me with a request for a non-disclosure agreement (NDA) for an upcoming meeting. After I prepare a draft NDA, I send it to outside counsel for review. When I receive a clearance on the NDA, I send it to the other party for execution.

During the rest of the week, I may visit one of our stores to make sure that our IP is correctly used. Often, I visit other stores to see if our intellectual property is being infringed. Periodically, I visit trendy stores and our competitors to keep abreast of the latest fashion and beauty styles. I do not have a normal desk job.

My varied career as an IP paralegal is exciting. I may be asked to review garments for trade dress, copyright, and trademark issues. Frequently, I review photos of store display windows for any IP issues.

One of the many tasks I handle is to send potential counterfeit merchandise to loss prevention and research and development to test for authenticity. Counterfeit merchandise will bear our company's label, but it will sell for less. We have to monitor that activity constantly to prevent the value and quality of our merchandise from being affected.

I attend style review meetings for upcoming seasons, meet with designers for review of graphics for clothing, and perform preliminary screenings for phrases that will be imprinted on our graphic tees and other items.

PRACTICAL TIPS, SHORTCUTS, AND TRICKS OF THE TRADE:

GENERAL ADVICE

- **Listen, listen, and listen.**
- **Patience is key.** We are trained to do, but sometimes we need to stop and absorb what is being told or given to us before we proceed.

- **Find a mentor.** This is most important. Networking, building relationships, and seeking mentors are essential career tools for everyone. I would not be where I am today without a supportive mentor. I actively sought out my mentors who often turned out to be the attorneys for whom I was working. There are also peers I have known throughout my career who served as mentors to me.

- **Become active in trade associations if you are interested in the IP field.** This is the secret. If you are interested in being a trademark practitioner, the International Trademark Association is a good organization to join. It does not matter what your level of expertise is. The organization has programs and committees that suit all levels of expertise and is supportive of trademark paralegals. You can work your way up in the organization as I did.

- **The world is your oyster.** You can do anything you want if you are open and work hard. It never occurred to me that I could not do something. When I wanted to learn something new, I just went to my manager and asked if I could do it.

- **Check your baggage.** If you have had a bad experience in a previous employment situation, do not let that experience influence your actions in a new position. Judge each experience individually.

- **Accentuate the positive.** You have the knowledge and skills you need to be successful. Keep up with the latest progressions in your field and find a way to apply them to your current job or the position you hope to have. Take risks, make decisions and stand by them, seek transfers or assignments to lateral positions directly related to the goals of your organization, perfect your writing and speaking skills, and recognize your cultural background as your strength not a weakness.

- **Blow your own horn.** Make sure your manager knows what you can do. To get ahead, you have to let people know who you are and what you have done. If the clients compliment your work kindly ask them to send a note to your manager.

SYSTEMATIC PROCEDURES

- **Use checklists.** Use checklists for searching, clearance, prosecution, post-registration, maintenance, and procedures for policing, and name clearance.

■ *When you see a need for a form or checklist, make your own.*

LEGAL RESEARCH SHORTCUTS

The following resources are useful in trademark law: *U.S. Trademark Law: Rules of Practice, Forms, Federal Statutes and Regulations, Trademark Manual of Examining Procedure* (TMEP; by the United States Patent and Trademark Office, USPTO), and the United States Patent and Trademark Office *Acceptable Identification of Goods and Services Manual* (which can be found at http://tess2.uspto.gov/netahtml/tidm.html).

> Writing Tips
> ■ The secret to writing anything is to remember that your words may come back to haunt you.
> ■ Discovery may include most documents.
> ■ Be concise, clear, and brief.

DOCUMENT PREPARATION

During the course of an opposition proceeding, you may have to provide copies or *certified copies of all existing trademark registrations*. Rather than spend the time and energy pulling this material together, it is better to provide copies of major representative countries along with a report of all existing trademark registrations and applications. For example, if you have an opposition pending in India, evidence of registrations of your marks in all British Commonwealth countries will carry more weight than copies of registrations from South American countries.

INVESTIGATIONS

It is imperative to find a good IP investigator.

E-FILING WITH (USPTO):

The ability to file or submit documents electronically or online is a fairly recent development in trademark prosecution. In the past, trademark owners filed applications manually with the understanding that the date of the application would either be the date of receipt by USPTO (acknowledged by return receipt of a pre-addressed postcard) or the date of deposit by express mail with the United States Postal Service (USPS).

Before e-filing, the process was complex and fraught with details—and attendant possibilities for human error. Paralegals are typically responsible for drafting applications and cover letters and for preparing the drawing page and specimens if needed. The person responsible for signing the application is often not at the same location as the law department. In the case of a law firm, clients are in other locations. The application is forwarded to the appropriate person(s) for review and signature, and then returned to the paralegal for further processing.

TIME IS OF THE ESSENCE

E-filing has simplified the process and significantly reduced chances of errors and the time required to file applications. The beauty of e-filing is that applications can be filed in any place, as long as there is access to the Internet. If an emergency arises, it can be done instantaneously.

ADVANTAGES OF E-FILING

USPTO prefers applicants to file applications for registration of a mark electronically, using the Trademark Electronic Application System (TEAS; available at www.uspto.gov/teas). The USPTO Web site lists many advantages of e-filing compared to filing on paper. Some of these advantages include:

1. The ability to file 24/7. This makes it possible to receive a filing date on days that USPTO is officially closed and extends the time for filing on any given day until midnight Eastern Standard Time. Trademark applications filed by express mail no longer receive the date of deposit with the USPO as a filing date, whereas documents filed electronically receive the date that USPTO receives the transmission.

2. Virtually instantaneous filing receipts and serial numbers.

3. Flexibility in payment options: credit card, deposit account, or electronic funds transfer (EFT), or E-Check.

4. Significant savings on postage, fax charges, and/or courier delivery costs because electronic applications are created, reviewed, and filed electronically using the Internet.

5. More accurate filing receipt information, because it is transferred directly from the database containing the information entered by

the applicant and does not need to be manually entered again at USPTO.

6. More efficient processing of applications because they are in a standard format recommended by USPTO, which allows for faster review by an examining attorney or paralegal.

7. Automatic confirmation via e-mail of receipt of all submissions.

On-line Filing with USPTO (TEAS and PrinTEAS)

1. To help meet ever-increasing workloads at USPTO, the office strongly encourages e-filing. The downloadable paper forms formerly available on the USPTO Web site have been replaced with links to TEAS, where applicants can file directly online, or access PrinTEAS to complete the application online, then print it out and mail it.

2. While a PrinTEAS filing is on paper, it is in a format that is able to be scanned preferred by USPTO over a traditional paper form. The PrinTEAS form allows for faster processing of the application and decreases the amount of paperwork to be prepared by the legal assistant.

3. For a stylized or design mark, or for submission of a specimen, TEAS requires attachment of a JPEG image file. For a mark in typed format, the mark can simply be entered via computer keyboard.

4. On the other hand, with PrinTEAS, applicants can attach an image file in the Mark Information section to create a drawing page. This is not required, however, and applicants can check a box indicating that they do not have an image file, and then attach the image manually. For a mark in typed format, it can be entered directly via computer keyboard.

5. If applicants are unable to submit an application directly online, PrinTEAS still provides advantages to both the applicant and USPTO. It offers online help with each data entry field by simply clicking on the field name. In addition, PrinTEAS, as with TEAS, features a validation function that provides an error message if mandatory fields have not been completed (and warning messages if other expected, although not mandatory, fields have not been completed).

6. The IP paralegal handles correspondence with USPTO.

7. The latest version of TEAS features a checkbox near the applicant's e-mail address that signals USPTO to correspond with the applicant via e-mail. Consequently, office actions will be sent via e-mail rather than regular mail. Certain items (e.g., a Notice of Allowance) will still be mailed via regular mail.

8. If the box is not checked, then all correspondence will be routed through the USPTO by regular mail. It is highly recommended that law firms or corporations set up group e-mail addresses for corresponding with USPTO. Applicants can add anyone, such as the paralegal, responsible attorney, or docketing clerk to the group address for whoever needs to be copied. Thus when someone leaves the firm or corporation, his or her name can simply be deleted from the group and new people can be added, eliminating the need to constantly change the address with USPTO.

PRACTITIONERS' ACCEPTANCE

Although USPTO was first to implement the e-filing system, many international trademark offices are adopting e-filing as a twenty-first-century IP business model. Not surprisingly, practitioners have had varied responses to TEAS and the concept of e-filing. Some prefer the old-fashioned pen and paper filings as a proven method, while others appreciate the uniformity of applications and the convenience of obtaining a filing receipt within 90 seconds of filing an application or other TEAS document.

It is not time-consuming, and the validation function prevents errors with the application. The system allows immediate updating of the firm's trademark docketing system, populating all of the necessary fields, and most importantly, the serial number and filing date. In addition to trademark applications, 90 percent of the documents relating to applications and registrations required by the USPTO are filed electronically.

TECH REQUIREMENTS

Certain technological capabilities are needed to file documents electronically. The correct Web browser settings, scanning equipment, and a method of electronic payment are requisite. Images of design marks, composite marks composed of a word and design, and specimens of use must be converted into JPEG files to be attached to TEAS documents. Lack of the equipment necessary to capture images electronically may preclude firms or companies with limited technology from using TEAS.

Overall, the flexibility of moving between manual and e-filing seems to be appreciated by those with heavy trademark filing deadlines and varied technological capabilities. An outline of TEAS technical requirements, TEAS forms, and an on-line TEAS Form Wizard are available at the USPTO Web site. The TEAS Wizard will assist users during the application process by prompting them to provide relevant information. TEAS will not allow an application to be accepted without providing the required information.

APPLICATION REQUIREMENTS

Whether filing on paper, with TEAS, or PrinTEAS, applicants must meet statutory trademark application requirements in order for USPTO to begin the examination process. Minimum requirements for receiving a filing date for an application are as follows:

1. Name of the applicant
2. Name and address for correspondence
3. Clear drawing of the mark
4. Listing of the goods or services
5. Filing fee for at least one class of goods or services

When the marks have been used in interstate commerce prior to submitting the application, applications may be filed on an intent-to-use basis or on a use basis. When filing the application, information concerning the attorney(s) of record may also be entered into the system, although it is not required. If applicants wish to include additional information concerning the mark (i.e., prior registrations, disclaimers, or a description of the mark), TEAS provides a radio button for Additional Statement with a list of options.

A USPTO attorney examiner will review each trademark application substantively, and it is subject to public review during an opposition phase. Depending upon whether the application was filed on an intent-to-use basis or an actual use-in-commerce basis, the applicant must submit proof of actual use of the mark in interstate commerce by filing trademark samples known as **specimens of use** for examination and approval prior to receiving federal registration of the mark.

Applicants may also electronically file specimens along with a statement of use, and there is a Help wizard to guide users through the form. The filing fee is a processing fee that will not be refunded, even if registration of the mark is denied. It is prudent to conduct a search and clear the mark prior to filing an application to prevent losing the filing fee and wasting an application.

SIGNATURE OPTIONS

The USPTO does not require signed applications at the time of an initial filing. However, if the original application is not signed, applicants are required to provide a completed application later. Authorized persons to sign on behalf of the applicant may be:

- A person with legal authority to bind the applicant.

- A person with firsthand knowledge of the facts and actual or implied authority to act on behalf of the applicant.

- An attorney who has actual or implied written or verbal power of attorney from the applicant.

Signature options with TEAS include an electronic signature that is a name or code of the applicant's choice between two slashes (e.g., /jane doe/ or /xyzl23/). The applicant's title and position are also required in the signature block. Pen and ink signatures may be scanned as JPEG files that are then attached to the application.

TECHNICAL LIMITATIONS AND REQUIREMENTS

Each TEAS form has a session limit of 60 minutes. If the form is not completed within this time, the form will not be validated and the entire process must begin again. It is a good practice to complete, validate, and download forms for modification prior to logging on in order to prevent loss of time and work product.

Images must be in JPEG format, and the image files cannot exceed two megabytes per attachment. Animated GIF files are not accepted.

OTHER DOCUMENTS

In addition to trademark applications, pre-registration forms that can be filed electronically are the Statement of Use/Amendment to Allege Use, Request for Extension of Time to File the Statement of Use, and a Response to an Office Action. Post-registration forms that can be filed are the Combined Declaration of Use and Incontestability under

Sections 8 and 15, Declaration of Use of a Mark Under Section 8, Combined Declaration of Use in Commerce/Application for Renewal of Registration of Mark under Sections 8 and 9, and a Declaration of Incontestability under Section 15. As with the application form, there are Help and Validation functions to guide applicants through the TEAS process.

CHANGE OF CORRESPONDENCE AND ASSIGNMENT

These forms have recently been added to the TEAS system. The ability to file a change of correspondence electronically can be helpful if a group moves to a new facility. Before e-filing, it would take a day or so to manually prepare the forms, cover letters, and postcards to send to the USPTO. With TEAS, it takes only a couple of hours to record the changes electronically. Confirmations can be printed out for paper filing systems.

CORRECTING MISTAKES

As with any system, mistakes can occur when filing electronically. Fortunately, USPTO will accept an electronically filed preliminary amendment stating the proposed correction. (See http://eteas.uspto.gov/.) Preliminary amendments cannot be filed until at least 15 days after initial filing of the application. Prior to that time, the serial number will not appear in the USPTO database (even though the number was assigned at the time of the e-filing).

For other types of mistakes, such as citing the wrong trademark, there is nothing that can be done. Since the filing fee is a processing fee, it will not be refunded. The only alternative is to file a new application. Many who file electronically wisely print out the form and review it prior to submission. Reading a printed form, versus staring at the computer screen, can make the final review process much easier and is a smart precaution.

WHO ACTUALLY DOES THE WORK?

Responsibility for e-filing falls squarely on many trademark paralegals. Often they are required to complete either the PrinTEAS or TEAS form and print out or e-mail it to the attorney for review prior to submission to USPTO. If paralegals are given authority to e-file the application after review of all pertinent information, then they are ultimately responsible for any mistakes or errors. That is why it is important to print a draft of the application prior to submission. The TEAS system also allows applicants to download the form onto their computers, thus removing the restraint of the 60-minute timing-out of the session. Another benefit of downloading the application form is that applicants can pre-populate certain fields and then update the form as needed. This is particularly useful for paralegals who work in corporations, essentially working for only one client. It minimizes the margin for error and reduces the time needed to prepare and file the applications.

MADRID PROTOCOL APPLICATIONS

In November 2003, the Madrid Protocol Implementation Act of 2002 (MPIA) became effective. This act enables the owner of a United States application or registration to seek protection of its mark in any of the 57 countries party to the Madrid Protocol by submitting a single international application through USPTO to the World IP Organization.

Similarly, an international owner may request extension of the protection of their mark to the United States. The USPTO has proposed that Madrid Protocol filing be submitted through the TEAS system. If implemented, United States owners will have no choice but to use e-filing if they want to benefit from the Madrid Protocol.

E-FILING BASICS

- Prepare a checklist for the application basics.
- Secure .jpg (jpeg) images of the mark or specimens as needed.
- Select either an electronic or pen and ink signature method.
- Select a payment method and have a deposit account, electronic funds account, or credit card information available.
- Refer to the TEAS Wizard for assistance in completing the application.
- Confirmation of e-filing is sent in a message titled "SUCCESS!"
- Contact USPTO if such notification is not received.
- Immediately record or notify docketing of e-filing details to adequately monitor the status and deadlines associated with the application.

END NOTES

Reprinted with permission of the *National Association of Paralegals (NALA)*, and co-authors Deborah Hampton, Candida Hinton, Grace Jennings, and Ellen Lockwood, CLAS. The article originally appeared in the November 2003 quarterly journal of *Facts & Findings*. The article is reprinted here in its entirety. For further information, contact NALA at (http://nala.org/) or phone 918.587.6828.

Part III

LEGAL RESEARCH AND WRITING

CHAPTER 9

CELIA C. ELWELL, RP

PACE Registered Litigation Paralegal
Oklahoma City, OK

CELIA C. ELWELL, RP

"Celia Elwell is a former staff member in my chambers and a long-time professional acquaintance of mine. She is a knowledgeable and conscientious paralegal professional with in-depth insights into the essence of trial and appellate process. Ms. Elwell demonstrates an amazing aptitude for the law and has well-developed legal research and writing skills."

Hon. Marian P. Opala
Justice, Supreme Court of Oklahoma

EDUCATION/HONORS/CERTIFICATIONS:

- University of Oklahoma Department of Legal Assistant Education (ABA-approved two-year certificate program), 1986
- PACE Registered Paralegal, 1999
- Co-author, *Practical Legal Writing for Legal Assistants* (Egan, MN: West Publishing Company, 1996)
- *PACE Study Manual* (Co-author, Legal Writing chapter)
- Adjunct Instructor and Paralegal Seminar Lecturer (various areas of law), University of Oklahoma, Department of Legal Assistant Education, 1986–2001

PROFESSIONAL ASSOCIATIONS:

- National Federation of Paralegal Associations (NFPA)
- NFPA PACE Assistant Coordinator of Education, 2000–2004
- NFPA Internet Communications Co-coordinator, 2001–2004
- NFPA PACE Coordinator, 2004
- NFPA PACE Development Committee (Domains, Item Writing)
- Oklahoma Bar Association Standing Committee on Legal Assistant Services
- Chair, Subcommittee that drafted the Minimum Standards on Education and Experience, adopted by the Oklahoma Bar Association in August 2000
- Member, Kansas Paralegal Association, 1993–present
- Kansas Paralegal Association Primary Delegate, 2003
- Kansas Paralegal Association Secondary Delegate, 2002
- Kansas Paralegal Association PACE Ambassador, 2006–2007
- American Trial Lawyers of America, 2003–2004
- Advisory Boards, University of Oklahoma Department of Legal Assistant Education Advisory Committee, 1986–2001
- Oklahoma State University at Okmulgee, Oklahoma, Business and Office Occupations Advisory Committee, 1990–1994
- American Association for Paralegal Education (AAfPE), 1993–1999
- *Pro Bono:* Mentors, PACE Candidates, paralegals, and paralegal students

YEARS EXPERIENCE:

22

COMPANY AT-A-GLANCE

Complex and Civil State and Federal Litigation
Celia C. Elwell is a highly experienced paralegal and a respected paralegal author who freelances in Oklahoma City. You may reach her at:

1714 Barb Drive
Norman, OK 73071
E-mail: pacecce@cox.net or cceparalegal@hotmail.com

PRACTICE AREAS:

- State and Federal Complex Civil Litigation
- Family Law
- Product Liability
- Personal Injury
- Employment/Labor Law and Arbitration
- Product Liability
- Wrongful Death
- Civil Rights/Constitutional Law
- State Appellate Law and Procedure
- Municipal Law

INTRODUCTION TO LEGAL RESEARCH AND WRITING/ OVERVIEW OF JOB RESPONSIBILITIES:[1]

This overview will take a hypothetical case from beginning to end. Some assignments will be normal tasks that would be typical for every case. Others would be necessary depending on the facts and complexity of the case. Remember that, depending on the client's ability to pay or the type or complexity of a case, you may need to keep the costs

---

[1] Portions of this chapter are adapted from Practical Legal Writing for Legal Assistants 1st edition by ELWELL/SMITH. 1996. Reprinted with permission of Delmar Learning, a division of Thomson Learning: www.thomsonrights.com. Fax 800 730-2315.

and billing to a minimum. In those instances, you would not spend as much time as indicated on some of these tasks. If I can, I delegate or modify tasks to plug into whatever litigation support software is available.

I. CASE MANAGEMENT

A. Identify the legal issues, the parties, and facts of the case.

1. Conduct a conflict of interest check.

2. Docket the statute of limitations and any deadlines for filing a complaint or response pleadings.

3. Conduct a search for the proper name of any company and its registered agents to identify the proper parties and to whom a summons should be addressed.

4. Locate opposing party's address using information from the client, the phone book, Westlaw® people search, and Internet search engines.

5. Start background investigations on parties if needed. For companies, this might involve research of the company's financial information. I always like to include a review of the company's Web page; I may find that we need to include sister companies as parties to the lawsuit, more information about the company's finances, mission statements (used as evidence in fraud cases), and other pertinent information. One of the best sources of information about a company is in its "mission statement" or the "about us" section on its Web site.

6. Conduct an Internet search for relevant articles about the event involving the lawsuit (e.g., a newspaper article about a car accident or the indictment of a corporate officer of a company that is party to the lawsuit). Create e-mail alerts using news trackers to continue searching the Internet for any relevant information.

7. If electronic discovery is relevant to your case, send a notice to any possible party or witness that litigation is anticipated and all relevant e-discovery should be properly maintained. (See the following Internet articles for advice and strategy: *The Plaintiff's Practical Guide to E-Discovery* by Craig Ball at www.craigball.com/articles.html, Electronic Discovery

Blog at www.ediscoverylaw.com, and Discovery Resources Blog at www.discoveryresources.org.)

8. Research verdicts and settlements.

B. Develop case strategy. (See the Discovery Shortcuts section later in this chapter.)

1. Identify and research the legal theories of the case.

2. Determine the necessary facts needed to prove your client's case (i.e., to support each element of proof, claim, or defense).

3. From this information, determine discovery strategy.

4. As more facts and evidence are obtained, identify potential motions *in limine* (typically, a motion to exclude evidence before trial, or at least to require opposing counsel to raise the question of admissibility outside of the presence of the jury during trial. Conversely, but much more rarely, an advocate may use it to move for admission of evidence before trial if she anticipates an objection to the evidence. See *Hon. Robert E. Bacharach, Motions in Limine in Oklahoma State and Federal Courts*, 24 Okla, City U.L. Rev. 112, 114: 1999.)

5. If you are going to use legal technology in the courtroom during trial or at hearings, now is the time to start working with whoever will design and create those presentations, whether in-house or outside the firm. (See Resources on Courtroom Technology and "*Effective Use of Courtroom Technology: A Judge's Guide to Pretrial and Trial*," published by The Federal Judicial Center; a copy can be found at http://www.fjc.gov/public/home.nsf/autoframe?openform&url_r=pages/1100.)

C. Review Documents

1. If not already produced, identify what documents your client needs to produce so that you and your attorney can determine what information should be sought in discovery from opposing parties.

2. Review the client's documents together with the research you have compiled on the parties. As discovery continues and more information is available, the case strategy will be

revised and augmented as the issues become more narrowly defined.

3. Create a master set of documents that are Bates stamped and indexed. Depending on the attorney's preference, the documents may be three-hole punched and placed in binders.

4. During the document review, tag any document that may hold a privilege. Once privilege has been determined, pull the document and place it in a separate file. In that document's place, leave a colored piece of paper to make it easy to locate the omitted page. In compliance to any applicable court rules, create a privilege log.

5. Note information gaps, missing documents, or inconsistencies.

6. Begin your exhibit list.

D. Witness Files

This can be a file or notebook, depending on your attorney's preference. Notebooks work well with descriptive dividers and an index, but it often depends on the case's complexity and/or volume of documents.

1. Using the documents provided by the client and based on your research, create witness files for the key players. These files will contain the attorney's notes on that person or entity, all background research, newspaper articles, financial or other relevant information, and Internet alerts. This should also include research to determine whether the person or entity has been involved in other litigation.

2. Make copies of documents that relate to, or could be sponsored by, the witness. Create a list of those documents and put the copies in the witness file. Often more than one witness may be linked to one particular document, that is, another witness may be linked to that same document. It is important to cross-reference each witness to each document, and each document to each relevant witness clearly.

3. Begin your witness list. Include the witness's contact information, social security number (if known), and a summary of anticipated testimony.

E. Draft initial pleadings. (See checklist Figure 9–1.)

F. Prepare your discovery strategy with your attorney before drafting discovery.

　1. Identify the legal theory (or theories) for your client's problem (or the client's defenses, if any), such as a statute of limitations.

　2. Determine the needed facts to prove your client's case (i.e., to support each element of proof, claim, or defense).

G. Answer the following questions to develop a discovery plan for each case.

　1. What facts are needed to prove our client's case against the other side (or defeat the other side's claims)?

　2. What information am I missing in Question 1 above?

　3. Which discovery methods would be best to get the information and evidence needed from Questions 1 and 2?

　4. What facts or witnesses (already known) do I need to find through formal discovery to be used as evidence? Formal discovery will substantiate in usable form those facts already known to you and help to fix the opposition's position.

　5. How much can the client pay for discovery? (This will determine which discovery methods will be used.)

　6. Determine your discovery method and the order in which to use it.

The best application of several discovery methods is to combine them and use each when its particular benefits apply. Ordinarily, conduct discovery in this order:

a. Interrogatories

b. Requests for Production of Documents

c. Depositions

d. Requests for Physical or Mental Examination

e. Requests for Admissions

First, using the discovery strategy outlined earlier, you would serve Interrogatories on the opposing party to identify documents you may wish to obtain and to lay a foundation for questions to be asked at depositions. Next, using a Request for Production of Documents, you would obtain the documents identified by the responses

FIGURE 9-1

Checklist for Drafting Initial Pleadings—Complaint, Answer, Counterclaims

■ Be sure that all deadlines, including the statute of limitations, have been properly docketed.

■ Double-check to make sure you have followed all court rules, local court rules, and administrative court orders.

■ Verify that the lawsuit is being brought in the proper court and that you have identified all "real parties in interest" in the lawsuit.

■ Verify the name of the court, the name of the parties, and the case number (if one has already been assigned).

■ Proofread each fact and allegation. Satisfy for yourself and your attorney that a reasonable inquiry has been made and that all facts are true.

■ If you are drafting a petition or complaint, make sure that you have included the proper jurisdictional paragraph, including the amount of money damages requested, as well as any required paragraphs for venue or other procedural requirements.

■ Have special matters been pleaded with sufficient particularity and detail?

■ Does the prayer for relief (demand for judgment) meet the court's requirements?

■ Is it necessary to make a separate demand for jury trial and, if so, has it been included?

■ Is it necessary to made a demand for an attorney's lien and, if so, has one been included?

■ Is a verification necessary? If so, has it been drafted, signed by your client, and notarized so that it may be attached to the pleading when it is filed?

■ Have all exhibits been marked and attached?

■ Has all private information, such as social security numbers, been redacted (blacked out so as to be unreadable) according to any applicable court rules?

■ Have you accurately calculated the filing fees and obtained a check for the court clerk? Have you included the cost of issuing each summons?

■ If you have been served with a summons and complaint, docket the answer date immediately.

■ Determine all possible defenses to the allegations in the complaint, including cross-claims to any other defendant named in the lawsuit.

■ Determine whether all "real parties in interest" have been named and whether any third-party defendants should be added to the case.

to Interrogatories. Once you receive and digest those documents, draft additional questions regarding those documents for your attorney to ask in Depositions. When the Depositions are complete, you can use Requests for Admission to validate disputed facts.

As a rule, when you want to serve an adverse party with Interrogatories and to take his Deposition, it is better to take the Deposition after his answers to Interrogatories are received. Because responses to Interrogatories are sometimes prepared by counsel without much, if any, interaction from the client, facts recalled by the opposing party at his deposition might deviate from the answers given to Interrogatories. Even if opposing counsel is smart enough to prepare his client for the deposition by giving him the Interrogatory answers to study beforehand, his oral answers could differ because he cannot refer to his Interrogatory answers at the Deposition. This means that your attorney can frame her questions at the deposition to exploit any weaknesses in the deponent's answers and to follow up on those leads.

Here is a quick exercise on how to use discovery to your best advantage. Your client, Defendant Linda B. Careful, claims that Plaintiff, Happy Jack Careless, drove his car across the centerline into the path of Linda's car causing the collision. You know there was a passenger in Happy Jack's car. You already have photographs taken at the scene of the accident showing the position of the vehicles in relation to the road. How would you use all five types of discovery in this lawsuit?

1. Submit Interrogatories to Happy Jack (making sure to ask for the identity of his passenger).

2. In an inspection Request for Production for Tangible Things, demand access to Happy Jack's car to check it for the location and extent of damage.

3. By order of the court, require that Happy Jack have a physical examination by any doctor you may choose.

4. In Requests for Admissions send to Happy Jack's counsel copies of your photo, together with a request for authenticity determining the photo to be a fair and accurate representation of the accident scene. (You could send the Request for Admissions simultaneously.)

5. Using the information gathered from the discovery you have already obtained, take the deposition of Happy Jack and his passenger.

H. Prepare your document.

Before drafting the complaint, exhaust all administrative remedies. Once you have the final draft of the complaint, proofread it carefully to be sure that the facts in the complaint are true. An excellent way to catch errors is to read the sentences backward.

I. Begin the Pretrial Discovery Process

1. Depending on your case's jurisdiction, there may be pretrial procedures that must be followed and/or filed with the court, such as Fed. R. Civ. P. 26 disclosures or discovery plans. Check your court's rules and local rules for these requirements, and the details of drafting and service.

2. Prepare discovery according to the discovery strategy to find the evidence necessary to win using a dispositive motion or at trial.

3. Supplement your list of witnesses and exhibits.

4. Identify and investigate expert witnesses.

   a. Obtain the expert's resume or curriculum vitae.

   b. Thorough research—identify each case in which this expert has been used or consulted, the opinion given in each case by the expert, and whether the expert has ever been disqualified.

   c. If the expert has ever been deposed, if possible, obtain a copy of the deposition.

   d. Obtain trial transcripts, when possible, to obtain the testimony given by any expert in the case. Further, check the court's final order in the case to determine whether the expert's testimony had any significant bearing on the court's and/or jury's final decision.

   e. Use databases provided by sources, such as The Defense Institute and the American Association of Trial Lawyers.

   f. Create a witness file or notebook for each expert. Include the report produced by the expert required by Fed. R. Civ. P. 26.

5. Summarize depositions. Add the deposition transcript, summary, and deposition exhibits to the deponent's witness file or notebook.

J. Prepare for Summary Judgment or Trial

1. Prepare and file a motion for summary judgment. In many jurisdictions, the motion, supporting brief, and attached exhibits will become the record on appeal. Always keep that in mind when preparing your summary judgment motion, brief, and exhibits.

2. Prepare and exchange or file any documents required by your court rules or the court's scheduling order, such as witness and exhibit lists, expert reports, or a settlement statement, motions *in limine*, and proposed jury instructions.

3. Call the judge's clerk to determine the judge's preference for the format of exhibit lists, numbering exhibits, exhibit notebooks, and the protocol for the use of litigation support technology.

4. Prepare the pretrial memorandum for the pretrial hearing. *The pretrial order is your roadmap for trial.* All claims, defenses, witnesses, and exhibits must be listed, or they will be excluded from trial. Ensure that a witness exists to sponsor every exhibit you list. My preference is to list witnesses and exhibits in the order in which they will be used at trial. Some judges will insist that the numbers used for each exhibit in the pretrial order dictate the number used to mark the exhibit for trial. Find out *before* submitting the final pretrial memorandum to the court.

5. Contact clients and witnesses to arrange for meetings to prepare for trial.

6. Prepare exhibits for trial. Determine whether any exhibits will be used as demonstrative aids, meaning that they are not intended to be admitted into evidence during trial; usually demonstrative or visual aids may include poster boards with illustrations, easels, PowerPoint presentations, (blown-up) photographs, models used for illustrations, and so forth; and take whatever steps are needed to create them.

7. Visit the courtroom to determine the location of electrical outlets and the courtroom's technology capabilities.

8. Prepare trial subpoenas and witness fees.

9. Make travel arrangements for any out-of-town witnesses.

10. Contact witnesses and tell them which day their testimony is anticipated.

11. Prepare trial notebooks for each attorney. Each notebook usually includes:

    a. the pretrial order

    b. the contact list for witnesses

    c. the final witness and exhibit lists for all parties

    d. all orders relating to discovery, summary judgment, and/or motions *in limine*

    e. *voir dire* (the preliminary oral examination of a prospective juror conducted by the attorneys to all parties prior to the actual trial)

    f. a seating chart for the jury

    g. proposed jury instructions (A charge is an instruction to the jury on the law, given by the judge after the closing argument.)

12. Pack boxes for trial. Include pleading files, witness files/notebooks, and trial notebooks. Include the rules of civil procedure and court rules, exhibit stickers, all necessary office supplies, a sewing kit, buttons, safety pins, antacids, Band-Aids™, aspirin, batteries, and a roll of quarters for pay phone emergencies. If you are using electronics of any kind, bring backup, including projectors, external drives, discs, computers, cords, and so forth.

13. Arrange for the delivery of sandwiches or lunches at the courthouse or the office during trial.

14. Reserve a conference "war" room to be used for trial preparation, meetings before trial, and during court recesses.

K. The Trial

1. If you sit at the counsel table, assist with control of exhibits.

2. Note whenever an exhibit has been (a) offered into evidence, (b) objected to, and (c) admitted into evidence.

3. Note all objections to testimony or exhibits and the court's ruling.

4. Coordinate witnesses' arrival before their anticipated time to testify.

5. Keep the counsel table neat and uncluttered.

6. Coordinate the presentation of technology used at trial.

7. Take copious notes.

8. Remind your attorney to "make a record" for appeal.

This is only a rough outline of the steps taken throughout a case from the beginning through to trial. No doubt, I have omitted many important elements that you would normally include. I have not found any two attorneys who prepare for trial alike. I always learn a new "trick" or "tip" every time I prepare for trial from whoever is involved.

TYPICAL WORKWEEK:

I am not sure there is such a thing as a typical workweek, which is one of the things I really like about being a paralegal. Because the majority of my work is civil litigation, most assignments are time-driven, depending on the deadlines in each case. Depending on the type of litigation, a typical workweek would begin with a review of the firm's calendar or docket. Even though I work with specific attorneys, I often help other members of the firm to cover deadlines if needed. It helps if you have a good idea of what is supposed to happen that day, that week, and the upcoming week.

I try to keep a running to-do list of assignments that I have been given and the deadlines for each. These are what I will try to accomplish first. Because I have interruptions with brief or lengthier assignments throughout the day, it is necessary to keep in mind the deadlines for each assignment and prioritize the work accordingly. If I receive too many demands on my time, or the demands compromise my ability to reach any deadline, I ask the attorneys who made the assignment to determine between themselves whose work will come first.

Job responsibilities vary depending on my caseload and the status of my assigned cases. In litigation, your workload is often either feast or famine. Your workload is heavy with deadlines, and you are working as fast as possible to put out fires, or you hit a lull where it seems there is not much to do.

PRACTICAL TIPS, SHORTCUTS, AND TRICKS OF THE TRADE:

1. Create "cheat sheets" or outlines as quick references for the statutes, court rules, or forms that you most frequently use. If you practice in both state and federal court, you might want to create a cheat sheet that tells you at a glance which statutes or court rules apply to various requirements.

2. If you do not have access to litigation support software that stores and provides easy access to information, such as the case style, certificate of mailing, and the pertinent data for opposing counsel (e.g., firm names, bar numbers for each attorney, addresses, telephone and fax numbers, and e-mail addresses, create a paper and electronic file for each case/client that contains this information. This list should contain the names, work addresses, and office numbers of all counsel in the case, as well as the paralegals in your office, clients and/or client representatives, experts, and other witnesses.

3. As the case proceeds closer to trial, include home phone numbers and/or cell numbers. If you name the folder with the number "1" before the name, it will automatically stay at the top of the list of the files for that folder. Keep a copy handy on the inside of the pleading file and trial notebook and/or attorney notes file. This list should be included in your trial notebook so that your team may reach any person on the list at a moment's notice during trial preparation and trial.

4. Create your own form file. Immediately delete anything that becomes outdated or inaccurate.

5. Set up a pleading shell for each case that has the proper formatting for that court, as well as the most current certificate of service. If you get new parties to the case or an attorney's address changes, immediately make the change to the pleading shell. Picking an older document and doing a Save As feature through your word processor may not have the most current certificate of service attached.

6. Send client a copy of everything received in the case.

7. Check your attorney(s) calendars daily and up to a week ahead of time. Set reminders for yourself and/or for your attorney and check them frequently.

8. Subscribe to the state bar journal. Read the opinions to keep up with recent changes in case law. Changes to court rules are also published here. Keep a copy of everything you send in the case. If you send discovery documents to experts or produce to the other side, I recommend indexing the documents before they are produced and keeping a master copy of what you sent them in a separate file or, at the very least, a list of which Bates numbers were produced to whom and when.

9. Bates number every discovery document produced in a case, even a small case. When producing documents to the other side, identify in a letter the Bates numbered–documents produced that can help you answer whether a document has been produced.

10. Keep a discovery log indicating which Bates numbers have been produced and on what date by which party.

11. Never give anyone the master set of documents received from the other side or produced by your client, especially in cases where several attorneys are involved. Make work copies for the attorneys to use instead.

12. After the attorney has given you the assignment, paraphrase the assignment by repeating the instructions in your own words while referring to your notes, if any. If you do not know how to do any part of an assignment, ask for instructions that are more complete or for a form the attorney has used and likes.

13. Keep files and notebooks organized and current.

14. Be scrupulously fair when keeping track of the time spent on a client's case. Padding your time is unprofessional and unethical.

15. Use Microsoft® Outlook® or other software to create your own to-do list with reminders and ticklers.

16. Always memorize any contact with a client, witness, opposing counsel, or the court for the file.

17. Create a scheduling order file or an alphabetized three–ring binder with a hard copy of the scheduling order for every case in which you are involved.

18. Organize your Internet Favorites by categories and subcategories to make them easy to locate.

19. Bookmark the Internet Web site to each court in which you or your firm may practice, as well as the court rules, state and federal statutes, evidence and discovery codes, and case law.

20. Bookmark and categorize links to factual and legal research, such as people finders, dictionaries, thesaurus, financial information, expert witness locators, search engines, legal blogs, court reporters, process servers, and travel information. Make periodic checks to delete obsolete links.

21. Err on the side of caution when it comes to legal ethics.

22. If you do not know how to do something, admit it. It saves time and mistakes.

23. Always insist on a comfortable chair.

24. Never put anything in an e-mail that you would mind seeing on a billboard posted outside your home, your office, or your church.

25. Take the initiative to improve your skills and knowledge, whether by attending continuing legal education seminars, online tutorials, courses, or personal study.

26. Network, network, network.

27. Be honest. If you make a mistake, say so; do not try to lay the blame on someone or something else.

28. Hone your proofreading skills. Never depend solely on spell-check. Proofread each letter, number, and punctuation mark. When proofreading, use the original source rather than a copy you may find on the word processor.

29. When sending a confirmation letter to the parties about scheduling a deposition, make sure you state who has the responsibility of getting the court reporter and the conference room. Send a copy of that letter to the court reporter if it is your client's responsibility, and carbon copy (cc) the court reporter on the letter. Always keep a copy of that letter nearby in case the court reporter fails to show.

30. Sloppy grammar and punctuation give the impression of a lack of professionalism.

31. Always return business telephone calls and e-mails the same day, if possible.

32. Regardless of the provocation, be kind, polite, and professional.

Writing Tips: Let us start with the basics. This is true of all writing, not just legal writing. We have all read long, cumbersome sentences and paragraphs. How many of us have had to reread something because we did not understand it when we first read it?

Our minds work like a sieve. Pretend your words are water falling on dry dirt. They bounce on top of the dirt at first, and then slowly begin to soak in. However, the water does not flow straight down—it percolates through the dirt, bouncing off a piece of dirt here, a bit of rock there, until it finally gets to the root of a plant. Whenever we write something that is hard to understand, like a long sentence or paragraph, or whenever we use an unfamiliar word, the reader either gets the meaning slowly, or worse—not at all. This is why our writing must be as clear and concise as we can make it, regardless of the topic.

Writing in the active voice is one way of making sure that your writing is clear and concise. Using the active voice means that the subject and verb are close together and those modifiers are close to what they modify. The active voice tells the reader *who the subject is* and *what the subject is doing*. In the **passive voice**, the subject has something done to him, her, or it. Here is an example of the active voice:

"The flower delivery van left the flowers at the hotel."

Change it to the passive voice, and you get the following:

"The flowers were left at the hotel by the delivery van."

When you use the active voice, you find out up front who or what did the acting, and immediately afterward, you find out what he, she, or it did. Active voice is clearer because you get right to the point. The reader does not have to wade through verbose sentences to get your meaning. Exemplary legal writing takes the reader systematically through all the logical points of the document until you reach the end.

Whenever we cite an authority, we must explain to the reader why that authority is relevant by recounting the facts, then the law, and then comparing each to our client's case so that the reader can see the relevance between the two cases. Leave nothing to chance. Do not ever assume that the reader will understand it. Lead the reader point by point until you reach the conclusion. You want the reader to be nodding his head subconsciously in agreement with every point you make.

A case is "on all fours" when the facts are similar or analogous to the facts of your client's situation. All case law is fact driven. To determine its ruling, a court will look at the facts of your client's case and find case law that has similar facts. The court will apply the law in that case to your client's specific fact situation, analyze the result, and come to a conclusion. We call this process IRAC (issue, rule, application, and conclusion).

Rarely do you find a case that has exactly the same facts as your case. Usually you will notice gaps, similarities, and differences in the authorities you find during your legal research. To distinguish a case, you emphasize the similarities or the differences. If you want to use the case to argue that it does apply to your case, then you emphasize the similarities and argue that the differences and gaps in the fact pattern are negligible. On the other hand, if you are arguing that the case is not relevant, you emphasize the differences and fact gaps.

CLIENT INTERACTIONS AND INTERVIEWING:

Whenever you are interviewing the client or a witness, you may use the following approach. First, tell the person that no matter what, tell the truth. Tell them, "The truth cannot hurt us. Do not try to help the case by saying something that is not true. You will do more harm than good. In addition, if opposing counsel asks you whether we talked before you gave your testimony, say 'yes.' If opposing counsel asks what we talked about, tell him that I told you to tell the truth. If you are concerned about giving your testimony, please let us know beforehand so we can address your concerns."

Next, prepare the client or witness for different types of questions: Tell the witness that he or she should try to answer questions using only "yes" or "no." Caution the witness not to elaborate, even if the witness feels that he or she has something important to add. If our attorney wants the witness to elaborate, he or she will ask the witness to explain and give the witness the opportunity to give a more complete answer. It is important to tell the witness to always stick to the facts and to never speculate or guess. Tell the witness that, if he or she simply does not know the answer, to say "I don't know." Also tell the witness that it would not be unusual for an attorney to ask the witness the same question more than once; the attorney is attempting to see whether the witness' story is consistent or will change if challenged.

Tell the witness that attorneys will often ask questions that call for multiple answers. The question may have several parts, and the answer to the first question is 'yes,' the answer to the next question is 'no,' and the answer to the third question is 'no.' If the response is only say 'yes,' then essentially the witness has answered 'yes' to all three questions. There are several ways the witness can address this situation. First, the witness could say that the attorney had asked several questions, and which one did the attorney want the witness to answer? Or, the witness could simply say that the attorney had asked several questions and would the attorney please ask each question separately. Regardless of how the witness responds, the important point is that the witness thinks before speaking. And, if a witness is not sure of the question or did not understand the question, he or she should ask the attorney to restate the question or simply state that he or she did not understand the question.

Most people who are being deposed are nervous and anxious, even if they have no big part to play in the lawsuit or have nothing to hide. Sometimes it helps to calm them if you remind them that, if they feel confused, it is all right in most jurisdictions to ask for a short break and that request should be made to their attorney. At most depositions, coffee, water, soft drinks, and bathroom facilities are always available. Provide a map to the place where the deposition will be held and tell them where to park. Tell the witnesses that they will be reimbursed for their mileage and parking expenses.

Above all, please stress the following: "You may call me 24 hours a day, seven days a week at 123-4567, if you have any questions or concerns about the deposition. And you may reach Mr. Attorney at 111-4444." Some clients or witnesses may wish to bring family or even clergy to depositions for moral support. If the Rule of Sequestration has been invoked, no other potential witnesses may be in the deposition room. A party to the lawsuit has the right to attend any deposition.

COMMUNICATIONS IN THE OFFICE

You need to understand ideas, instructions, and questions, whether oral or written, or they are not effective. As with Murphy's Law— what can be misunderstood will be. Here are some helpful hints:

PARAPHRASING

When you receive instructions or assignments, listen carefully. Whenever possible, take notes, but only if you can do so accurately. After the speaker finishes, it is a good time to ask questions. Then paraphrase your understanding of the assignment by repeating the instructions in your own words, while referring to your notes, if any. The supervising attorney can then determine whether you have misunderstood the instructions and make whatever corrections or explanations necessary.

CLARIFICATION

After the attorney has given complete instructions for the assignment, think before you speak or ask questions. Do not try to guess the attorney's meaning or intentions. If you are not sure, it is better to ask for clarification than to guess. There is no such thing as a stupid question.

1. Take a minute and think about the assignment.
2. Did you fully understand the assignment?
3. Do you know where to find the files you will need?
4. Are there unanswered questions as to whom to contact or how to obtain certain information?
5. Do not be afraid to say, "I don't know." If you do not know, say so. It is always better to admit you do not know it rather than to flounder around trying to figure it out. At best, you will produce a substandard work product and, at worst, something so wrong is completely unusable and embarrassing to both you and your supervising attorney. Even the most qualified, experienced, and highly paid lawyers and paralegals do not know how to do everything! When we receive an assignment beyond our experience, it is hard to admit it.

PRIORITIZING ASSIGNMENTS

Many people find it extremely difficult to say "no" to any assignment, even though their workload is already overwhelming them. It would be difficult to turn down a senior partner's assignment; however, it may be impossible to accept that assignment and keep the commitments you have already made to other attorneys in the office.

What do you do? Here is an example of what can happen when work assignment priorities become an issue. On Monday, one of the firm's associate lawyers gave you an assignment to summarize 15 depositions before the end of next week. On Wednesday, the senior partner asks you to monitor and take notes during a criminal trial in a lawsuit that relates to a case in your office. The trial should last until the end of the following week. You know you cannot summarize all of the depositions and monitor the criminal trial. Whenever you are working on one assignment and another attorney asks you to do another project, ask for the deadline. There may not be a conflict in getting both assignments done on time.

However, if there is, let the second attorney know about your prior assignment, mentioning that you would like to take on the assignment but you have other projects, and say what those deadlines are. Discuss the new assignment's deadline, and how that will affect the other assignment you already have. If there is a conflict, the attorneys should decide whose assignment has priority and set the deadlines for the new and the old assignments.

COMMUNICATION WITH SUPPORT STAFF:

Here are some suggestions on supervising or sharing a secretary or other support staff:

1. Aim toward quality of performance.
2. If you gave the secretary the wrong address, admit the error was your fault and apologize for causing the secretary extra work. This attitude encourages a better work atmosphere because support staff is not made to feel that they will be blamed, regardless of who or what is at fault when something goes wrong. The emphasis is on solving the problem and learning from the experience to upgrade the quality of performance.

PROMOTE THE TEAM CONCEPT

1. Your productivity and effectiveness will increase whenever you and support staff work together as a team, utilizing each other's strengths to the office's advantage.
2. Build your support staff's self-image.
3. The single most effective technique of good management is to make people feel good about themselves and their contribution—that they are worthwhile and important. Productivity and quality of work performed are directly tied to any employee's self-image. Therefore, take into account not only your support staffs' abilities and skills, but also their personalities and how this combination of factors affect desired performance.

4. Be considerate when you give assignments.

5. Give clear and adequate instructions.

6. Although it may be convenient for you to leave details, such as addresses and titles, for the secretary to figure out, this may be giving you a reputation for not knowing what you are doing. Sloppy or incomplete instructions increase the opportunity for mistakes and program you and your support staff for failure.

7. Never ask a support staffperson to stop working on someone else's work and start on yours. Do not place someone in this awkward position. I would not appreciate it any more than you would. Some offices use a system, such as "first in, first out." Other offices' policies dictate that the persons sharing the secretary or the office manager make the decision. If you have a rush project and there is work ahead of yours, diplomatically request permission to bump your work to the top of the stack from the people with whom you share the secretary or from the office manager. In law offices, emergencies and deadlines are a fact. It is better to establish an office policy in advance on how to handle these crises than to force the secretary to make these no-win decisions.

What do you do if a support staffperson continually bumps your work to the bottom of the stack or just balks at doing your work? Most paralegals have encountered this situation sometime during his or her career. Unfortunately, some secretaries or other support staff resist receiving instruction or assignments from a paralegal, regardless of the tact or consideration used. In these situations, it is helpful simply to talk privately with that person about the problem. Perhaps you are unaware of some misunderstanding or some other small slight. If so, apologize and try to get the relationship back on track. It may be that this person feels that your instructions or your work style is creating unnecessary and time-consuming work. If that is the case, suggest a compromise. Ask the person for ideas of how you could work better together, and be receptive to suggestions.

If simply trying to talk it out does not seem to have any effect, it may be that both of you are in a struggle for control. If you cannot amicably meet at some common ground, then approach the problem in another way. This problem can be overcome with patience and professionalism. Usually, the supervising attorney or office manager explains to the secretary or support person that he or I do not work for a specific person, but for the firm. By not cooperating or doing a paralegal's work, that person is refusing to do the firm's work. This problem usually disappears when management makes it clear that such an attitude is not acceptable.

If the problem persists despite management intervention, avoid doing anything that escalates the tension between you and your secretary. Be courteous and professional. The paralegal director/manager, office administrator, or supervising attorney should decide what steps should be taken to rectify the problem like any other office rule.

Unfortunately, some paralegal directors/managers, supervising attorneys, or law office administrators, who are uncomfortable handling personnel issues, may fail to acknowledge or handle this problem. If that happens, you probably cannot change that person's attitude. Should you find yourself in this situation, avoid confrontations; these only give the other person an excuse to find fault with you. Be pleasant, courteous, and professional. Try to compromise as much as you can without forfeiting quality. Then, if all else fails, ask to be assigned to another secretary with whom it is easier to work.

Do not be disheartened if this problem happens to you. Talk about your problem with more experienced paralegals and find out how they dealt with it. Even if you do not find the solution to your problem, it will help to talk with other paralegals who have wrestled with this situation.

DEMAND QUALITY WORK

Minor errors in spelling, grammar, punctuation, or syntax reflect on you and the firm. You are responsible for catching errors, not your secretary or your proofreader.

TRIAL POINTERS:

Preparing for trial is preparing for the anticipated and the unanticipated. Ask yourself the following questions:

1. Have all the pleadings been organized and indexed?
2. Have the witness files been prepared and contain depositions, witness notes, and questions for examination and cross-examination?

3. Have the trial exhibit notebooks been copied, indexed, and marked?

TRIAL NOTEBOOK:

Many paralegals look forward to sitting with their attorney during trial and assisting with handling the documents and the client. While I enjoy being at the counsel table, I prefer sitting in the gallery. From the gallery, I can observe the jury, the witnesses on the witness stand, opposing counsel, and the opposing party (or parties), as well as my attorney. I can leave the courtroom to contact witnesses when it becomes close to the time for them to appear in court to testify. I can soothe the restless nerves of witnesses while they wait. If necessary, I can even run back to the office to grab a file.

END NOTES

Elwell, Celia C., and Robert Bar Smith. *Practical Legal Writing for Legal Assistants.* (Egan, MN: West Publishing Company, 1996).

Part IV

COMMERCIAL REAL ESTATE

CHAPTER 10

SUSAN M. CUSTER
REAL ESTATE PARALEGAL
GLAST PHILLIPS & MURRAY, P.C.
Dallas, TX

"As a paralegal, Susan is indispensable to the real estate practice. While the attorney must address legal issues and negotiations with competence, I find that the client is more often appreciative of Susan's organizational skills, attention to deadlines, and the closing process, which are fundamental to 'getting their deal done.' Her participation is more likely to be seen as value added than the subtle turn of a word by the attorney."

Scott Jackson, Attorney
Glast, Phillips, & Murray, P.C.

EDUCATION/HONORS/CERTIFICATIONS:

Paralegal Certificate, Southern Methodist University, School of Continuing Education, 1988

PROFESSIONAL ASSOCIATIONS:

- Dallas Area Paralegal Association (DAPA) Board of Directors (six years)
- DAPA President, 1999
- President-Elect, 1998–99
- Programs Vice President, 1996–98
- Director at Large, 1994–96
- Scholarship Committee Chair, 1993
- El Centro Paralegal Committee, 1998–99
- Southeastern Paralegal Institute Committee, 1998–99

FIRM AT-A-GLANCE:

Glast, Phillips, & Murray, P.C.
Dallas, TX
Phone: 972.419.8300
Fax: 972.419.8329
Other Locations: Houston, TX; San Antonio, TX

MANAGING PARTNER:

Troy D. Phillips

ATTORNEYS (PERMANENT):

84

PARALEGALS (PERMANENT):

FIRM PRACTICE AREAS:

- Commercial Real Estate
- Litigation
- Corporate Securities
- Estate Planning
- Intellectual Property
- Business Law
- Family Law
- Bankruptcy
- Employment Law
- ERISA/Employee Benefits and Executive Compensation
- International Law
- Tax Law

INTRODUCTION TO COMMERCIAL REAL ESTATE LAW

This chapter outlines commercial real estate transactions from a developer's perspective, primarily in the representation of real estate entrepreneurs and equity partners in the development, purchase, sale, and related financing of income producing properties. For those working for banks and institutions financing these transactions, this chapter will be helpful in that you can "reverse" the checklists and see what types of documents you will be producing and reviewing. Note that production of loan documents is not covered here. However, there are general tips and caveats that will work for you regardless of your practice area.

PROFILE:

"I started working in the legal profession when I was nineteen years old. I had just gotten married with a baby on the way. My mother-in-law was a legal secretary and worked for a circuit judge in Dallas. She took me to work with her one morning, showed me how to use a Dictaphone and type pleadings, and then that afternoon she took me to my first job interview.

"After my daughter was born, I worked as a legal secretary for about seven years, and then was informed that our law firm was dissolving. Parker Nelson, my primary attorney who specialized in commercial real estate, decided to go out on his own and asked me if I would go with him. He offered to send me to paralegal school at Southern Methodist University if I accepted. Needless to say, I jumped at the chance!

"We eventually joined Calhoun, Gump, Spillman & Stacy, a downtown firm, and were there for about thirteen years. During that time, I worked in many different practice areas: bankruptcy, intellectual property, business, and corporate law, while keeping current with real estate law. This diversity kept me employed during a time when real estate was slow, and most real estate paralegals were changing practice areas out of necessity.

"In July of 2000, we joined Glast, Phillips, & Murray P.C., where I am now working, primarily with J. Scott Jackson in the real estate section. Although there were many people who trained me and showed me the ropes, my mother-in-law never lets me forget that she is the one who got me started!"

OVERVIEW OF RESPONSIBILITIES:

Our primary practice area is representation of real estate entrepreneurs and equity partners in development, purchase, sale, and related financing of income-producing properties. (We do not handle lender representation.)

I. Acquisition/Sale of Real Estate

  A. Initial Contract Review

    1. Review real estate sales contract immediately upon execution and calculate critical dates. Note non-standard provisions.

    2. Prepare critical dates outline/checklist and send to client.

    3. Post critical dates on follow-up calendar.

  B. Contract Administration

    1. Follow up with attorneys, client, title company, and surveyor to ensure that documents required by contract are provided on a timely basis and note it on checklist.

    2. Prepare any contract amendments or extension agreements as required and post revised critical dates.

    3. Prepare and process estoppel certificates and subordination agreements.

C. Title Review (for Acquisitions Only)

    1. Examine title commitment, all title exception documents, and survey and note how they affect the property.

    2. Prepare title objection letter and make sure it is delivered to the seller and other parties as required by the contract.

    3. Note commencement of time based upon issuance of title objection letter and post on follow-up calendar.

    4. Process title curative matters, such as having blanket easements located and limited to specific areas, and then amending the easement documents accordingly.

D. Closing

    1. Review contract again to make sure that all required documents are prepared.

    2. Prepare draft of closing documents and their figures and submit to opposing counsel for review.

    3. Prepare authority documents for client to buy/sell and make sure that the title company has any entity documentation that they require.

    4. If the client is taking title in a new entity, form the entity with the secretary of state and prepare ancillary formation documents; have all signed by client and post any annual meeting requirements on the follow-up calendar.

    5. Organize documents for closing and prepare the title company closing instruction letter.

    6. Oversee execution and delivery of closing documents, either in person or by messenger delivery.

    7. Confirm closing and funding.

E. Post-Closing

    1. Follow up with the title company and obtain copies of all closing documents.

    2. Prepare closing checklist for document binders and note outstanding items.

    3. Finalize closing binders and send to client. Note follow-up items and post on follow-up calendar. Deliver documents to client as received.

II. Financing/Construction Loans (General)

    A. Review construction loan documents. Check negotiated revisions and process through closing. Prepare summaries for client.

    B. Process architect and contractor's contracts.

    C. Work with developers on zoning and platting issues.

    D. Assemble documents as required by lenders and work through lender checklists with client to facilitate closing and funding.

III. Leases

    A. Review leases and prepare lease abstracts or summaries.

    B. Post any critical dates on the follow-up calendar.

    C. Prepare drafts of leases for review.

IV. Foreclosures

    A. Review loan documents to determine notice requirements and other parameters.

    B. Prepare notice letters to debtor, notices of sale, and if required, appointment of substitute trustee (also serve as substitute trustee, if requested).

    C. File and post the foreclosure notices with the county clerk's office.

    D. Either conduct the foreclosure sales or prepare appropriate documentation for the substitute trustee to conduct it.

    E. Prepare post-sale document binders.

V. Business Entities

    A. Check entity name availability with appropriate secretary of state.

    B. Prepare entity documents and file with the secretary of state.

    C. Order minute book, if required, and prepare ancillary entity documents, including any stock certificates, applications for employer identification numbers, and S-election forms, if required.

    D. Prepare assumed name certificates, if required, and file with appropriate jurisdictions.

    E. Prepare foreign qualification documents, if required, and file with appropriate jurisdictions.

    F. Prepare instruction letter sending documents to client for execution and return.

    G. Post any meeting dates on follow-up calendar.

    H. Annual meetings.

      1. Prepare annual resolutions if by unanimous consent and send to client for execution and placement with the entity records.

      2. If conducting an annual meeting, assist client with preparation of meeting notices and attend meeting to act as secretary, if required; prepare meeting minutes and have executed and filed with the entity records.

    I. Prepare drafts of partnership agreements.

    J. Transfers of stock or partnership/LLC interests.

      1. Prepare appropriate documents for filing with the secretary of state.

      2. Prepare amendments to entity documents and resolutions to effect transfers.

TYPICAL WORKWEEK:

- I start each day checking in with my assistant to prioritize her assignments and determine her availability for other work. Then I check my e-mail and messages to see if there are any priority projects. There is not really a "typical" workweek because my time is prioritized based upon closings and other deadlines, some of which are not known at the start of the week.

- Routine assignments include preparation of deeds for closing and reviewing title work received for each tract of property. I review the easements affecting the property and note their parameters, I review the survey to determine compliance with parking requirements, ADA compliance, and so forth, I review title documents to determine restrictions and their impact on development of the project. We then meet with the client to discuss any issues that will affect the development or use of the property. I contact the title company to discuss required title endorsements and the deletion or modification of certain items on the title commitment, and prepare a title objection letter based upon my title review.

■ I review settlement statements, prepare closing instruction letters to the title companies, and check the status of the purchasing entity to ensure good standing. If the purchasing entity is not formed, then I form it and prepare the other organizational documents and authority documents that will be required by the title company, including any foreign state qualifications. I also prepare and file UCC forms (Uniform Commercial Code) with the secretary of state, prepare releases of lien, and send them to the lender for execution. I may also prepare leases for certain owners to continue occupancy of the properties for a short period after closing.

■ Many transactions do not close according to schedule for various reasons, and in these instances I prepare contract amendments and extensions.

The key to managing it all is to prepare a closing checklist at the onset and maintain it throughout closing.

PRACTICAL TIPS, SHORTCUTS, AND TRICKS OF THE TRADE:

■ **Attend a qualified, ABA-approved paralegal program.** Paralegal school helped me to understand *why* I was doing the tasks that I was assigned to do. Before obtaining my paralegal certificate, I just did what I was told—the way I was told to do it. Now I can see the big picture, I know *why* things must be done, and *how to do it* correctly. That is empowering. I feel like I can do almost anything.

■ **Make certain that you understand the assignment and its parameters.** Often the attorneys have allocated a certain amount of time (i.e., money) for a task. If it will take you longer to complete the assignment than they allowed, let them know immediately so that they can communicate with their clients. Make certain that your attorneys know your schedule and the time frame within which you can complete their assignments.

■ **Do not be offended if attorneys give you menial or very basic assignments in the beginning.** They are trying to get a feel for the quality and timeliness of your work. Give those assignments the proper priority and do them well. Once they get to know you and the quality of your work, you can ask for and will be trusted with more challenging work.

- **Remember that every day you go into the office you are marketing yourself.** Your "clients" are the attorneys and their clients. Make certain that you present a professional appearance and that you have an upbeat, positive demeanor. Whether or not anything is ever said to you, people notice if you are competent, professional, and easy to work with. I cannot tell you the number of job offers I have received from opposing counsel after we close a deal.

- **When you are feeling overwhelmed,** remember that the attorneys (in most instances) do not care if you personally do the work—they just want it to get done. Ask about getting assistance or out-sourcing all or a portion of the project.

- **Be the "go to" person.** Keep up with technology and information available to you so that you are able to get information quickly and efficiently. You will be a valuable asset to your firm. Also, be versatile and willing to learn new skills. In a tight economy, these skills could make the difference between staying employed or not.

- **Take responsibility for your own education and career growth.** Sometimes this means working late on your own time to learn a new skill. Take advantage of on-site training or continuing education offered by your firm and paralegal associations.

- **Join professional organizations.** They provide you with opportunities to network with other paralegals and vendors, and provide you with opportunities for continuing education. It can be a real lifesaver to call a colleague with experience when you have a tough project and need information quickly. In addition, it is good to get feedback from your peers on how they handle projects or situations. It is helpful to know the vendors and the services they provide.

MORE QUICK TIPS:

- **Checklists.** Paralegals would all be lost without them. Develop a system for handling the routine tasks; even though they vary from file to file, you will have a good starting point.

- **Follow up on stored files.** Stored or filed files without a follow-up date tend to be forgotten. Mark everything until the file is complete and ready to close, with reminders for critical dates and ample lead time to make certain that things are done in a timely manner. At any given point, we have 30 or more active files.

- **Communication.** Always copy your supervising attorney and the client on your e-mails or other communication so that they know the status of your work. Devise a report form for this purpose and use it on a weekly basis.

- **Form file.** When you are new to the job, keep copies of any revisions to your documents that were made by the attorney. If it is not obvious why the revisions were made, ask and make a note. Then when you do a similar project, you can refer to the prior one and not repeat the same mistakes.

- **Questions.** When working on a project, work through it as much as you can, make a list of questions that you need answered before you can complete the project, and then ask your attorney about them at one time, instead of constantly interrupting every time you need an answer. Your attorney's time is valuable, usually billed out at two to three times your hourly rate. Respect that, and use the attorney's time efficiently.

REMEMBER:

- **Always check everything before a letter or document goes out.** Do not get so involved in the content of the letter that you forget to check the obvious. Computers and forms are great, but it is embarrassing to send out a letter with an old date on the header of page two, or worse, the incorrect subject line or addressee.

- **Be proactive.** Never assume that someone else is doing his or her job. One major action you can take to differentiate yourself from others is to be proactive. Many people send out a request, and they do not give it a second thought after that because the ball is in someone else's court. They just hope the other person does their job, and they send them the items they requested. You cannot take a chance that someone else will do his or her job. You must follow up yourself.

■ **Follow up.** Never assume that someone is going to respond to your requests. When a request goes out, give the person a few days to receive it and answer it, post that date on your follow-up calendar, and then call, write, or e-mail them. You need to get the job done, and you cannot do that by being passive. If you get no response after several attempts, report to your attorney so that he can decide how to handle it from there.

■ **Keep track of what you have reviewed.** As you review contracts, highlight those portions that you have included in the contract summary so that you can tell at a glance what you have and have not covered. The system works well also when you are implementing comments that someone has marked on your draft. Highlight the changes as they are made so that you can quickly ascertain if any revisions were omitted.

ORGANIZATIONAL METHODS:

Step 1: Get an overview of the entire project so that you can see how your tasks fit in with the whole project. You need to understand the desired results. There is a difference between keeping up with the details and killing the deal with minutia.

Step 2: Prepare a checklist outlining the necessary steps to complete the project.

Step 3: Break down each of the steps and decide who will handle each portion.

Step 4: Prepare an estimated timeline for completion of each step.

Step 5: Obtain and provide forms for use with preparation of documents required by each step.

Step 6: Follow up and update checklist.

SUSAN'S HANDY TIPS:

Remember these checklists will become dated and are starting points only, as no one checklist can anticipate every detail of a closing. Make sure your attorney reviews your checklist so the legal and ethical points will be covered.

TECHNOLOGY TECHNIQUES:

■ Some secretaries of state offer online filing for entity documents, assumed name certificates, and UCC filings. Check the Web pages to determine what you can and cannot file online. This is the fastest, most efficient way to form an entity or check UCC records, often with same day results.

■ It is amazing how much information is available on the internet. We use LexisNexis® to obtain entity information, but most secretaries of state have their own Web pages with varying levels of information available to the public at no charge.

■ Likewise, property records are in the public domain. Most tax assessors have web pages where you can search a property by owner name or street address. Try to obtain this information first before you resort to other services. When you find a great resource, save it as a favorite.

■ When you are using an online service, such as Westlaw® or LexisNexis®, where you are either charged by the minute or by the search, be careful when an attorney requests "everything you can get" on an individual or company. Explain how much information is available and how much it will cost before proceeding. This will prevent you from running up a large bill that was not anticipated.

SYSTEMATIC PROCEDURES:

Several years ago, I read about a technique of document assembly in a State Bar of Texas publication that I found helpful. I customized these procedures for forming entities, for dissolving them, for simple loans, and for foreclosures. You can develop the system for any procedure that is forms-oriented. You can use this system if you are repeating the same information in different documents.

First, assemble all of the documents that you prepare from start to finish. For example, for a corporate formation, this includes the following documents:

■ Articles of organization
■ Bylaws
■ Organizational minutes

■ Other ancillary documents

■ Final letter sending all of the documents to the client

Highlight all of the variable information in these documents, and then prepare a numbered list of variables, with number "1" being the entity name, "2" being the principal address, and "3" being the registered agent, and so on. Then using the Merge feature in Microsoft® Word®, you can prepare forms with merge codes for each of the numbered variables. When a new file comes in, complete the data to create the data file, and then merge the data file with the appropriate documents. This creates consistency and eliminates typographical errors from document to document.

SUSAN'S HANDY TIPS:

Be careful that the data file is completely accurate because any error in a form will show up in all of the documents that you create.

We also prepare "standard" forms of resolutions, and for each entity that requires annual meetings, we set up a control sheet to monitor these actions.

WRITING TIPS:

1. Be succinct. You can lose your reader after the first paragraph. It is helpful to prepare an outline of the points you wish to convey.

2. Consider your goals and what you want to accomplish:

■ For example, when preparing minutes authorizing a transaction, consider what actions must be approved and by whom.

■ Does the transaction require director approval, shareholder approval, or both?

■ Start with an outline of the transaction, and then move to the specific resolutions that must be approved. Standard resolutions streamline processing the documents.

DOCUMENT PREPARATION:

1. Do not reinvent the wheel. Most attorneys have forms that they prefer you use, and you should always ask before you begin to draft a document.

2. If they do not maintain a forms file, start one yourself. This eliminates errors and greatly improves the quality of work produced.

We maintain a forms bank and add to it when we do particularly creative work or deal with unusual provisions.

3. If you are preparing a document from scratch, it is helpful to outline the history, or why the document is being executed, in the first section of the document, and then move to the substantive sections.

CLIENT INTERACTIONS AND INTERVIEWING:

> **PRACTICE TIPS** It is more effective for the paralegal to attend client meetings or conference calls so that the attorney does not have to spend time relaying the information to the paralegal later. This will also facilitate client interaction and help you accomplish the project more efficiently.

■ Questionnaires and checklists are helpful in getting the client to focus on certain aspects of the project. For example, when an attorney comes in and asks for your assistance in forming an entity, you can produce your data checklist and get all of the information that you need to complete the assignment. Your only time restraint will be the processing times of the various secretary of state offices and the sufficiency of the client's data.

■ Be persistent in following up with the client to give you the information you need.

■ Copy the client with e-mails and copies of letters.

TRANSACTION POINTERS:

In real estate acquisitions (unimproved land), the procedures are the same, but it is always a different deal with different challenges:

1. Meet with client to obtain deal points for transaction.

2. Prepare draft of contract based upon deal points provided.

3. After negotiation of the contract and the contract is signed, obtain a signed copy, and prepare the critical dates outline, and post to follow-up calendar.

4. Follow up with title company and/or surveyor to obtain title commitment and survey for title review.

5. Review title work and prepare title objection letter.

6. Determine title endorsements that will be required and negotiate them.

7. Determine what curative actions the seller, if any, will take. In addition, determine what actions the client must take if they wish to proceed based on title review.

8. Take any curative actions that the client requires, for example, discussions with utility providers to relocate utility lines or to obtain permission to build over them.

9. Review any additional documents provided by the seller, such as environmental reports, leases (for unimproved property there are often agricultural leases) to determine their impact on the property.

10. Once the client is satisfied with title and intends to proceed to closing, start preparing closing documents. The contract typically outlines the documents required. The title company also lists documents that they need to close the transaction. (See checklists previously provided.)

11. After your attorney approves the documents, opposing counsel and the title company need to approve them.

POST-CLOSING

- Title Policy. Always check the title policy to make sure that it reconciles with the title commitment that you received and that you received the endorsements that you requested. In checking one policy, we discovered that the title company had inadvertently recorded our lien documents in the incorrect county. This would have been a major issue later when we needed to foreclose if we had not discovered this error and corrected it.

- Closing Binders. Much work goes into closings, and while the client knows this, a closing binder is tangible proof of the work that you have done. It is simply good marketing to get them prepared promptly after closing, using three-ring notebooks or whatever type of binder the client prefers. Clients love having all of the documents in one place in an organized file after closing.

PRACTICE TIPS, SHORTCUTS, AND TRICKS OF THE TRADE:

CDs. We use a copy service that also scans in the documents in PDF format so that we have a hard copy in the form of a binder, plus a copy on a CD to deliver to the client. The CDs are especially helpful, because they can be maintained in your office long after the physical file has been sent off-site for storage. Often, clients will pull documents out of the binders and neglect to put them back, and then they have to call us to get a copy of the missing document.

CDs allow you to send documents from the binders as e-mail attachments without retrieving the physical file from archives whenever someone needs a copy. CDs can also be duplicated inexpensively if the client needs all of the documents to be delivered to another lender for some other purpose, such as re-financing of the project.

Binders. The contents, style, and format of the binders will vary depending upon your client and the preference of your attorney. We include most of the items on the checklist, including the contract of sale, any amendments, acquisition documents, title documents including any active title exceptions, loan documents, and entity documents for any entities you formed to acquire the property. We typically include everything unless the copying charges become prohibitive, such as lengthy environmental reports, or copies of leases in an apartment complex. again, it depends on your client's preferences.

WORK WORLD EXAMPLES:

ENTITY FORMATION ASAP

In commercial transactions, the company that signs a contract as the purchaser typically assigns its interest in the contract to another, newly formed entity that will actually take title and own the property. The purchaser does not want to form a new entity too early in the process, because it costs several thousand dollars to do so, and they do not wish to incur these expenses until they are certain they will go forward with the closing. This often leaves the paralegal scrambling at the last moments to form the entities that will take title as the purchaser (and if they are financing the acquisition, then these entities will be the borrower). The transaction cannot close until the purchaser/borrower exists.

WHAT YOU CAN DO TO EASE THIS PROCESS

1. Find out early on if a new entity will be formed, and its structure. For example, will they use a limited partnership, and if so, will the general partner be a newly formed entity or an existing one?

2. Find out if the new entity will be foreign or domestic, and if domestic, will it need to qualify to do business in another state?

3. Once you have this information, you can review the required forms for formation and qualification if necessary, and determine if the general partner will also need to qualify in another state. Most of the secretaries of state have these forms available online, so you can review them and discover the information that you will need to file these documents.

4. Confirm filing requirements that vary from state to state, and most importantly, ascertain how quickly these entities can be formed. Some states will file your formation documents immediately, while others take days or even weeks to process your documents. You do not want to hold up a closing because you did not get the entities formed in time.

5. If required by your lender, you may need to request certificates of good standing at the time of filing in order to receive them in a timely manner.

6. Find out if the secretary of state will accept facsimile signatures or if they require originals. Then confirm that your client will be available to sign the documents if necessary. Travel is necessary for most real estate developers, so you cannot assume that they will be available to sign documents when you need them.

REAL WORK EXAMPLES:

THE "BIG" CLOSING

- The work leading up to this closing was incredible. The day before closing, documents were still being negotiated, and opposing counsel decided that it would be more efficient if we were responsible for printing and assembling the documents. It took four of us working into the wee hours in order to have everything organized for a smooth closing.

- At closing, I was the ringmaster. We wound up with 436 documents, 4 counterparts of each, for a total of 1,744 documents—all requiring signatures. We had as many as seven different persons who had to sign some or all of the documents, and they did not all come in to sign at the same time. We color coded the signature tabs to keep up with whose signature was required for each document, and we had a master checklist with "mini-checklists" for each transaction that outlined who signed each document and the exhibits to be attached.

- We commandeered the conference room and set up tables with boxes of documents just outside. When clients came in, we were able to pull only the documents that they needed to sign so they could get in and out quickly. I had two secretaries handling all of the notarizations and checking the documents (as they were signed) for missed signatures, while I monitored the checklists. We closed the deal and had all of the documents signed and notarized in less than four hours. We then prepared document summaries of each of the documents and prepared 28 closing binders, had them duplicated, and then distributed to all of the parties.

Part V

RESIDENTIAL REAL ESTATE

CHAPTER 11

JILL J. HALE, PP, PLS, CLA
RESIDENTIAL REAL ESTATE (with responsibilities in Probate & Estate)
ROBERTS & CARVER, PLLC
Prescott, AZ

*"From the start of my legal career, Jill has provided encouragement and support.
When I was a young, wet-behind-the-ears lawyer, Jill showed me the ropes. She
has always been extremely knowledgeable and willing to share that knowledge.
Jill's goal-oriented style and compassion for others has set an example for me
throughout my career."*

Paul L. Roberts

EDUCATION/HONORS/AWARDS:

- The Paralegal Institute, Phoenix, AZ, 1979 (Diploma, Lawyer's Assistant, Litigation)
- Lamson Business College, legal secretary program, Phoenix, AZ, 1971
- Runner-up for LAT (*Legal Assistant Today* magazine) Paralegal of the Year, 2003
- Lamson Business College Merit Award for Outstanding Achievement, 1971
- Yavapai County Legal Secretary of the Year, 1981 and 1988
- Arizona Legal Secretary of the Year, 1981 and 1988
- NALS Continuing Legal Education Award, 1983, 1986, 1989, 1992, 1994, 1996, 1998, 2000, 2003, and 2006
- Arizona Award of Excellence, 1994
- Finalist for NALS Award of Excellence, 1994

PROFESSIONAL ASSOCIATIONS/CERTIFICATIONS:

- NALS Certified PLS (an advanced certification for legal professionals), March 1980, with recertification in 1994, 1999, and 2004.
- NALA Certified Legal Assistant, June 1992, with recertification in 1997, 2002, and 2007. CLA recertification requires 50 hours of CLE over a five-year period.
- NALS certified Professional Paralegal, December 2003

FAMILY:

Born in Wakefield, Nebraska, and moved to Prescott, Arizona. Married 33 years to Richard. Jill enjoys performing with the community theater, chamber singers, and a clogging team.

FIRM AT-A-GLANCE:

Roberts & Carver, PLLC
239 South Cortez Street
Prescott, AZ
Phone: 928.445.8824
Fax: 928.445.6231

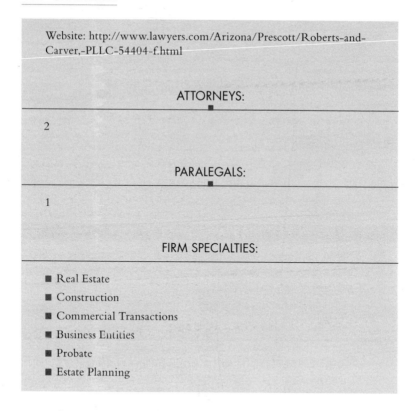

Website: http://www.lawyers.com/Arizona/Prescott/Roberts-and-Carver,-PLLC-54404-f.html

ATTORNEYS:

2

PARALEGALS:

1

FIRM SPECIALTIES:

- Real Estate
- Construction
- Commercial Transactions
- Business Entities
- Probate
- Estate Planning

INTRODUCTION TO RESIDENTIAL TRANSACTIONS:

As with most areas of the law, working in the real estate arena presents many challenges. The gathering of detailed information for each transaction starts the process. A detail-oriented person can thrive in this environment. One important thing to remember is that one must never rely on one's memory to be sure all items have been included. Checklists are vital. Use this sample real estate transaction checklist. (See Figure 11-1.)

Real estate transactions (both residential and commercial) and business asset sales lend themselves to the use of "boilerplate," or template, forms. However, each type of transaction has different requirements. One checklist does not fit all, and one contract form does not fit all. Once an initial form is chosen as the starting point, the form must be reviewed carefully to make sure each provision fits the current project. Then the checklist must be reviewed for other items that may need to be added.

Figure 11-1

REAL ESTATE SALE INFORMATION CHECKLIST

Seller

Name _____

Address _____

Telephone number _____

Fax number _____

E-mail address _____

Buyer

Name _____

Address _____

Telephone number _____

Fax number _____

E-mail address _____

How buyer(s) intend(s) to **take title:** _____

Our **office represents**   ☐ Seller   ☐ Buyer

Ask if client has consulted **accountant**   _____

Request **Commitment for Title Insurance**   _____

Desired **title company/escrow officer** _____
_____

Description of real property _____
_____
_____
_____
_____
_____

Address or identifiable location of real property _____
_____
_____
_____
_____
_____

Assessor's Parcel Number of real property _____

Description and approximate value of any personal property included _____
_____
_____
_____
_____
_____
_____

Liens or encumbrances on real or personal property, and how they are to be handled _____
_____
_____
_____
_____

Entire agreement clause   _____

Governing law clause   _____

Acceptance of joint tenancy   _____

Acceptance of community property with right of survivorship   _____

Closing:

Date   _____

Time   _____

Place   _____

Documents to be prepared:

☐ Contract for Sale/Purchase

☐ Articles to create entity

☐ Disclosure documents

☐ Deed of Trust and Assignment of Rents

　　　Trustee name _____

　　　Trustee address _____

☐ Direction for Deed of Release

☐ Deed of Release and Full Reconveyance

☐ Promissory Note

☐ Personal Guaranty

☐ Corporate Guaranty

☐ Security Agreement

☐ UCC Financing Statement

- ☐ UCC Termination Statement
- ☐ Deed (warranty, joint ten, com. prop. w/ROS)
- ☐ Affidavit of Real Property Value
- ☐ Bill of Sale
- ☐ Assignment of Lease and Consent
- ☐ Lease
- ☐ Disclaimer Deed from spouse
- ☐ Settlement Statement

Who assumes risk of loss during term and how loss or destruction will be handled

_____

Warranties by seller

- ☐ Title to real property marketable
- ☐ Personal property in good condition
- ☐ No law suits pending or threatened
- ☐ No judgment against seller or property
- ☐ Seller existing and in good standing   What state _____
- ☐ Other warranties _____

_____

_____

Warranties by buyer

- ☐ Property inspected
- ☐ Purchasing as is
- ☐ Buyer existing and in good standing   What state _____
- ☐ Other warranties _____

_____

_____

Consequences for failure to close

Seller _____

_____

Buyer _____

_____

Default terms (rights of each party) and attorneys' fees clause _____

_____

_____

Time of essence clause _____

Parties in interest/binding clause _____

Provisions and addresses for giving of notices _____

_____

  Include notice to escrow officer _____ _____

Hold harmless clause _____ Include hazardous waste language?

_____

- ☐ Phase I or other environmental assessment
- ☐ Use or other permits
- ☐ Buyer financing
- ☐ Approval of development agreements and entitlements
- ☐ Location of easements and access
- ☐ Determination regarding FEMA flood hazard area
- ☐ Water rights
- ☐ Determination regarding any existing leases, encroachments, liens, etc.
- ☐ Sale of other property by buyer
- ☐ 1031 exchange cooperation
- ☐ Other _____ _____

_____

Due diligence period _____

Required disclosures
- ☐ Seller's Property Disclosure Statement
- ☐ Affidavit of Disclosure
- ☐ Lead-based paint
- ☐ Swimming pool
- ☐ Other _____

_____

Allocation of purchase price, if any _____

Who pays costs of sale, escrow, recording, attorneys' fees
  ☐ Seller   ☐ Buyer   ☐ Split % _____

Escrow agent
  Name _____
  Company _____
  Address _____
  Telephone number _____
  Fax number _____
  E-mail address _____

Insurance coverage (fire, liability) during term and who pays _____

_____

Purchase price $ _____

Terms of sale

Earnest money/down payment $ _____

Payable by _____

Assumption of underlying encumbrance (description and amount) _____

_____

_____

Installments and other terms of sale _____

_____

_____

_____

_____

_____

Interest rate on note if amount carried back _____

Late payment penalty and start date _____

Default interest rate and start date _____

Additional provisions for contract

Who will be responsible for real and personal property taxes and assessments

☐ Seller ☐ Buyer ☐ Prorated to close of sale

Brokerage commission payable

How much _____

To whom _____

Who pays ☐ Seller ☐ Buyer ☐ Split % _____

Title insurance

☐ Standard	Who pays	☐ Seller	☐ Buyer	☐ Split % ____
☐ Extended	Who pays	☐ Seller	☐ Buyer	☐ Split % ____

Lender's policy needed ☐ Yes ☐ No

☐ Standard	Who pays	☐ Seller	☐ Buyer	☐ Split % ____
☐ Extended	Who pays	☐ Seller	☐ Buyer	☐ Split % ____

Contingencies:

☐ Approval of provisions of commitment for title insurance

Delivery date of commitment _____

☐ Confirmation of appropriate zoning

☐ Standard survey	Who pays	☐ Seller	☐ Buyer	☐ Split % _____
☐ Extended survey	Who pays	☐ Seller	☐ Buyer	☐ Split % _____

Although some of the laws of a particular state may apply to each type of sale or purchase in general, each project will also involve specific laws or rules that will differ from those that pertain to another type of transaction. A business asset sale may include Uniform Commercial Code (UCC) concerns for bulk sales or special security devices. A residential sale may include requirements that special disclosures be made, such as lead-based paint, asbestos insulation, septic or alternative wastewater treatment systems, or swimming pools. Commercial real estate transactions may include environmental concerns, zoning codes, and use permits.

THE PARALEGAL'S ROLE IN RESIDENTIAL REAL ESTATE:

Where does one start? As mentioned earlier, the first three steps to beginning a transaction are as follows:

1. Gather information using the appropriate checklist.
2. Choose a basic form of contract and other documents.
3. Carefully compare the contract form, the information gathered, and the checklist to make sure all necessary provisions have been included.

At Roberts & Carver, we process both commercial and residential transactions, as well as numerous business asset sales. Normally, I am included in the initial conference with the attorney and the clients. We gather some preliminary information before that first meeting, such as:

- Type of transaction contemplated (purchase or sale of raw or developed land)
- Purpose (residential or commercial development or a possible change in zoning for use)
- The name of the other party and whether a new entity will be required as part of the project.

Having these basics allows us to choose the appropriate checklist and perform a "conflict of interest" check to make sure that any of the firm's clients do not have a conflict with the potential clients. If your firm does not have a conflicts software program, research and talk to other paralegals in similar-sized firms to obtain recommendations.

Often, the client asks us to create an entity to be the buyer or developer in a project. We gather that information at the first meeting with the clients, along with details regarding the transaction. The attorney may ask me to leave the meeting briefly to check on the status of a business entity, the availability of a name for a new entity, or to verify the ownership or the tax status of a parcel of property. We need to make these determinations early in case a problem is evident from the outset.

PROFILE:

One event can change a life. I was a starry-eyed teenager from a rural Arizona town who had dreams of becoming a professional actress, but my father died when I was 16 years old, and my whole world changed. There was little money for college, and my mother needed me close to home.

The attorney for whom my mother worked as a legal secretary offered me a job in the law office as a file clerk and errand runner. Legal work was fascinating. After attending a legal secretarial course and graduating in half the normal time, I returned to the office where my mother worked and have been here for over 35 years. I am now employed as a paralegal.

After serving in offices at the local, state, and national levels of the National Association of Legal Secretaries (NALS), the association for legal professionals, I was national president during the 2001–2002 fiscal years. I continue to be active in NALS today, currently serving on a national committee to monitor activity across the country regarding certification and regulation of paralegals, as the marketing director of NALS of Arizona, and as immediate past president and newsletter editor of NALS of Yavapai County. I am also a member of a number of other professional, law-related associations. Belonging to multiple associations helps me keep abreast of trends in the legal field.

TYPICAL WORKWEEK:

DAY 1

1. Conference with client and attorney regarding preparation of estate planning documents; memorandum to file.
2. Call from client asking that a certificate of trust existence be faxed to a bank; arrange for fax to be sent by office assistant and memorandum to file.
3. Conference with attorney and draft letter to CPA regarding irrevocable trust.

4. Conference with attorney regarding change in corporate stock ownership for three corporations, finalize consents in lieu of meetings, and prepare new stock certificates and update stock transfer ledger.

5. Prepare documents to change statutory agent for two corporations and a limited liability company and prepare transmittal letters.

6. Check status of three corporations with the Arizona Corporation Commission, draft consent in lieu of annual meeting and letter to one client, draft annual report and transmittal letter for second client, and draft letter to third client regarding need for annual meeting.

DAY 2

1. Conference with clients and attorney to finalize stock ownership transfers for three corporations and memorandum to file.

2. Call from client with details for incorporating nonprofit corporation; check proposed name with the Arizona Corporation Commission and existence of trade name with the secretary of state and memorandum to file.

3. Review affidavit of publication from newspaper; prepare transmittal letter to Corporation Commission.

4. Draft warranty deed and prepare affidavit of property value for limited liability company.

5. Telephone conference with client and attorney regarding spouses' possible interest in corporate stock and prepare memorandum to file.

6. Conference with attorney regarding preparation of promissory note and prepare memorandum to file.

7. Conference with attorney regarding terms for business sale and prepare memorandum to file.

8. Conference with attorney and prepare draft contract for sale of airport lease rights.

9. Call from client regarding existing limited liability company and organization of two more limited liability companies and prepare memorandum to file.

10. Draft consent in lieu of annual meeting for corporation and letter to client.

11. Conference with attorney and review written consent from lien holder allowing property to be deeded to limited liability company and prepare draft letter to title company regarding title insurance.

Day 3

1. Review facsimile from CPA and signed documents from clients, update limited liability company records, and revise operating agreement and prepare draft consents and disclaimers.

2. Review signed real property documents from clients; conference with attorney and prepare draft transmittal letter to recorder.

3. Review court order regarding a probate; conference with attorney and prepare memorandum to file.

4. Prepare statements of change of known place of business for five limited liability companies and two corporations and prepare transmittal letters to Corporation Commission.

5. Review letter from sellers' attorney regarding draft contract for purchase of residential property.

6. Conference with attorney regarding organization of new limited liability company.

7. E-mail messages to and from title company; call to court regarding filing of affidavit of succession to real property and prepare memorandum to file.

8. Review memorandum from attorney; draft follow-up letter to clients regarding status of operating agreement for limited liability company.

9. Finish first draft of contract for sale of airport lease rights.

10. Review letter from IRS and prepare draft letter to clients regarding electronic payment of taxes.

11. Review signed documents from clients; prepare transmittal letter to Corporation Commission with articles of amendment to articles of organization for LLC; review promissory note; draft pledge agreement, UCC financing statement, and consent in lieu of meeting of members.

12. Review consent from lien holder and draft transmittal letter to title company.

DAY 4

1. Review information on Web sites at Corporation Commission, secretary of state, and county recorder; draft articles of incorporation for nonprofit corporation and prepare statement of trade name holder.

2. Review drafts of stock transfer agreement and partnership interest transfer agreement prepared by attorney.

3. Review corporate records supplied by new client and check on-line information at Corporation Commission and Registrar of Contractors, prepare memorandum to attorney, prepare application for registration of trade name and fictitious name certificate, conference with attorney regarding property ownership and plans and prepare memorandum to file.

4. Conference with attorney regarding septic system inspection requirement for residential property and prepare memorandum to file.

5. Calls from and to client regarding probate matter; call to court and exchange e-mail messages with escrow officer and prepare memorandum to file.

6. Review records for another corporation of new client and review on-line information at Corporation Commission and prepare memorandum to attorney.

7. Draft articles of organization and cover sheet for submitting two new limited liability companies; conference with attorney and prepare memorandum to each file.

8. Letter to title company regarding deed for subdivision property, call from client, and conference with attorney and prepare memorandum to file.

9. Conference with attorney regarding preparation of articles for new corporation and prepare memorandum to file.

10. Review information from client regarding existing limited liability company; draft articles of amendment to articles of organization and prepare memorandum to attorney.

11. Review information from client regarding two new limited liability companies; check name availability with Corporation Commission and draft articles of organization and filing cover sheets.

Day 5

1. Prepare annual reports and transmittal letters for four corporations.
2. Conference with attorney and draft letter to client with memoranda of status previously prepared for two corporations.
3. Conference with attorney and draft letter to client regarding execution of articles of organization for two new limited liability companies.
4. Conference with attorney and draft sample form of commercial covenants, conditions, and restrictions and mail to client for review.
5. Conference with attorney and review information from client and review on-line information at Corporation Commission, secretary of state, and Registrar of Contractors.
6. Draft articles of organization, statement of trade name holder, and filing cover sheet for new limited liability company.
7. Revise contract for purchase of residential property.
8. Review certificate of death for client, conference with attorney, prepare transmittal letter to recorder, and draft affidavit of termination of tenancy.
9. Conference with attorney regarding preparation of contract for sale of real property and memorandum to file.
10. Revise contract for sale of airport lease rights and prepare transmittal letter to client.
11. Revise consent in lieu of meeting and pledge agreement for limited liability company.

OVERVIEW OF JOB RESPONSIBILITIES:

I. Real Property and Contracts
  A. Meet with clients and attorneys
  B. Research property ownership
  C. Obtain copies of surveys, deeds, and encumbrances
  D. Research Uniform Commercial Code filings
  E. Research status of parties
  F. Review legal descriptions and title issues

G. Review and analyze documents, including deeds, leases, security devices, appraisals, surveys, plat maps, and subdivision maps

H. Assist with due diligence investigations

I. Prepare memoranda for attorneys

J. Draft contracts for sale or purchase of real property (both commercial and residential), business assets, and for subdivision lot sales

K. Draft deeds, bills of sale, security documents, easements, affidavits of value, leases, option agreements, and assignments

L. Draft correspondence and consent and disclosure documents

M. Draft covenants, conditions, and restrictions for residential and commercial developments

N. Assemble documents for public reports

O. Notarize documents as needed

P. Attend closings with attorneys and clients

Q. Process recording and filing of documents

R. Follow up after closings as needed

S. Telephone conferences with clients and other legal professionals

T. Telephone conferences with city, county, and state agencies

U. Review Legislative Service regarding any changes in statutes affecting real or personal property and report to attorney

II. Business and Corporate

A. Meet with clients and attorneys

B. Review and analyze documents and online information regarding status of existing corporations, companies, and partnerships

C. Reserve names for corporations, limited liability companies, and contractors

D. Corporations

1. Draft organizational and governance documents, including articles of incorporation, certificates of disclosure, bylaws, minutes, consents, share certificates, and stock transfer ledgers

2. Draft stock buy-sell agreements

3. Assist with initial tax matters

4. Draft correspondence necessary for filing, publication, and transmittal of documents

5. Maintain records of approximately 190 corporations, including meetings with shareholders, directors, and officers, preparation of minutes of annual and special meetings, consents in lieu of meetings, resolutions, annual reports, annual valuations, stock ownership changes, contracts for sale or purchase of stock, amendments to governance documents, and any needed correspondence

E. Limited Liability Companies

1. Draft organizational and governance documents, including articles of organization, operating agreements, day-to-day operations agreements, and member ownership records

2. Assist with initial tax matters

3. Draft correspondence necessary for filing, publication, and transmittal of documents

4. Maintain records of approximately 70 limited liability companies, including meetings with members and managers, preparation of minutes of annual and special meetings, consents in lieu of meetings, resolutions, annual valuations, changes in members and managers, amendments to governance documents, contracts for sale or purchase of membership interests, and any needed correspondence

F. General and Limited Partnerships

1. Draft organizational documents, including partnership agreements, certificates of limited partnership, and certificates of general partnership

2. Assist with initial tax matters

3. Draft correspondence necessary for filing, recording, and transmittal of documents

G. Draft dissolution documents for corporations and termination documents for limited liability companies

H. Draft documents for state trade name and trademark filings and work with patent and trademark attorney for national filings

    I. Telephone conferences with clients and other legal professionals

    J. Telephone conferences with city, county, and state agencies

    K. Review Legislative Service regarding any changes in statutes affecting business entities and report to attorneys

III. Estate Planning

    A. Meet with clients and attorneys

    B. Research property ownership

    C. Telephone conferences with clients and other legal professionals

    D. Telephone conferences with city, county, and state agencies

    E. Obtain copies of vesting documents evidencing asset ownership

    F. Obtain copies of documents evidencing encumbrances on assets

    G. Review and analyze documents

    H. Prepare memoranda for attorneys

    I. Draft trusts (revocable, irrevocable, and special needs), wills (regular, pour-over, and those incorporating a testamentary trust), health care powers of attorney, durable general powers of attorney, special powers of attorney, and living wills

    J. Provide instruction documents to clients to assist with trust administration

    K. Draft documents to transfer assets to trusts and assist clients in completing all transfers

    L. Process recording and filing of documents

    M. Draft correspondence

IV. Probate and Estates

    A. Meet with clients and attorneys

    B. Telephone conferences with clients and other legal professionals

    C. Telephone conferences with city, county, and state agencies and courts

    D. Review and analyze documents

    E. Prepare memoranda for attorneys

F. Draft pleadings for various types of probate matters, including informal and formal filings, and affidavit of succession to real property

G. Draft documents for non-probate matters, including collection of personal property by affidavit and removing joint tenant owners from titles

H. File probate documents with court

I. Research asset ownership and assist personal representatives (executors) with marshaling assets

J. Draft inventory and arrange for appraisals if needed

K. Help with creditors' claims

L. Assist personal representative with payment of claims and distribution and/or sale of assets

M. Work with CPA regarding estate tax returns

N. Draft documents for conservatorship proceedings if a minor is to receive assets

O. Draft accountings for court

P. Draft probate closing documents and assist with final distribution of assets

TIPS, SHORTCUTS, AND TRICKS OF THE TRADE:

- Never stop learning.
- Be open to change.
- Take advantage of opportunities as they come along.
- Use checklists for everything.
- Share your knowledge with your colleagues and help others.
- Be a team player.
- Join a professional association.
- Be prepared for many challenges.
- **Write it down!** Do not leave anything to memory. Write down instructions from attorneys, clients, and others. Make a note or memorandum regarding every telephone call and attorney/client conference. Include the date, time, people involved, and client matter. Carefully record all deadlines and other important dates. Keep a written log of all projects.

- **Be cheerful and nice to the other staff.** We work together as a team. In a small office, no one is "too good" to make copies, answer the telephone, or help as needed. We keep an eye on costs and try to have the least expensive person do tasks they can do, but that is not always possible.

- **Learn the preferences of each attorney as quickly as possible.** Understanding how each attorney works is an integral part of creating a good working relationship between paralegal and attorney. When you are employed by more than one attorney, you must often work with each in a different way to meet expectations and cope with personality differences. It is important to become familiar with desired turn-around time on projects, different work styles, and expected styles of product.

- **Think ahead and anticipate projects and needs.** At the end of each day, organize and prioritize work for the next day. As you work on projects, prepare reminders for additional items that will be needed and the date by which those need to be completed.

- **Be mindful of your responsibility to your employer.** Do you know what makes your salary "worth it" to the firm? This may include the little things like being on time to work and keeping personal matters to a minimum during the workday. However, it also includes a desire to learn, the ability to think ahead, as well as caring about the firm's reputation and about the other people in the firm.

- **Continue your education.** This includes joining a professional association for the networking, personal, and professional development opportunities. Attend seminars. Take classes. Read professional magazines and textbooks. Read the newspaper on a daily basis.

- **If you are not sure, ASK!** I have worked with some individuals who wanted to appear to "know it all," so they plowed ahead in the dark, too embarrassed or egotistical to ask for assistance. That is not helpful to you, your co-workers, you employer, or the clients. In fact, proceeding with things when you are not sure can lead to a malpractice suit for your firm! On the other side of the coin, if someone asks you for information or assistance, be as helpful as possible, with either the answer or a resource. Be a mentor!

■ **Log in all projects** on the date received and mark them off as they are completed, whether in draft (and number of the draft) or final, to whom the product was delivered (attorney or other staff, mailed, delivered, etc.), and the date. Confirm instructions with the attorney. The Tasks section of Microsoft® Outlook® is excellent for this.

■ **Collect similar items to do together,** if possible, such as copying projects, checks to be written, files to be taken to the file room in exchange for files that are needed from there. (Remember this is a small office with only a part-time office assistant/runner.)

■ **Think of how projects circulate in your office** and around the firm so that "in and out" and deliveries can be as efficient as possible. Do a flow chart to eliminate loss of productivity.

■ **Always use checklists** to make sure a step has not been missed. Establish a checklist if there is not one available for a certain type of project.

■ Gather all the information needed for a project before starting a draft.

■ Locate a similar type of document to use as a starting point.

DOCUMENT PREPARATION:

■ Use checklists and use previous documents to make new templates or forms. Make sure you are clear about the instructions.

■ Organize topics within a document, such as a contract for sale or purchase, in logical order.

■ Learn the capabilities of your computer program and utilize them.

■ Know how to assemble information from many different documents by copying and pasting, and you need to be able to make the entire paragraph and cross-reference numbering work properly.

■ *Proofread carefully!*

- When you prepare the next draft, proofread the entire document again.

- Understand the *why*, not just the *how*, with all projects. This will facilitate your work and help you be more creative.

- Organize first. Be completely familiar with the case or matter. Make a list of needed contacts or information. Understand the type of matter so you know what is needed. Use a checklist if available (or make one as you go for the next time).

- Document everything.

- Be courteous to everyone. You never know when you might need his or her assistance in the future.

- Get to know people in various governmental offices, title companies, banks, the courts, and other places that you might need to contact from time to time.

CLIENT INTERACTION AND INTERVIEWING:

- Enjoy your contact with clients. Always be courteous. Keep a smile on your face and in your voice, if appropriate. (You may have to temper that in probate and domestic relations situations, but you can still be relaxed and friendly.)

- Use an interview sheet and/or a checklist with blanks so you make sure you get all the information needed for a certain type of matter.

- If you tell a client or someone else that you will follow up or do something, make sure you do.

INTEROFFICE COMMUNICATIONS:

- Be cheerful and courteous (even before you have your morning coffee)!

- Ask—do not demand.

- Anticipate the needs of others and help when appropriate.

- Use in-person communication in the office rather than e-mail or telephone if possible.

- Body language says a lot.

- E-mail especially may be interpreted incorrectly.

TECHNOLOGY TECHNIQUES:

- Know the equipment and the capabilities of each piece of equipment thoroughly, including the computer, scanner, copier, fax, digital camera, and telephone system. Read the manual or take a class if necessary.

- Learn to use (and use efficiently) as many functions of your word processing software as possible, including how to do tables of contents, tables of authorities, numbered paragraphs, outlines, and cross-references.

- Learn the keyboard shortcuts of the various computer programs you use. Keep your fingers on the keyboard whenever possible, as moving from keyboard to mouse and back uses up time.

- Even though I set up all of the systematic procedures we use in the office, such as filing, timekeeping, work logs, ordering supplies, copying, mailing, faxing, telephone messaging and logs, personnel training, and checklists for most of the areas in which we practice, there is always room for improvement. If you have an idea, make sure to share it.

- If possible, always have the file available and open when doing a project or even just writing a letter. There may be information in the file that has changed since the last time you prepared an item for that client.

- I use checklists for everything, even tasks I have done hundreds of times.

- I do research first in organizing each project. Review statutes and rules, if applicable, as they change often.

- Check the status of entities and titles.

- Know more than one word processing program. We have both Word and WordPerfect on our computers because people work in different programs.

- Learn the best ways to convert files from one type of program to another and when document clean up is necessary.

- If you need help with any software item, try the Help feature first. If that does not work for you, do not hesitate to ask. Everyone in the office is happy to help solve a problem. That is how we learn together and help each other. Of course, you can always find a good computer book at the library or bookstore.

■ Do a Google search for your problem on the Internet. You can Google anything—just type in your question; it is amazing.

WRITING TIPS:

■ Attend a class or seminar or read a book on efficient writing (cutting extraneous words and using plain writing rather than legalese).
■ Organize information and your thoughts before starting to write.
■ Know the attorneys' preferences regarding how they like projects and memoranda organized.

TRIAL POINTERS:

■ *Organize and prepare.*
■ Use checklists.
■ Know how each attorney likes things organized for trial.
■ Understand the why, not just the how. Find out why various items are organized a certain way in a trial notebook for different cases. Ask the attorney what she is looking for during *voir dire* (the process of election of juries) and why.

If possible, anticipate every need:

■ What are the preferences of each judge?
■ Help the attorney do a practice run.
■ What technology is available in the courtroom?
■ What do you need to bring?
■ Make sure all the cords are included.
■ Make sure everything will connect as needed.

REAL WORK EXAMPLES:

There are clients with whom I have worked since the day I walked in the door as a green 19-year-old. Sadly, many of the early clients have passed away now. Others have grown up before my eyes. One such client stands out. His parents purchased a business through our office at least 30 years ago. He was a teenager then, and my boss helped him with a traffic citation (the client had a sports car and a lead foot). Now that young man has grown into a very successful businessman in his own right. Having those sorts of long-lasting relationships with clients—seeing them succeed—is one of the most rewarding parts of working in the legal field.

Some of the most difficult cases have been divorces when the parties have used the children as ploys. On the other side of family law, some of the most rewarding matters in which I have been involved are the adoptions, including a couple of adult adoptions.

We had one client who ripped a file in half because he did not like the advice given to him by one of the attorneys. There was another client who punched a hole in the wall when he was told to leave the building after he was verbally abusive to the receptionist (my mother). I am very proud to work for attorneys who stick up for their staff in that manner. We have employees who have been here for many years because of that support.

DETAILS OF TWO TRANSACTIONS

Sale of Residential Real Property

We met with clients and attorney to gather the details of the transaction. We represented sellers of residential real property being sold to buyers who have been lessees of the property. After we reviewed all documents provided by clients, including deed to the property and the current lease, we confirmed there was no lien against the property. Buyers were current under the lease.

We reviewed statutes and local ordinances regarding sales of residential real property not located inside the city limits. We discussed desired contingencies with the attorney, including approval of commitment for title insurance and approval of survey by buyers. Then we discussed desired warranties by sellers and by buyers. The sellers' warranties included good title and no pending litigation or claims. The buyers' warranties included that, because they had been lessees for a number of years, they were familiar with all aspects of the property and were buying the property "as is."

I drafted contract for sale and related documents, including the affidavit required for residential property located in the county, warranty deed, and promissory note and deed of trust needed for carry-back by sellers. As soon as the contract for sale was signed by all parties, the contract and accompanying documents were delivered to the title company to open escrow and order the commitment for title report. I followed up at the closing date to make sure the sale closed and requested a copy of the executed documents and settlement statement. I confirmed that the deed of trust was recorded.

Sale of Business with Lease-Option on Real Property

We met with attorney and clients regarding a sale of business and a lease with option to purchase on real property on which the business was conducted. The owner of the business assets was a corporation. The owners of the real property were individuals who had leased the property to their corporate entity. We represented the sellers. We reviewed the list of assets to be sold. The list of assets included the name of the business, which was also the name of the seller corporation. We reviewed the deed to the property and the lease between owners and corporation. We confirmed that the corporation was in good standing with the state of Arizona. In addition, we confirmed that there were no liens against the real property.

It was determined that the sale of the business and change of our client's corporate name would close in 90 days and that, at the same time of the closing, a lease with option would be executed for the real property. I drafted a contract for the sale of the business, a contract for the sale of the real property, a lease agreement, and an option to purchase. The method to exercise the option to purchase at the end of a two-year period was by the buyers' signing and delivering the contract for sale on the real property. In the meantime, the two-year lease would govern.

The sale of the business was for cash at close and handled without an escrow. We prepared the necessary bill of sale and transferred documents for vehicles. Immediately after the close of sale, we filed for a change of name for the seller corporation and assigned the registered trade name to the buyers. The transaction also included an employment contract for the seller's son to continue to work in the business for one year, along with a requirement that the sellers finish certain work that had been started and not yet completed. We prepared reminders for the two-year lease-option. The option was property exercised; then we prepared the warranty deed and affidavit of property value and recorded those documents to complete the sale.

END NOTES

New PLSs have mandatory recertification requiring a minimum of 75 hours of continuing legal education in a five-year period. Those certified before 1992 were "grandfathered in," but may recertify voluntarily.

Part VI

CORPORATE AND BUSINESS

SIOBHAN S. SMITH

Senior Corporate Paralegal Specialist
STEPTOE & JOHNSON, LLP
Washington, D.C.

"If anything, Siobhan probably underplays her responsibilities as a top-flight corporate paralegal. The head of our corporate department confided in me that he gives her work that he would not even trust to a third-year associate. Siobhan works for around 20 different lawyers in the course of the typical year; every year she gets nearly perfect performance evaluations from them. They do not rate anyone else in the corporate group so highly. She is enthusiastic about her profession, smart, and meticulous in her work. She is also universally liked and highly regarded by her peers. She is a joy to have on my staff, and simply the best corporate paralegal I have ever worked with."

Christy Stouffer
Manager, Practice Support and Paralegals
Steptoe & Johnson, LLP

EDUCATION/HONORS/CERTIFICATIONS:

- B.S., Paralegal Studies, University of Maryland, University College, 1993, *magna cum laude*
- Paralegal Certificate, University of Maryland, University College, 1992

PROFESSIONAL ASSOCIATIONS:

- Member and former Board Member, National Capital Area Paralegal Association
- Member, National Federation of Paralegal Associations
- Speaker, Georgetown University Paralegal Program

PRO BONO ACTIVITIES:

- Mentor and Spanish Instructor, Adopt-A-School program through the firm
- Train, mentor, and supervise new paralegals
- Volunteer, Scott Montgomery Elementary School Mentoring Program, Washington, D.C.

YEARS EXPERIENCE:

14

FIRM AT-A-GLANCE:

Siobhan is a senior corporate paralegal specialist based at the Washington, D.C., location of the firm of Steptoe & Johnson LLP, from May 1991, to the present. She is currently working in the firm's London office.

Steptoe & Johnson LLP
Washington, D.C.
Phone: 202.429.3000
Fax: 202.429.3902
Web Site: www.steptoe.com

Other Locations:

Brussels
Chicago
London
Los Angeles
New York
Phoenix

MANAGING PARTNER:

Roger E. Warin

ATTORNEYS:

450+

PARALEGALS:

90+

FIRM PRACTICE AREAS:

- Corporate Securities and Finance
- Energy
- Environment & Natural Resources
- ERISA, Labor and Employment
- Government Affairs and Public Policy
- Immigration
- Insurance and Reinsurance
- Intellectual Property
- International Regulation and Compliance
- International Trade
- Litigation
- Property
- Tax

- Telecom, Internet, and Media
- Transportation
- Worldwide Arbitration and Dispute Resolution

Paralegal Program at Steptoe & Johnson, LLP:

Behind almost every pleading, filing, production, and transaction, the paralegals at Steptoe & Johnson, LLP, are working at full capacity to help produce top-notch work products. Our goal as paralegals, among other things, is to assist the attorneys to research, to investigate, to organize, to manage, to juggle, and to produce. What makes being a paralegal at Steptoe so unique is that the attorneys and paralegals truly work as a team. We are all here for one thing—to assist the client in every way possible. The attorneys and paralegals at Steptoe work together toward that end...and we do this with a smile. We enjoy what we do. Although we may need to pull an occasional all-nighter, we know that there is no greater reward than turning out a great work product, and knowing that it is simply the best. You experience a professional "high" when your Herculean efforts support a win in the courtroom or a seamless corporate transaction. Though the paralegals are not the parties signing the documents, or in front of the bar arguing before the court, we are vital to the practice of law.

—Siobhan S. Smith, Paralegal Specialist

INTRODUCTION TO CORPORATE AND BUSINESS

Our firm advises clients in numerous areas of law. I work in Corporate, Securities, and Finance where I assist the attorneys on corporate transactions, securities filings and compliance, corporate governance, and research.

PROSPECTUS VS. COMPLAINT

For some, the idea of sitting and reading a prospectus is quite horrid—for me, it is just the opposite. Reading what a company has done or intends to do, its ideas, its goals, its transactions, and its intended acquisitions is far more real to me than reading a complaint. The idea that you can actually form a company on-line now, in a matter of minutes in some jurisdictions, is a true sign of technology at its best.

The corporate field has numerous facets, including transactions, securities, and governance. It also affects other areas of law, such as contracts, real estate, bankruptcy, and many others. For example, in order to purchase real property, investors often form a limited liability company (LLC) to effect the purchase, thus taking advantage of some personal liability protection. This field can truly affect every person, such as the small-scale Mom-and-Pop diner just set up on the corner or the energetic entrepreneur looking to start her own business. On a larger scale, you may have corporations merging with other corporations or your local bank acquiring a new bank (and therefore requiring you to learn all the new bank's technicalities)—someone has to prepare the documents to finalize those transactions. *That* is corporate. It is intense, it is intellectually challenging, and it is extremely rewarding.

OUTLINE OF JOB RESPONSIBILITIES:

- Form corporations, limited liability companies, partnerships, nonprofits, and so on.

- Draft charter documents, board consents, employer identification number (EIN) applications

- Research statutory requirements for various jurisdictions

- Confirm availability of corporate name, domain, and cursory trademark search

- Prepare and coordinate formation filings with secretaries of state

- Meet with attorneys and clients

- Research other companies

- Qualify companies in foreign jurisdictions

ETHICS CAVEAT:

Siobhan does very sophisticated and high-level drafting work. She undoubtedly requires little actual supervision to do this work with her education and years of experience. Despite this, lawyers are required under the ethics rules on supervision to review the documents she prepares before they are filed or submitted to a client. The level of review depends on all the factors involved, including the degree of expertise that the paralegal has.

Therese A. Cannon, Attorney at Law and author of *Ethics and Professional Responsibility for Legal Assistants*

CORPORATE GOVERNANCE

- Prepare and coordinate the filing of corporate annual reports
- Draft annual board and shareholder consents or meeting minutes
- Draft special consents
- Maintain corporate minute books
- Prepare and issue stock
- Create corporate "Guide Books" for clients

SECURITIES

- Prepare and coordinate filings with the Securities and Exchange Commission (SEC)
- On-line securities research and due diligence
- Blue Sky (State Securities) research and filing preparation

TRANSACTIONAL

- Due diligence
- Prepare closing checklists
- Draft transactional consents, officer's certificates, disclosure schedules, and other documents as necessary
- Coordinate closings
- Prepare, index, and organize closing documents and coordinate their distribution
- Extensive client/outside counsel contact
- Research companies involved in the transaction
- Form new entities for mergers and acquisitions as needed
- Corporate legal research
- Prepare and coordinate the filing of UCC Financing Statements
- Prepare corporate dissolutions, state withdrawals, and coordinate filings regarding documents

TYPICAL WORKWEEK:

I have attempted to write this section many times, with a straight face, no less. Alas, there is truly no such creature in this practice area—there is absolutely, unequivocally, no such thing as a typical workweek for a corporate paralegal.

Monday mornings are my favorite time of the week. Typically, the fire alarms do not sound before 11 A.M. Thus Monday mornings allow me to recap the prior week's projects and create a *fresh* to-do list with expected priority levels. This week, I have 24 items. These items are comprised of items that are important, yet not time sensitive. They include items such as ordering corporate minute books, scheduling board meetings, updating calendar items, researching current statute changes or research in general, preparing for seminars, and reviewing client press releases. I create the list, and then the phone starts ringing.

Each day I work on a priority basis, and in between, I squeeze in my work for each client. Today I worked on Client A and reviewed the current closing checklist for open items, edited and updated documents, e-mailed parties to determine the status of open documents, and drafted board and shareholder consents regarding the stock purchase agreement. I forwarded these to Attorney A, reviewed the stock ledger of target, performed additional due diligence regarding the target, prepared stock certificates for closing, drafted officer certificates, stock powers, and receipts for the closing.

For Client B, I contacted Attorney B regarding the status of client information necessary to obtain the EIN and documents, prepared IRS Form SS-4 in final, and coordinated filing of EIN on-line with the IRS, and then contacted the tax attorney concerning issue with foreign officers.

I also worked on Client C's securities filings by following up with Attorney C regarding additional states that have been added to the private offering, researching Blue Sky statutes in additional jurisdictions, creating a Blue Sky chart to reflect the state notice filing requirements, reviewing current offering documents, and preparing draft Regulation D, Form D filing.

The next day, I worked on Client D's matter. I received a client/attorney call regarding the need for immediate formation of a new corporate subsidiary. It was necessary to confirm the name availability in domestic jurisdiction, as well as prepare draft documentation (certificate of incorporation, organizational minutes/consent for initial board, and bylaws) for the corporation. I then forwarded these documents to the attorney, participated in client/attorney call; decision was made to change corporate structure. I prepared limited liability company formation documents and foreign qualification documents for three jurisdictions, confirmed availability of the domain name, performed a cursory trademark search, and contacted the trademark attorney regarding the research results.

That afternoon, I had to review edits from the draft consents for Client A's closing and coordinate obtaining good standing certificates and other ancillary documents for the closing. I also made numerous calls with inside and outside counsel regarding the transaction.

For Client B, my assignments included the review of EIN filing evidence, scanning and forwarding to the client and Attorney B, confirming other open items with attorney concerning increasing the board size, and creating necessary committees.

With the closing set for tomorrow, I had to prepare documents in final, organize documents for the closing, update closing checklist, proof and edit final documents, and meet with the clients and Attorneys A, X, Y, Z regarding the closing documents (18 hrs).

Later, we found out that the closing was rescheduled for Monday. (Breathe.) I made new edits to certain agreements, but one party was not available for signature (so I adjusted pertinent documents).

I prepared for the private offering for Client C scheduled to close next Wednesday, and made a calendar note: 15 days to make federal and state filings. I drafted letters to relevant states and finalized Form D for filing with the SEC post-closing.

I received a call from Client E regarding receipt of the Notice of Revocation of Authority to Transact Business regarding one its subsidiaries. I downloaded and prepared a draft of the annual report, and forwarded it to Attorney E and the client for review and approval. I then filed it on-line with the client's approval, and then coordinated obtaining a good standing certificate for the record book.

I prepared for the Attorney F/client conference call, set for Tuesday morning regarding a new acquisition. I researched the target company.

I performed the following additional tasks:

Client G: Client e-mails regarding issuance of new class of stock, prepare amendment to charter, consents, and stock certificates; and e-mails with Attorney G regarding documents.

Client H: Confer with Attorney H regarding UCC search results, preparation and filing of UCC-3 with the secretary of state.

ETHICS CAVEAT:

In high-stakes matters like corporate acquisitions, paralegals and others working on these matters must be especially vigilant about protecting the confidentiality of the matter.

Therese A. Cannon, Attorney at Law and author of *Ethics and Professional Responsibility for Legal Assistants*

Client A: Minor edits to closing documents, meet tomorrow morning to review and finalize any open issues.

Client B: Review Bylaws and draft consents regarding new Audit and Finance committees and to increase the board size, forward documents to Attorney B.

Client C: Edit Form D and forward to Attorneys C and X for review and comment, contact the SEC to confirm current filing requirements.

Client D: Coordinate filing the LLC formation documents in the domestic jurisdiction.

Client E: Confirm filing evidence and forward documents to Attorney E/client.

Client H: Review and forward filing evidence.

Friday, 4:00 P.M.—Attack To-Do list! Although anyone who works in a law firm knows that 4 P.M. tends to be the bewitching hour, I honestly believe that at 4 P.M. every day there is a silent alarm that rings in every attorney's ear. Screaming for attention are all the projects they have on tap to complete prior to C.O.B. (close of business). My motto: Smile and Nod. Everything will be done—just breathe.

Friday, 7:00 P.M.—Status of To-Do List: Only 14 items remain—not bad!

GENERAL ADVICE:

Working as a corporate paralegal is a bit like herding cats. Advice I often offer to new corporate paralegals is, "Communicate, communicate, and communicate some more!" If an attorney requests that you perform a certain task, and it is taking longer than expected, call or e-mail—just communicate! That said, I do not mean write a novel. Attorneys bill by the hour, and they do not want to hear you complain or narrate your issues (just get to the bottom line). Explain the issue and suggest a solution in a concise manner. Brevity is best. Time is money—and while you may want to explain the problem *ad nauseum*, my advice is always that *less is more*. In addition, a good attitude goes a long way with both the attorneys and the government agencies we work with on a daily basis. It is true—the person on the other end of the line will know if you are smiling.

ORGANIZATIONAL METHODS:

CLOSING CHECKLISTS

Organization is key in any practice area, but especially so in corporate transactions. In a transaction, for example, it is imperative to keep the documents organized and be familiar with the substance of the documents. Every transaction requires a closing checklist that details the documents in the transaction. One thing I do to make the transactions run more smoothly is to make comprehensive closing checklists. For example, be sure to include all signatories to each agreement on the checklist, and add every schedule, exhibit, and side agreement so that absolutely nothing is overlooked. At any given time, any party to the transaction will see what documents they must sign and for what deliverables they are responsible. I merely set up my checklists in a Word table, and then ensure the checklists are all-inclusive. No item is too small.

MINUTE BOOKS

Place all originals in plastic slip covers, as well as the cover page to the book. This will help maintain the integrity of the original documents, and allow for easier scanning at a later date.

TECHNOLOGICAL ADVANCES:

I do significant research and many filings on-line. The corporate practice is technologically evolving daily. Two years ago, we were thrilled to find that some states were moving to on-line corporate status. To date, all state jurisdictions now have the ability to confirm corporate status on-line, and many have gone to on-line annual report filing; even the Internal Revenue Service offers on-line filing. Wherever possible, on-line filings are necessary. The move to paperless annual reports and filings is imminent. I make a point of reviewing the state's on-line capabilities whenever possible. I have certain secretary of state Web sites bookmarked for easy access and set up accounts when necessary. Clients wholly appreciate the benefits that come from increased technological advances and my keeping abreast of the current knowledge and techniques. Often the jurisdiction will offer a reduced fee for on-line versus paper filings.

In addition to on-line filings, there is a growing need for attorney/client intranets. In this regard, the attorney, the paralegal, and in-house counsel all have continuous access to the same corporate documents. This is especially helpful for larger clients that have numerous subsidiaries. At any time, a client is able to review a particular subsidiary, determine when the next annual report is due, or confirm the shares held by that entity.

Similarly, there are commercial services that will provide, for a fee, complete databases for companies, which will enable a company to have all the corporate details readily available, and even provide stock certificate templates and full shareholder details. The current fervor over corporate misconduct is driving many of these technological advances. Commercial services assist companies by providing creative services, while at the same time they can assist the company to more accurately and efficiently heed the statutes and regulations that govern the company.

Lastly, there are services, such as LIVEDGAR® (for a fee) or IncSpot®, that enable the corporate paralegal to research SEC or corporate state filings, within seconds, rather than relying on "in-person" research. Now researching in person seems archaic with the ease and cost-effectiveness of on-line research.

VIRTUAL CLOSING:

Another technological advance in corporate transactions has been the ability to scan closing documents to other counsel, especially with Adobe® software; one can now scan a document into a PDF format that provides a much cleaner document than a fax version that was oftentimes illegible. Documents can be provided and uploaded by either party into a virtual dataroom to allow any party to the transaction to review relevant documents at any time. It is no longer necessary to meet in a large conference room to close a transaction. We can close it via e-mail, or even set up a virtual closing where both parties can comment on documents at the same time.

LEGAL RESEARCH SHORTCUTS:

Because in corporate law, we are researching numerous state codes regularly, I have bookmarked my favorite research sites and most-used state codes. I can pull up any state corporate code/statutes/regulations in seconds. I can search the codes by keywords, and this eliminates long research hours. One of my favorite state statute Web sites is www.findlaw.com. Statutes are easy to download, read, or print.

Researching Blue Sky statutes is also quite common for corporate paralegals. Because the statutes tend to be fluid, I have bookmarked Web sites for many states, and yet always review the statutes each time I have an assignment such as this. I create Blue Sky charts to detail the notice filing requirements for the relevant jurisdictions. Although the attorney must also review the statutes for each assignment, I often refer to a previous chart to draft a current chart, thus saving time in chart preparation. Lastly, before the filings, I verbally contact each state to confirm any jurisdictional nuances.

One common challenge I face is private company research that arrives at a dead end. There is so much information on public companies from many different sources. It is the smaller companies that are often the most difficult to locate a wealth of information on. Again, I search the basics: Google, company Web sites, the Better Business Bureau, Dun & Bradstreet®, LexisNexis®, on-line phone books, and so on. One of the most wonderful resources we have at our firm is a team of fantastic research librarians. They are always a significant source of information. Although there are fee services that will provide additional information, even investigative in nature, but, more often than not, you will face Freedom of Information Act issues and will need to address privacy concerns. Perseverance is the key here. Often I will ask a colleague for ideas, and sometimes it gives me a fresh perspective—a new set of eyes.

WRITING TIPS: The most important thing I have learned as a paralegal is that less is more.

- **Write simply and directly.** In the past when I drafted board minutes, I would try to write my notes verbatim. For many reasons, this is neither efficient nor practical, and it is usually best to keep it simple. The "heretofor's," "therein's," and "aforementioned's" are overused and not particularly appealing. I strongly suggest losing them whenever possible.

- **Mimic Good Writers.** Another aspect of my job is to proofread agreements and corporate documents for the attorneys. I have found that the best way to learn to write better is to mimic those who do!

- Lastly, proof, proof, and *proof* your work again.

INVESTIGATIVE/INTERNET TIPS:

- **Companies:** Often attorneys ask me to research or investigate a company involved in a potential transaction. I have a typical checklist I use that involves substantially free services. Typically, I will track down a company's Web site and glean what details I can, and then I search SEC filings, state filings, corporate research sites, and I always run a Google search to see what interesting details surface.

DEVELOP GOOD COMMUNICATION SKILLS AND KNOW YOUR ETHICAL BOUNDARIES:

As a paralegal, conferring with clients directly is sometimes similar to walking a tightrope. It is imperative that a paralegal *not give advice* or even appear to do so. Although we may have the answers to the clients' questions, we have to refrain from answering them unless it relates to items that are not advice driven but perhaps factually driven. I confer with clients on a daily basis. They call or e-mail me directly with corporate questions. I always confer with an attorney in the group and make sure that the client is aware of this.

It is extremely important that an e-mail signature reflects a paralegal's title, as well as the signature block to any letter on the firm's letterhead. It is simply good practice to "cc" (carbon copy) attorneys on e-mails to the clients, and to make sure the attorneys are aware of conversations with their clients through e-mails and memoranda. Lastly, and certainly one of the most important things I can stress is that following through with both the clients and the attorneys is an absolute must. Return e-mails and voice-mails ASAP. Everyone appreciates good communication.

ETHICS CAVEAT:

Siobhan's advice about communications with clients is excellent, and her explanation of what is and is not legal advice is accurate and helpful.

Therese A. Cannon, Attorney at Law and author of *Ethics and Professional Responsibility for Legal Assistants*

CORPORATE PRACTICE TIPS:

In the corporate legal practice, there is never a dull moment. Each day brings tasks that are wholly different from the day before. There are certain tips I teach to new paralegals that I mentor and others (including the new corporate associates). These are what I consider good tips for any position, and I have them posted in big, bold letters on the wall of my office:

1. Do your job, and do it well.

2. Keep it simple.

3. Promise only what you can deliver. Then deliver more than you promise. (Author unknown)

4. With kindness and a smile, you can lead an elephant by a thread. (Persian proverb)

5. Always follow through.

TEN TIPS FOR A SMOOTHER CLOSING:

Corporate paralegals may not necessarily work with the hundreds of boxes of documents that their colleagues in litigation do, but we do organize multitudinous documents for due diligence purposes, investor packages, and transactions. The goal is to keep everything completely organized and clearly labeled.

1. Organize the closing room. Make sure all document folders match the corresponding items in the closing checklist and that they are organized. The result: when any party walks in the conference room, there is obvious order.

2. Color-code files and signatories. In a transaction with multiple parties that will only be arriving for the closing, it makes for a much smoother "signature party" if each party has a particular colored flag and knows exactly what documents they need to review and sign, as well as how many items they will need to deliver at closing. I also color-code the closing categories, such as "Pre-Closing," "Deliverables at Closing," and "Post-Closing."

3. Ensure that there are ample office supplies for every need and that they are placed around the room for easy access by all the parties. In addition, plan for additional visitors by ensuring that keys and security codes are ready as needed.

4. Confirm that laptops, desktop computers, conference phones, and any other media needs are ready hours before a closing so that any issues are resolved before parties arrive.

5. Coordinate a notary if need be. (It is always helpful for the notary to have the notary identification particulars already in the documents so that the notary merely needs to sign and seal at closing.)

6. Create a separate section of files that are just for your use for additional copies of closing checklists, deal contacts, secretary contacts, notes, and so forth.

7. Sometimes you may not have the names of the parties that will be signing at closing (and therefore will not have them included in the signature blocks of the deal documents). Many office supply stores can create a rubber stamp of the signatory's name and title in a day. This is just an alternative if you are not able to edit the deal documents accordingly.

8. If possible, leave the signature pages of the deal documents unnumbered and without document identification in the footers. At the bottom or top of the signature page(s), write the name of the document (in brackets, bold, or italics) to help you clearly identify the correct signatures and their corresponding documents. For example: [Signature Page to Asset Purchase Agreement].

9. Create an "electronic library" for the transaction; create an e-mail folder for the transaction that contains subfolders of draft agreements as of particular dates, documents that are final and ready for signature, fully-executed agreements, and any other deal-specific folders.

10. Expect the unexpected, and always remain calm. Closings are often intense but relatively friendly events. Occasionally, you will experience opposing counsel that may be somewhat contentious. Remain professional at all times.

DEAL CONTACTS:

Another transactional must is a document I create and call "Deal Contacts." I have all the parties and their counsel contact information in one document that is accessible to all the parties of the transaction. This eliminates the inevitable hunt for phone numbers, e-mail addresses, and so forth.

CORPORATE GOVERNANCE:

Organization is also important in corporate governance. When I need to set up a company for a new client, I prepare a corporate checklist to ensure that I have the basic items necessary to form the company. I created this checklist to eliminate the need for me to remember every detail when the attorney and I are meeting with the clients. This checklist asks for many items, such as confirming the corporate structure, the initial capitalization, the client contact information, initial director(s) and officers, and even details of the location of the corporate minute book. Other issues always arise, but this keeps things simple. It has been a wonderful aid to our group. (See Figure 12-1.)

Because of the Sarbanes-Oxley Act of 2002, it is even more imperative that the corporate paralegal maintain complete, accurate, and organized files on the corporate clients the firm represents. For example, one way corporate paralegals could further assist their attorneys regarding compliance issues is to maintain organized electronic files, such as files for correspondence, filings, agreements, and transactions. At any time, a client or attorney should be able to call upon the paralegal to determine annual meeting dates, last filings made, or the corporate secretary's contact information. Thus, if the corporation is at the receiving end of an internal or external corporate fraud investigation, the firm's records are accurate, complete, and at your fingertips.

Figure 12–1
CORPORATE CHECKLIST

No.	Item	Notes	Comments
1	Type of Entity	LP, LLP, Sole Proprietor	
2	For Profit/Not for Profit		
3	Name of Company	Business/Corporate "ending"	
4	Domestic Jurisdiction		
5	Qualify in any other jurisdiction?		
6	Statutory Agent		
7	List of Directors (or Managers/Members) and Addresses		
8	List of Officers and Addresses		
9	Total Authorized Stock		
10	Par Value		
11	Will this be an S Corp?		

12	Incorporator or Authorized Person		
13	Purpose		
14	Articles of Incorporation		
15	Bylaws		
16	Organizational Minutes		
17	Order Corporate Seal and Stock/Minute Book?		
18	Will S&J maintain?		
19	Stock to issue and consideration		
20	Fiscal Year		
21	Min and Max Number of Directors/Managers		
22	Obtain a Fed Tax ID Number (SS-4)		
23	Mailing /address of Company		
24	County where business is located		
25	SSNs of D&Os		
26	First date wages are/will be paid		
27	Highest number of employees expected in the next 12 months		
28	Principal activity (brief)		
29	Is principal business manufacturing?		
30	To whom are most of the products sold? (public/business)		
31	Business phone/fax		
32	Main contacts at company with phone numbers		
33	Attys at S&J		
34	Check for name availability (domestic and foreign)		
35	Reserve Name (if fee is charged?)		
36	Operating/Partnership Agreement (LLC, LP, Partnerships)		

JURISDICTION DETAILS:

Another item that I prepare related to corporate governance is a spreadsheet that details each jurisdiction where a company transacts business, when the annual report is due, and relevant state identification numbers and dates. Again, the idea here is to offer attorneys and clients immediate answers to basic corporate information without necessitating an in-depth review of their corporate files. Clients truly appreciate these timesaving systems created to keep them organized.

In addition to the "homemade" spreadsheet option, there are many services that, for a fee, will integrate and organize your corporate details and will produce spreadsheets or reports on a company's shareholders, foreign jurisdictions, director and officer terms, and so on (e.g., Corporation Service Company, CT Corporation, and Corporate Focus™ by Two Step® Software). I highly recommend these services for the larger companies; however, it is certainly possible to maintain entities properly without such a service. With companies becoming more accountable for their every action, a service that provides companies with these organizational abilities is certainly worth reviewing, regardless of company size.

CORPORATE INFORMATION SHEET:

Similar to the charts previously mentioned, I also create a corporate information document that I place in the front of each company's corporate minute/record book. This details the main contact at the company, the company's officers and directors, the authorized shares and available share balances, the tax ID, jurisdictional IDs, and any other pertinent information. One sheet + easy access = a quick response time. (See Figure 12-2.)

CORPORATE INFORMATIONAL GUIDE:

Many clients are large corporations with numerous subsidiaries that are qualified to do business in multiple jurisdictions. Given the need to keep all this information completely organized, I often create a corporate informational guide for clients. Some may be only a page, whereas others could easily be 20 pages. It details all the companies at a glance, contains their organizational chart, and also complete subsidiary details. For one client in particular, the in-house counsel adds to their guide regularly, and the attorneys that represent this client here at the firm all have copies they refer to and maintain. At any time, all of us have the important corporate details readily available.

Fig. 12-2
CORPORATE INFORMATION SHEET
USA AEROSPACE, INC.
12345.0001 - SHK

CONTACT INFO:

Mr. Company President

USA Engineering, Inc.   Mr. Treasurer - Billing and Accounting

123 Lexington Avenue   Ph: 212.123.4321

New York, NY 10022

212.123.4567   Mr. President's Assistant

212.123.4568-fax   212.123.0000

comppres@usa.com   assist@usa.com

DOMESTIC: Delaware, 02/30/2020, 3123456
FOREIGN: California, 02/30/2020, 2123456
               Virginia, 02/30/2020, 4123456
               Maryland, 02/30/2020, 5123456

EIN: **20-1110000**

ANNUAL SH MTG: April

DIRECTORS: Mr. X, Mr. Y and Mr. Z

OFFICERS: Mr. President, President
                Mr. Treasurer, Treasurer
                Mr. Secretary, Secretary

STOCK: Cert 1,100 shares to USA Satellites, Inc., 02/30/2020 ($ 100,000
                initial cap) Total Authorized Shares: 1,000 common, $.01 par

DIRECTORS / OFFICERS INFO:

DIRECTORS / OFFICERS	RESIDENCE/PHONE	NOTES
Mr. President Director - Chair, President comppres@usa.com 203.536.1234-cell	123 Main Street Old Greenwich, CT 06870 Home Phone: 203.123.4567	SSN: 123-45- 6789 Home fax: 203.123.4568
Mr. Treasurer, Treasurer		
Mr. Secretary, Secretary		
Mr. X, Director		
Mr. Y, Director		
Mr. Z, Director		

ELECTRONIC LIBRARY:

After any transaction, I compile the final versions of all the transactional documents into what I call an "electronic library" of the deal, archive it in my e-mails, and save it to CD for the clients and counsel. Many outside copying services provide a complete duplicating service, as well as scanning services, and will provide you with a CD of the final executed documents for all the parties. Then, at any time, we can retrieve documents for future transactions with the same parties or for other similar transactions, thereby eliminating the need to reinvent the proverbial wheel.

THE RULE OF OFFICE COMMUNICATIONS:

Similar to client interactions, I think communications in the office should follow the "less is more" rule as well. One thing I have learned is that partners in law firms do not necessarily want all the gory details about their filings. They want to know when you made the filing and when it is effective. Instead of e-mailing the attorneys with explanations of slow messengers, half-witted file clerks, or terrible traffic, send very simple, one to two-line e-mails: "Your filing was delivered at 10 A.M. to the Virginia State Corporation Commission. Attached is a PDF of the filing evidence." Like clients, attorneys' time is money. Do not waste it. What is the good side of this? Fewer keystrokes and less chance of foot-in-mouth issues.

SOFTWARE NECESSITIES:

For me, the full version of Adobe Acrobat™ is an absolute must in this position. With the full version, you can edit, write and save PDF forms. For example, recently the SEC created a new Regulation D—Form D; however, the Securities and Exchange Commission ("SEC") did not provide the form in a writeable format. Because the firm provides Regulation D advice to clients on a regular basis, we truly needed this as we had pending filings. I was able to take the new SEC form and create a writeable document for use with all the clients.

In addition, working knowledge of Microsoft® Excel® is important to maintain stock ledgers, sort through escrow accounts, and so on. Keen Microsoft® Word® skills and the ability to search on the Internet are a given.

Additionally, there are other on-line services that are necessary for certain areas of law: LIVEDGA® (securities), Corporation Service Company (CSC), and IncSpot® (corporate) each hold a vast array of information. For example, IncSpot has current forms, databases, links to secretaries of state offices, tax sites, insurance and banking sites, UCC search links, domain name information (WhoisIt™) and more. You have immediate access to a veritable plethora of updated information. It is usually the first Web site I log onto every day.

CORPORATE CHEAT SHEET:

One other item I created for our firm is what I call my "corporate cheat sheet." This lists basic information that all new corporate attorneys and paralegals need to know. It has links to certain research sites, and it contains corporate lingo that may appear obvious but, surprisingly, is not always. In addition, it has information on our local jurisdictions that we contact on a regular basis. I strongly feel that the more I can teach others, the better service we can provide to the clients. (See Figure 12-3.)

You have to love to learn in this field. A good attitude, a fifth gear, and a healthy dose of humor are the secret. Do your job, and do it well. Keep it simple. Less is more. Lastly, smile—a lot!

REAL WORK EXAMPLES:

EXAMPLE 1: PERFORM DUE DILIGENCE AND REVIEW DOCUMENTS AT A NUCLEAR POWER PLANT

The Situation: Of all the assignments that have landed on my desk, my most interesting assignment was the one that landed me inside the fence of a nuclear power plant for a week. Before I officially became a paralegal in the corporate practice, I was involved in litigation and other practice areas at my firm, essentially working on whatever large project the firm had at that moment. (Our paralegal program at that

Figure 12-3
CORPORATE CHEAT SHEET

1.	Corporations are *incorporated*.	Limited Liability Companies (LLCs) are formed.
2.	Corporations have a Certificate of Incorporation or Articles of Incorporation.	LLCs have a Certificate of Formation.
3.	Corporations have Bylaws.	LLCs have an Operating Agreement or LLC Agreement.
4.	Corporations need to have "corporate endings" (unless granted special permission by the secretary of state), such as Inc., Co., Company, Corporation, etc.	LLCs need to be designated with "LLC" in the name or "Limited Liability Company." (The LCC can be with or without periods; we prefer not to use them.)
5.	Registered Agents/Statutory Agents/Resident Agents. There are numerous agents, the main two national agents are: Corporation Service Company (CSC) and The Corporation Trust Company (CT).	States require that each company maintain a relationship with a registered agent, including appointing one in the original Certificate of Incorporation or Qualification/Registration (if foreign) documents filed with the secretary of state.
6.	Corporation Service Company 2711 Centerville Road, Suite 400 Wilmington, DE 19808 New Castle Country 800.9279800 www.incspot.com	The Corporation Trust Company 1209 Orange Street Wilmington, DE 19801 New Castle Country 800.677.3394 DC-Team 1:202.393.1747 www.ctadvantage.com
7.	I need a company's 8-K/10-Q/S-1, where can I find it? http://www.sec.gov/edgar/searchdgar/companysearch.html	www.sec.gov (Edgar Filings); www.gsionline.com (call 800.669.1154 for support); look on the company's Web site, they often have links to recent filings.
8.	I need to look up a company, where should I start? All jurisdictions have on-line databases to look up companies. CSC's IncSpot has direct links to each state database, or run a search for 'secretary of state' in the jurisdiction you need to search.	Try the search engines first to locate the company Web site. If you can pinpoint where they do business or the principal business address, they you can locate them on that state's database, and then locate the corporate state's database, and then locate the corporate status of the company, when they were incorporated, etc.

9.	9. What is corporate status? What is a Certificate of Good Standing? This is typically whether the company has filed their annual reports and paid their franchise taxes. A Certificate of Good Standing indicates that all corporate formalities have been adhered to, and that the company is "active" and in "good standing." Most states have corporate status or standing available on-line for free.	Before entering into any transaction, you should confirm the corporate status of the entities involved. Look up the company on the secretary of state Web Site; if not available online, call and confirm via telephone.
10.	10. DE (Most companies are formed in DE, ease of use, court system, etc.) 302.739.3073 www.state.de.us/corp/default.shtml	**MD** - Maryland Department of Assessments and Taxation 410.767.1330 http://www.dat.state.md.us/sdatweb/charter.html
11.	11. DC - Dept of Consumer and Regulatory Affairs 202.442.4432 - www.dcra.dc.gov Search for a company: http://mblr.dc.gov/corp/lookup/index.asp	**VA** - State Corporation Commission 866.722.2551 - www.virginia.gov Search for a company: http://www.scc.virginia.gov/division/clk/diracc.htm
12.	12. forms: 13. www.irs.gov/formspubs	Tax ID/EIN Application: Form SS-4 This can be completed and filed on-line.
13.	14. SEC: www.sec.gov Filing-202.551.8090 8.00 A.M.–5.30 P.M.	Securities and Exchange Commision 100 F Street, NE Washington, DC 20549
14.	15. Closings - Mergers and acquisitions, stock purchases, asset purchases, and so forth are all transactions. Transactions are a series of negotiations over an agreement and its affiliated agreements. The transaction "closes" when all agreements are approved and fully executed. Some transactions are two-fold,	Closing Binders – All the documents that support a transaction are compiled, indexed, and tabbed into volumes of closing documents for distribution to the relevant parties. It is the paralegal's responsibility to ensure that all of the documents are complete with

(Continued)

Figure 12-3
CORPORATE CHEAT SHEET (*Continued*)

one closing on the main purchase agreement, the latter closing of the entire transaction (that may be months after the first closing). The paralegal's role is drafting some of the more minor documents, obtaining the documents supporting the agreements proofreading the deal documents, and orchestrating the closing.	schedules and exhibits, that the documents are fully executed, and that each party to the transaction receives the agreements that are relevant to them.
15. 16. Transaction/Securities/IP/Tax/Other Attorneys (we work with regularly): Scott Katzman, Bob McLaughlin, Fil Agusti, Harold Freilich, Ellen d'Alelio, Caroline Gaudet, Don Meiers, Chris Tai, Savery Gradoville, Alfred Mamlet, Stan Smilack, Julie Vinyard, Joby Bascon, Margaret Lin.	Corporate Paralegals Siobhan

time consisted of approximately 20 paralegals for 250 attorneys.) My assignment was to travel with three attorneys and to coordinate a huge due diligence/document review pursuant to a document production request.

My Strategy: To get behind the fence at the nuclear power plant meant drug testing, hours of briefings on how the nuclear power plant worked, and many safety briefings. To coordinate such a voluminous due diligence/document review required much organization, coordination, and regular communication with the attorneys. Checklists and planning were extremely important to save duplication.

What I Learned: I have to admit, although the project was interesting, it was a bit unnerving—all the while, I wondered if I was the only one there who jumped at every whistle or loud noise. Even though they had inherently dangerous jobs, the employees at the plant were quite inspiring. I recall being in awe of the men and women who performed their jobs with incredible expertise and detail. I was ready to get back to my office and hear the dull sounds of my printer and not the whistles and nerve-wracking sounds at a nuclear power plant. Coming home was a joy. I still wonder how the employees do their jobs day in and day out.

Example 2: Orchestrating a Huge Closing

The Situation: Another interesting experience was orchestrating a closing that filled our firm's large conference center that seats 100+ persons. We prepared for the closing, confirmed every detail, coordinated with numerous counsels, as well as organized and proofread a room full of documents. I do not believe we slept for the final three days; but it closed, and it went like clockwork.

What I Learned: That experience was my very first taste of the corporate transaction field. That was all it took. I loved the excitement.

All Assignments: Meeting Time Challenges

Other than the research road blocks, the most frequent problem I face is lack of time, coupled with lengthy to-do lists. Ideally, we could all sit and work on one project, one paper, one letter, one document at a time, and steadily check off our to-do list, one by one. However, realistically you must prioritize, organize, and herd the cats. Note: I am writing this at 2 A.M., the to-do list is long, but not overwhelming, and I will finish everything.

END NOTES

Reprinted from the firm's Web site: http://www.steptoe.com/professionals-search-paralegals.html.

Part VII

FAMILY LAW

CHAPTER 13

JENNIFER ARNOLD, NCCP, CP

Family Law Paralegal
WAKE FAMILY LAW GROUP (PLLC)
Raleigh, NC

"In my opinion you couldn't find a more talented or deserving candidate for the 'Top 15 paralegals' designation than my [I am still her paralegal] paralegal, Jennifer Arnold."

Nancy L. Grace
Attorney at Law

EDUCATION/HONORS/CERTIFICATIONS:

- University of North Carolina at Wilmington, B.A. in political science, 1995
- Meredith College, Legal Assistants Program, Specialty—Civil Litigation, 1998
- Certified Paralegal (CP), 1999
- North Carolina State Bar Certified Paralegal, 2006

PROFESSIONAL ASSOCIATIONS:

- National Association of Legal Assistants (NALA)
- North Carolina Bar Association (NCBA)

PUBLIC SPEAKING, PUBLICATIONS, AND AWARDS:

- Speaker for the NC Association of Women Attorneys annual conference, "Using Legal Assistants Effectively," 2002
- Recipient of the James G. Lye Award for Outstanding Paralegal Service, presented by the Wake County Volunteer Lawyers Program, 2003
- Author, "The Role of a Paralegal in a Family Law Case," NC *Academy of Trial Lawyers, Legal Assistants Division,* October 2003; *Discovery, NCATL Trial Briefs* publication, 2004
- Speaker for the *Institute for Paralegal Education* Advanced Skills Seminar, "Exploring Essential Issues in Domestic Law for North Carolina Paralegals." Speaker on the issues of Equitable Distribution, Post-Separation Support, Alimony, Child Support, and Ethics.
- Speaker at the North Carolina Bar Association's Practical Skills Seminar, September 2004, Web-Based Research and Supervision of Paralegal and Support Personnel.
- Guest speaker, Family Law, Certified Legal Assistant exam review course, Meredith College, 2004
- Adjunct instructor for the Meredith College Legal Assistant's Program, co-instructor at five-course series for local law firm on civil litigation, 2005
- Speaker at the North Carolina Bar Association's Practical Skills Seminar, September 2005, Supervision of Paralegal and Support Personnel.

■ Adjunct instructor for the Meredith College Legal Assistant's Program, co-instructor on appellate practice.

FIRM AT-A-GLANCE:

Wake Family Law Group
4350 Lassiter at North Hills Avenue, Suite 360
Raleigh, NC
Phone: 919.787.4040
Fax: 919.787.4811
Website: http://wakefamilylawgroup.com/

PRACTICE AREAS:

■ Family Law—all issues
■ Pension Division
■ Mediation/Arbitration
■ Litigation
■ Family Law Appeals

PRACTICE AREAS:

■ Family Law, which may include the following issues: premarital agreements and marital separation agreements, custody and child support issues, division of property (equitable distribution), post-separation support, and alimony.

■ Pension Division, which may include preparation of the first draft of a pension division order (federal and state pensions, as well as private sector).

■ Civil Litigation/Appellate Procedure, which may include preparation for trial, assistance during trial, and post-trial appeals.

INTRODUCTION TO FAMILY LAW

A typical family law case involves many different issues that can be interrelated. The attorney may ask the paralegal on such a case to handle many diverse tasks. From custody to property distribution, the family law paralegal faces a wide range of cases at a generally fast pace. The average family law attorney carries from 50 to 100 cases, and each one has its own unique set of facts and deadlines. A paralegal in this area of law often has to wear many different hats including, but not limited to, therapist, organizer, and financial analyst. If the paralegal works for several lawyers, she must also learn how each lawyer wants things done.

One of the most difficult aspects of family law is handling the client's emotions. The paralegal must manage these emotions as part of the case. The client may be especially sensitive about one issue over another for reasons that the paralegal may not be aware of without asking. Getting behind the client's motivation for wanting a certain item of property, or a specific day of visitation, is necessary. Part of the attorney/paralegal function is to help the client break through the emotion to see the practical angle to their case. This field of law is much like practicing medicine—you cannot get too emotionally attached or involved with the clients you help serve, because you may lose perspective.

OVERVIEW OF JOB RESPONSIBILITIES:

■ Calendar maintenance and scheduling

ETHICS CAVEAT:

Calendaring is a critical duty. The lawyer and paralegal have an ethical obligation not to miss important deadlines that may impair a client's rights or position.

Therese A. Cannon, Attorney at Law and author of *Ethics and Professional Responsibility for Legal Assistants*

■ Client appointments and telephone conferences
■ Telephone conferences with opposing counsel
■ Hearings/trials
■ Depositions
■ Mediation and arbitrations
■ Settlement conferences
■ Prospective client appointments

- Professional meetings and CLEs
- Preparation of all court documents
- Preparation of cases for trial
- Preparation of documents for appeal
- File maintenance

RESEARCH:

- Pull all cited cases in appellant's brief in preparation for the appellee brief.
- Initial case law search on issues to use in preparing brief.

ETHICS CAVEAT:

When researching case law, be sure to address and distinguish to the extent possible controlling law that contradicts the client's position. Not reporting the existence of opposing controlling cases is an ethical violation and may subject the lawyer to sanctions by the court.

Therese A. Cannon, Attorney at Law and author of *Ethics and Professional Responsibility for Legal Assistants*

- Research the Code of Federal Regulations (CFR) regarding requirements when including survivor benefits in a COAP.
- Research case law for trial arguments.
- Web site research on pension plans (private, state, and federal)
- On-line research as to asset/debt values (equitable distribution)
- Cite checking/Sheppard's Citations

DRAFTING OF DOCUMENTS:

First Draft Pending Attorney Approval

- All pleadings, motions, and orders (primarily pretrial orders and consent orders)
- Discovery requests and responses
- Settlement agreements and premarital agreements

- Mediation and arbitration agreements
- Deeds
- Pension Division Orders: Qualified Domestic Relations Order, Retirement Benefits Court Order, Court Order Acceptable for Processing
- Some appeal briefs
- Merit Systems Protection Board petitions (initial application and reconsideration)
- Letters to clients, opposing counsels, plan administrators, and other third parties

---

ETHICS CAVEAT:

When writing to clients under your own signature, be sure to use the appropriate paralegal title and to include legal advice only if the lawyer has approved it and you are relaying it at the attorney's request.

Therese A. Cannon, Attorney at Law and author of *Ethics and Professional Responsibility for Legal Assistants*

- Motion and orders for extension of time
- Notice of hearings and calendar requests (and deposition notices)
- Subpoenas
- Equitable distribution spreadsheets
- Financial affidavits
- Equitable Distribution Inventory Affidavits
- Trial exhibits
- Last will and testament and power of attorney
- Child support worksheets

DOCUMENT REVIEW AND ANALYSIS:

- All account statements
- All financial records as they relate to financial issues in a case
- All income documents
- All expense documents

- Some depositions transcripts
- Client notes
- Property documentation
- Discovery responses (RPDs, RFAs, and INTs)
- Initial disclosure production (property and support issues)
- COAP questionnaire and supporting documents (calculation of the marital share as well)
- Other pension division documents

GENERAL:

- File maintenance and sorting
- Initial prospective client intake calls
- Opposing counsel calls on all issues
- Client calls on all issues
- Potential co-counsels
- Potential clients
- Assist with updating forms and reference materials
- Preparation and updating of client information letters
- Tracking of receipt of signed legal services contract and trust account deposits

ETHICS CAVEAT:

Paralegals generally enjoy client contact. However, remember not to answer questions that would be tantamount to giving legal advice, such as, "How do you think my case is going to turn out?" or "Should I [take a particular action]?" Be sure to identify yourself as a paralegal when you take a call from opposing counsel. Remember, when you speak to a prospective client, do not make statements that amount to entering into the lawyer-client relationship. Interviewing, providing, and taking information are excellent paralegal tasks, but do not commit the firm without approval and the go-ahead from the lawyer who should set the terms of the agreement, including fees.

Therese A. Cannon, Attorney at Law and author of *Ethics and Professional Responsibility for Legal Assistants*

TYPICAL WORKWEEK:

- Meet with attorney to brainstorm about interrogatories and request for production of documents needed in a case.
- Finish the first draft of the Equitable Distribution Inventory Affidavit (EDIA; list of all assets and debts in a case) and responses to interrogatories and request for production of documents for attorney review and discussion.

ETHICS CAVEAT:

When doing document productions, be sure you screen carefully for privileged documents so that you do not inadvertently disclose any protected documents, thereby threatening the privileged status of these documents.

Therese A. Cannon, Attorney at Law and author of *Ethics and Professional Responsibility for Legal Assistants*

- Call to Certified Public Accountant (CPA) (expert in case) regarding the results of his report on the value of a marital asset and to inquire as to whether he will need the parties' tax returns (back up data used to prepare his report) in case this issue goes to court and he needs to testify.
- Telephone call with client regarding her conversation with the opposing party and her concerns.
- Review and respond to e-mail from opposing counsel regarding the distribution of household goods. Review the Microsoft® Excel® chart prepared by opposing counsel that sets out the proposed distribution. Telephone call with client regarding whether it was received and that his immediate review is needed. Revise the property list with errors already identified and fax list to opposing counsel.
- Telephone call with prospective client; set up an appointment with an attorney for an initial consultation.
- Send e-mail to opposing counsel to follow up on the status of their review of the qualified domestic relations order and the custody consent order.

ETHICS CAVEAT:

When using e-mail with opposing counsel, be sure not to send any documents that have not been cleaned to remove previous drafts that can be accessed by the tracking function.

Therese A. Cannon, Attorney at Law and author of *Ethics and Professional Responsibility for Legal Assistants*

- Meet with attorney to review the first draft of the EDIA and the discovery responses. Make edits to same in preparation for the meeting with client. Meet with client to go over the EDIA and discovery responses. Make edits after meeting with client. Final meeting with the attorney to go over the revised draft of the documents and to brainstorm about any possible pitfalls with the responses. Make all final edits; prepare it for filing and hand delivery today.

- Telephone call with client regarding the issues he notes with the household goods list. Edit the property list and send e-mail to opposing counsel with the revised consent order (revised by the attorney) and property list exhibits. Meeting with attorney regarding the proposed order sent to opposing counsel.

- Telephone call with prospective client, set up appointment with an attorney for an initial consultation, and meet with attorney regarding the appointment set up and the issues in the case.

- Telephone call with *pro se* opposing party regarding the status of him signing the forms to transfer stocks to our client as set out in the settlement agreement previously signed.

ETHICS CAVEAT:

Be especially careful when working with opposing parties who are representing themselves so that there is not even an appearance of your taking advantage of the situation or that you are giving them legal advice.

Therese A. Cannon, Attorney at Law and author of *Ethics and Professional Responsibility for Legal Assistants*

- Send e-mail to opposing counsel regarding the status of signing and filing the acceptance of service for the complaint previously sent.

- Review and respond to professional e-mails regarding committee work.

- Meet with attorney regarding the status of settlement in the case. Review the e-mail to opposing counsel from attorney regarding it. Sit in on attorney's call with client to discuss the proposed consent order and household goods list. Cross-check the revised consent order received from opposing counsel against the last version sent to them.

- Telephone call with opposing counsel and attorney regarding the location of property on the date of separation and today.

- Review the EDIA and discovery responses received from opposing counsel. Meet with attorney regarding the objection also received. Fax these documents to our client. Send e-mail to opposing counsel regarding the possible waiver language in a consent order. Meeting with attorney regarding her call with opposing counsel to further discuss the language. Review the first draft of the report received from the CPA (expert).

- Task list meeting with attorney to go over all of our cases and to discuss work and deadlines.

- Review the Court of Appeals decision received in a case. Meeting with attorney regarding the dissenting opinion. Telephone call with the Court of Appeals to confirm the deadline for filing a notice of appeal to the Supreme Court.

- Review the Court of Appeals' decision received in another case.

- Telephone call with client regarding the status of preparing and filing of the complaint in her case and the tape recordings she has that may be relevant. Discussed the chain of custody of the tapes.

- Review the e-mail from opposing counsel regarding the revisions to the consent order.

- Meeting with *pro se* opposing party for him to turn over the stock transfer forms he has now signed.

- Meet with client to go over her proposed budget and list of all assets and debts along with date of separation values. Go through all documents provided by client and prepare list for client of further information needed from her. Start financial affidavit and date of separation equitable distribution spreadsheet.

- Prepare note to opposing counsel to accompany the stock transfer form for client to sign. Provide instructions on submitting it to the plan administrator.

- Review the discovery requests received from opposing counsel. Begin to go through the initial disclosures produced from opposing counsel to determine what documents are still necessary pursuant to court rules.

- Work on the date of separation spreadsheet for another case.

- Review and respond to e-mail from opposing counsel's paralegal regarding the revisions to the consent order. Telephone call with her regarding further settlement issues.

- Review the affidavit received from a witness in a case. The affidavit is an attachment to an exhibit to a petition for reconsideration to the Army Board for Correction of Military Records.

- Review the letter from the attorney to client regarding the status of the case.

- Meet with attorney regarding my call with opposing counsel's paralegal yesterday regarding settlement issues. Review the newest version of the consent order received against the last version sent to them to make sure that no edits are missing. Meet with attorney regarding the revisions made. Telephone call with opposing counsel regarding questions on the revisions she made. Telephone call with client regarding the revisions requested by opposing counsel. Telephone call with opposing counsel's paralegal regarding possible language for the consent order. Revise the consent order. Meet with attorney to review the revisions. Send e-mail to opposing counsel to accompany the revised consent order.

- Meet with attorney regarding client's budget and asset/debt spreadsheet. Discuss the amount needed for alimony and possible property distribution issues.

- Review and respond to professional e-mails.

- Telephone call with client regarding opposing party's desire to divide the 401K prior to the filing of the complaint for divorce and the potential problems with this approach, as discussed previously with attorney and identified in attorney notes. Begin the letter to opposing counsel regarding the documents needed from their client.

- Telephone call with client regarding the discovery requests received from opposing counsel, the deadline for it, and draft responses needed. Meet with attorney regarding it.

- Telephone call with prospective client; set up initial consultation with attorney.

- Meet with attorney regarding the status of work in a case. Continue work on the documents that will go to Vital Records.

- Send reminder e-mail to co-counsels regarding the responses needed from them both as to the direction of the case and what language they can agree on being included in the Court Order Acceptable for Processiong (COAP) we are preparing.

- Review e-mail from opposing counsel regarding issues in the case. Send e-mail to client regarding the questions raised by opposing counsel and input needed.

PRACTICAL TIPS, SHORTCUTS, AND TRICKS OF THE TRADE:

ORGANIZATION AND TEAMWORK—THE SECRETS TO BEING A SUCCESSFUL FAMILY LAW PARALEGAL

I lecture and write about the use of spreadsheets in family law as a way to summarize the equitable distribution portion of the case in one document. You can use this document to prepare trial exhibits, inventory affidavits, and court orders. Beyond equitable distribution and all other family law claims, keeping an organized file and office leads to an organized mind. I am less likely to forget tasks and deadlines if I am on top of the documents in my office. Family law is too fast-paced to spend time looking for information.

Teamwork is the most important piece of the attorney/paralegal relationship. When the teams meet regularly to discuss the status of cases and changes in court rules, the office runs more smoothly. Everyone is much happier. Each team member should present a report regarding the status of her work, what work is pending, what calls she has to make regarding the case, and any new issues discovered. When there is a checks-and-balances system, cases are handled efficiently.

The team should divide the work evenly. If one member is overloaded and another is not, this will lead to problems in general attitude and the quality of work produced. Get to know your attorneys and learn to anticipate their needs.

ETHICS CAVEAT:

This is an important point because ethical lapses and failure to act competently are often the result of excessive workloads and inadequate supervision.

Therese A. Cannon, Attorney at Law and author of *Ethics and Professional Responsibility for Legal Assistants*

FAMILY LAW LITIGATION TIPS:

Family law that involves litigation generally has the same elements as any litigation case, but with a different focus. There are pleadings, discovery, subpoenas, depositions, witnesses, trials, and other litigation processes. As a rule, paralegals should be involved in all aspects of the case and prepare the first drafts of most documents. The following sections will discuss the specifics of a family law case without going in depth as to the general litigation process.

FILING THE COMPLAINT

Most states and counties have their own domestic court rules, domestic forms, and filing coversheets. After the complaint has been finalized and you are preparing it for filing, make sure you are including all of the required attachments and coversheets. For example, does your county require a special child support coversheet in addition to the domestic civil coversheet? Below is a list of supporting documents that you may need to file in addition to the complaint and summons in your county. Make sure you check your local rules before sending the complaint to the clerk for filing. Neither you nor your attorney wants the complaint rejected because required forms are missing.

GENERAL

1. Domestic Civil Coversheet
2. Affidavit of Judicial Assignment
3. Equitable Distribution Inventory Affidavit

4. Notice of Equitable Distribution Mediated Settlement Conference

5. Notice of Equitable Distribution Scheduling and Discovery Conference

6. Notice of Initial Disclosure

7. Affidavit as to Status of Minor Child to establish jurisdiction

8. Custody Mediation Coversheet

9. Notice of Custody Mediation Orientation

10. Financial Affidavit and Income Information

11. Employer Wage Affidavit

12. Verified Complaint

You may be able to find your county's local rules on-line. Try searching for "local rules." Some examples of Web sites are www.nccourts.org, www.courtinfo.ca.gov, www.courts.state.tx.us/, www.flcourts.org, and www.courts.state.ny.us. When filing documents out of the county, make sure you look at that county's local rules. Each county may have its own requirements. What works in your county may not work elsewhere. You can expect that each county also has its own timeline for completed work in a case. There are generally quick deadlines in the first 120 days, so make sure you have looked closely at the rules and calendared the deadlines with two-week ticklers as a reminder. You do not want to jeopardize the case or spend your client's money on missed deadlines.

EQUITABLE DISTRIBUTION (ED)

Whether the case is litigation-bound or headed for settlement, you will need to compile a list of all marital assets and debts. Spreadsheets can be invaluable during this process, as well as the best start to the document-gathering portion of the case. A spreadsheet can be created in office suite software programs, such as Word, WordPerfect, and Excel.

You should start this document with the first equitable distribution (ED) document that you receive from your client or opposing counsel. You will want to identify the value of an asset or the amount owed on a debt as of the date of separation (DOS). You may also need to consider looking at the current values of any assets or debts with passive growth or loss in the event that the growth or loss is divisible between the parties. Since the decline in the market in 2001, there has been more of a focus on passive loss than gain. Keep this in mind when analyzing account statements and looking for indications as to why there may have been a decrease in account balances.

The spreadsheet is a great resource to help you remember any questions or comments to address later in the case. For example, it may be important to remember the number of vested and unvested stock options, as well as their strike or grant price. You will also want to list the title owner of an asset as a reminder to prepare deeds and transfer titles in the future, if necessary. For clarification, specifically note the document you are using to reflect the value listed (e.g., CCB interest checking account in wife's name alone, acct. # 3234787031, and 4/1/03 statement). In addition, keeping track of the information you are expecting from others on the spreadsheet is a great way to quickly and efficiently identify what further documents are needed (e.g., client to get updated statement on this account, opposing counsel to provide last two years of statements).

> **PRACTICE TIP NO. 1:** Make sure that you note the date of marriage (DOM) and date of separation (DOS) on the top of your spreadsheet so that you will have a point of reference when looking at the dates for the values noted. Also, make sure you save the spreadsheet as a new version every time you edit it and change the revision date so that you can backtrack if needed.

> **PRACTICE TIP NO. 2:** You may want to keep a DOS statement or exhibits file in your case expanding (Redweld) file for the documents that you may need later. To save time, it is easier to pull one file folder of exhibits than a folder for every asset and debt.

There is extensive information to manage in an ED case, and your attorney relies on you to prepare the ED case for settlement negotiations or trial (in other words, know the file). The spreadsheet will enable you to know what is going on in the ED case at any time.

- Do we have the document we need to prove the DOS balance of the marital bank account?
- Do we have the current stock price to recalculate the value of the stock options?

- Is the value noted for the pension the accumulated contributions or the actual value?

All of these things are important for the attorney to know, and if you keep this information in one document, you can answer questions easily and not have to search the bankers' boxes worth of documents to respond. In addition, the spreadsheet can be a good starting point for you and your attorney to review the assets of the estate to determine if a house appraisal or a business valuation will be necessary. The earlier in the case that you and your attorney determine you need experts, the more prepared you will be as the case progresses.

> **PRACTICE TIP NO. 3:** Make sure that you have one column for Wife and one column for Husband so that you can shift items back and forth between columns as needed. This will be important when you are trying to get to the bottom-line number that is the ultimate goal when determining an equal or equitable distribution.

While you are putting together your spreadsheet, gather the DOS or current documents that you will need for trial. If you have noted the date of the statement for the value you listed on the spreadsheet, make sure you have that statement in the file. When the trial draws closer, it will be very easy to use the spreadsheet and all of the supporting documents behind it as the exhibits for the ED case. If you have been gathering the information all along, trial preparation will not be overwhelming or a last-minute struggle.

> **PRACTICE TIP NO. 4:** These types of spreadsheets make great trial exhibits. They are also good to have during mediation so that you can update numbers as the day goes on.

Handle household goods in either of two ways on the spreadsheet. You can make one entry for these items and assign each party a percentage or dollar amount of the total, or you can list each item individually. You will need to talk to your attorney about her approach to this part of the ED case. Some parties are able to amicably split up the household goods to their mutual satisfaction and not put a dollar amount on each item (the preferable way of handling the division). If this is the case, you will only need one entry on the spreadsheet, which will greatly simplify the case. If the parties feel the need to pick through each item and value everything from the small kitchen appliances to the bathroom accessories, you will want to consider a separate spreadsheet for the household goods.

The spreadsheet format can be much the same as noted above (i.e., one column for each party, one column for the item, a totals column, and a net value bottom-line calculation). It may also be necessary to list specific information about the item on the spreadsheet, such as chair inherited by wife from her mother or sofa bought with husband's separate funds. Remember that you can always delete specific information from the spreadsheet and save it as another version that can then be used as an exhibit or attachment to a consent order.

PRACTICE TIP NO. 5: Remember to note on your spreadsheet any information about where you got the value of the item listed. Did you perform an on-line search for values or was a professional appraisal performed? The reliability of your value may become very important if this issue were to proceed to trial or arbitration.

You may find it necessary to prepare additional spreadsheets as the case draws closer to mediation, arbitration, or trial. A spreadsheet for calculating the value of stock options might be helpful. You can prepare one that allows you to change the amount of the stock price based on the market that day in only one location and recalculate the value of the stock options (stock price minus grant price) with the most up-to-date numbers. You may also want to prepare a spreadsheet that will show mortgage payments made by one spouse on the marital residence after DOS (amortization table).

You will want it to calculate the amount of interest paid and the amount of principal reduction. This will allow you to give a credit for principal reduction to the party paying the mortgage after DOS if your attorney decides to take this approach. You will want to let the attorney know if your client has paid a significant amount of interest on a marital debt after DOS in case she wants to raise this issue as a possible distributional factor. A spreadsheet that illustrates this issue will make things much clearer for everyone involved.

If you have already prepared your spreadsheet, the next step in a litigation ED case will be much easier to tackle. In most states, the district court requires each party to file an Equitable Distribution Inventory Affidavit (EDIA). This form is essentially a list of all assets and debts and additional information about them. If you have already finished your spreadsheet, the EDIA will be much easier to prepare because you have already gathered most of the information requested in the form. You will find it easier to schedule a meeting with the client to go over the spreadsheet in detail to make sure that nothing has been omitted before preparing the EDIA. You may find it necessary to include the attorney at this point; she may address any questions the client has in this meeting. It is important that the client understand he will be signing an affidavit swearing that everything listed on the EDIA is all that exists in the estate. During that meeting, give the client the option to use the spreadsheet and prepare the first draft of the EDIA. What you should get back from your client is a handwritten draft of the EDIA that is easily typed in, edited, and prepared for filing. You will find the remainder of the ED case much less burdensome when you have spent the time to put together the spreadsheet in the beginning.

> **PRACTICE TIP NO. 6:** Allow your client to be an active participant in the EDIA preparation process. Who better to list all assets and debts than the one whose case it is? You will find the daunting task of EDIA preparation far less painful with the help of the client.

Analyzing documents is an important part of any ED case, especially when you have one side that has been less than forthcoming with information about what marital accounts may exist. Bank account statements and investment account statements can be especially helpful when trying to locate all of the assets. You need to look closely at account statements. Sometimes there can be more than one account on a single statement. Often, bank account statements may list overdraft or equity accounts.

You will also need to examine any deposits or withdrawals from the account. Often, the account statements will list the account number for the account of final destination or the account from which the funds came. Trace this account number to assets you are already aware of if you have not yet seen this account number; chances are you have identified an account not previously revealed. Canceled checks, if written by a detail-oriented person, might also have useful information.

> **PRACTICE TIP NO. 7:** Asking your client to analyze the other party's checks can be very helpful. Your client has the most invested in the case and is more likely to look for and recognize any strange out-of-place expenses.

- Who is the payee on the checks?
- Does the check note the account number on the bottom?
- The check was written from what account?
- What is the check number?
- Is it a new account or an old account? Detailed analysis can often be a lengthy process but one that is most often worth the time spent.

> **PRACTICE TIP NO. 8:** Someone's spending can be a sensitive or hot-button issue. A face-to-face meeting with a client can sometimes be more effective than a telephone conversation, especially when you are explaining the financial affidavit form and the work that you need them to do. Telephone calls can be too impersonal for a very personal process.

ALIMONY AND POST-SEPARATION SUPPORT

The family law paralegal plays an important role in the early stages of the alimony or post-separation support (PSS) case. Whether you are working with a supporting spouse or a dependent spouse, the financial affidavit (budget) can be the most important document in the case. The first detail that the attorney must determine after meeting with the client is whether the numbers show that there is a shortfall or an excess of income.

Once that is determined, the next question is, What point in time are you trying to reflect? Is it more important to show the marital standard of living or is the present situation more of a reality? Only your attorney can decide this strategy. You may find it necessary to prepare two separate scenarios: one that shows the marital standard that the ex-spouse is entitled to maintain, and another that shows the current situation that reflects a significant downscale in the standard of living. Once you and the attorney have had a chance to discuss the focus of the financial affidavit, your attorney (and you) should meet with the client. It is more effective to sit down with the client face to face to go over the financial affidavit form and to talk through what type of supporting information you will need them to provide for the first draft.

If you are dealing with a supporting spouse who already has a shortfall in her income, you will want her to provide all bank statements, checkbook registers, canceled checks, and credit card statements so you can track her spending and make sure that your argument that there are no available funds to pay the dependent spouse is airtight.

> **PRACTICE TIP NO. 9:** You might want to get a copy from your client of all documents that she used to calculate her monthly budget. You may feel the need to review her numbers prior to trial to make sure that the financial affidavit is airtight and subject to only limited examination by opposing counsel. Everyone is capable of miscalculation; you just do not want the other side to be the one to figure it out.

You may also want to ask for ATM withdrawal receipts to determine how much of the money your client spends is uncategorized, but nonetheless needed. Many people take money out of the ATM to pay for their everyday expenses, but they do not account for it like a check or credit card purchase. Talk to the client about tracking this spending for a period of time so that these expenses are not lost and can be accounted for when determining the amount of money available to pay the dependant spouse.

> **PRACTICE TIP NO. 10:** Playing the devil's advocate at times can be helpful. When reviewing your client's financial affidavit, objectively look at the numbers and ask yourself, "If I were opposing counsel, would I say that $500 a month for clothing is excessive?" Of course, I would never complain about $500 a month for clothing, but I am not on the other side. Think about the expenses from both points of view to plan and anticipate holes in the numbers.

When dealing with a dependant spouse, you will need generally the same information as previously mentioned for the supporting spouse, but, in addition, the client will need to consider the expenses that his spouse still pays (e.g., health insurance, life insurance, and car insurance). Most likely, your client will need to pay these expenses on his own in the future, and you will be cutting him short if you do not include these numbers when calculating the amount of shortfall he may have in his monthly budget.

Because the client will need to prepare the initial draft of the financial affidavit, he will need to provide you with a written summary of how he calculated the numbers on his affidavit so that, if this issue comes to trial, you will have the documents and information you need to prepare trial exhibits. You will also need to gather the last several months of pay stubs from your client for your files, but you may also be required to file this information with the affidavit. It might be necessary to look at the last several years of tax returns so that you can look at a range of your client's income to spot any unusual decreases or increases in income. Your client may have made more income than usual in the last month due to a one-time bonus or travel expense reimbursements. A footnote on the affidavit to describe the unusually high income might be necessary. A better strategy might be to include the last year's W-2 along with the pay stubs.

As the trial draws near, you may need to run some calculations with the help of a CPA to gross up the alimony amount for the dependant spouse. You and your attorney will need to consider whether to pay a professional to run these numbers or to run rough calculations on your own using your client's effective tax rate. The ultimate goal is to determine for your client how much after-tax money he will need in his pocket to pay for their reasonable living expenses. The other side of that calculation is to determine how much the supporting spouse is actually paying after taxes are deducted. If you decide to hire a CPA to run these calculations, make sure that he is available to testify in court, if needed.

Analyzing income numbers is also an important part of any alimony case. When you represent the dependant spouse, you want to make sure that you closely analyze the income of the other party to make sure that they are not trying to conceal income. Dividend or investment income may be one source to consider. If the other party owns her own business, you need to look closely at the personal expenses the business may pay on her behalf. She may be receiving in-kind benefits, such as a company car, or have other living expenses paid for by the company. Doing a set of interrogatories or request for production of documents may be beneficial to determine all sources of income for a supporting spouse.

You may also want to take a close look at business credit card statements and canceled checks for the types of expenses posted. If there is a large amount of information to go through or the businesses' books appear to be recorded incorrectly (or not recorded at all), you may want to consider seeking the services of a CPA to analyze the true income of the other party.

PRACTICE TIP NO. 11: The project may be too complicated for you to determine any concealed income. There are experts for these types of analysis, such as CPAs. Know when to talk to the attorney about hiring outside counsel. Realizing that you need assistance can be a great asset to the firm.

Child Custody and Visitation

A paralegal's role in a custody case can be limited, depending on whether settlement or litigation results. The first task for the paralegal is to put together a visitation calendar that sets out the current situation and one that sets out your client's proposal for settlement (or best-case scenario). These calendars can be an attachment to a custody order or an exhibit in the future for trial. They can be a guideline for calculating child support (discussed later in the next section). It is important for your client to have realistic expectations, and preparing a visitation calendar forces him to see the reality of his proposals. It also forces him to think about the logistics of how a given visitation schedule may actually work.

ETHICS CAVEAT:

Be sure when preparing witnesses not to tell them what to say. Over coaching can give the appearance that you are trying to get them to testify falsely, which is a serious ethical and legal violation.

Therese A. Cannon, Attorney at Law and author of *Ethics and Professional Responsibility for Legal Assistants*

The paralegal can work closely with the client to put together the visitation calendar to remind them of items they may have forgotten. Does the holiday visitation supersede the regular schedule? You may find it necessary to involve the attorney as you are working through the details of the calendars with the client because he may have questions that involve legal advice that only the attorney can answer.

PRACTICE TIP NO. 12: You can use a paper calendar or a computerized calendar (my preference). There are also Web sites that allow you to prepare visitation calendars on-line for a small fee.

If mediation or settlement fails in the custody/visitation case, generally the next step is trial or arbitration. Custody cases can require a fair amount of witnesses. The paralegal can handle the initial witness interviews to provide basic information to the attorney as to the possible testimony of the witness. This will allow the attorney to narrow the list of witnesses before becoming too involved in the witness preparation portion of the trial planning.

This is also an opportunity for the paralegal to check with all of the witnesses as to their availability the week of the trial. It may be necessary for the attorney to hold a video deposition prior to the trial if an important witness cannot be present. To avoid inconveniencing the witnesses anymore than needed, the paralegal may find it necessary to put them "on call" the week of trial. Coordinating witness appearances in court can be very stressful when considering everyone's schedules and the judge's decisions as to when and how the trial proceeds. The attorney should rely on you to handle the scheduling of witnesses so that she can concentrate on the trial.

> **PRACTICE TIP NO. 13:** Even a "friendly witness" may need a subpoena for their employer to let them off work. Make sure you talk to all the witnesses for your client's case about whether they will need a subpoena to attend trial and miss work. After all, you do not want to anger one of your witnesses by causing her to miss work without pay or take one of her vacation days to testify. An angry witness is usually not a favorable witness for your case.

CHILD SUPPORT

The visitation calendars (discussed in the previous section) will be helpful when it comes time to calculate child support after the custody decision. The first item you will need from both parties to run a child support worksheet is their gross income (yearly or monthly). You will want to look at a minimum of six months worth of pay stubs to make sure that you are accurately representing the income of each party. Be sure to include annual bonuses in your calculations. Watch out—some parties are paid every two weeks and others twice a month. This will make a big difference in your numbers if calculated incorrectly.

Keep in mind that you need to give your client an offset if he is responsible for another child outside of this case. Next, you will need to find out who pays health insurance for the child. Remember it is only the portion paid for the child that belongs on the worksheet (not the portion paid for self). You will need to talk to the attorney about whether extraordinary expenses apply in the case at hand. Does the child go to a private school or need special therapy? The worksheet should account for any day care expenses. Be careful to avoid including the summer months in your day care calculations for the school year.

You can assist the attorney by gathering all of the previously mentioned information from your client (and opposing counsel) and running the worksheet. You may want to run several worksheets with different scenarios if the settlement proposal is to switch the day care or extraordinary expenses to the non-paying party or you want to present several options to the court for trial.

PRACTICE TIP NO. 14: Your county may require the child support worksheet to be filed with any child support order. Check your local rules to make sure that all required attachments are included at the time of filing.

If one party has requested a deviation from the guidelines, the financial affidavit mentioned in the "Alimony and Post-Separation Support" section will be very important. Go over the child's expenses with your client to make sure that he has not undercut what he really spends. Often, the client will under calculate his true monthly expenses. The goal is not to inflate the budget, but rather to present an accurate picture of spending. The client may need to track her expenses for the child for a period of time to make sure that her numbers are not inflated or deflated. When the client requires a deviation, you will want to pay special attention to income. Make sure that you have fully examined the other party's income to catch any miscalculations or incorrect representations. The payor, as well as the payee, will tend to use the lowest income numbers possible. Obviously, you want to be an advocate for your client, but you do not want to get in the habit of manipulating the numbers.

PRACTICE TIP NO. 15: Remember to include provisions for payment through the Office of Child Support in child support orders. This is especially true for the cases where there are young children and you foresee non-payment in the future. This will allow someone else, other than you, to monitor the payment of child support over the years and allow your client to seek free assistance on collection of arrears from the Office of Child Support Enforcement.

ABSOLUTE DIVORCE

The paralegal needs to ask the attorney about their state's law regarding the length of the parties' separation before filing for divorce. In most states, there are two ways to handle an absolute divorce, either by summary judgment or testimony. After talking to the client, your attorney will need to determine the best approach. Be careful when setting the hearing because a testimonial divorce generally requires 5 days notice of the hearing, whereas a summary judgment divorce requires 10 days notice of the hearing. You will also want to remember to ask your female clients if they want to resume the use of their maiden name because that should be included in the complaint or answer and counterclaim.

Another item to consider if the divorce comes at the end of the case is including the withdrawal of the attorney in the divorce pleadings. This can be an easy way to finish the case and avoid the extra paperwork involved in filing a separate motion and order for withdrawal. If you include the withdrawal in the divorce, make sure that you file and process all pension division orders (qualified domestic relations orders and court orders acceptable for processing, etc.) as required by any ED orders or settlement agreements. This is especially true in states where the court does not deal with all issues at one time (bifurcated proceedings). You do not want to leave any loose ends.

The well-utilized paralegal can be the right hand of the attorney and a valuable asset to any family law firm. The most important role of the paralegal is being a reliable member of the attorney/paralegal team. You and your attorney will want to work together to develop systems that make cases run more efficiently. Your attorney should tell the client that his office will use a team approach on his case.

A family law paralegal is the first line of contact for the client with the volume of cases in family law. The first step in the client/paralegal relationship will be working together to gather and analyze documents, regardless of the claims raised. That is the common thread in almost all family law cases. Even though you cannot give legal advice, your role in the family law firm is extremely important and valued. Pay close attention to detail, keep an open mind, get used to a fair amount of client contact, and you will prosper in family law.

PRACTICE TIP NO. 16: You and your attorney will want to make sure that your client's ED and alimony claims have been reserved or resolved at the time of the divorce because, once the divorce is granted, any ED or alimony claims that have not been reserved could be lost. This only applies to states where not all issues are resolved at the time of the divorce.

CHALLENGES IN FAMILY LAW:

- Getting all the financial statements needed when the date of separation was over five years ago. Financial institutions only keep electronic records available for a couple of years. Once electronic records are no longer available, it will be necessary to contact the document retrieval department of the company for paper statements. This can be a lengthy process.
- Keeping information on divisible property current (passive gain or loss as an example).
- Working through the logistics of valuing marital property that is in another state.
- Getting pay and benefits information from employers.
- Serving defendant's with complaints outside of the state or country.
- Obtaining present value calculations on retirement benefits without hiring a CPA.
- Client's emotions making their decisions in the case.
- Making sure that all loose ends are tied up after settlement or a court order (e.g., deed transfers, title transfers, pension division orders, exchange of property, and transfer of dependency exemptions).
- Staying on top of the numerous phone calls during the day. Family law has significant client contact.
- Knowing the different types of law that family law overlaps with, such as real estate law, business law, elder law, and estate law.
- Keeping current on the changes in statutes, court rules, and case law. There are new Court of Appeals and Supreme Court cases released every month.
- Controlling the high-stress levels due to the fast pace of family law.

ETHICS CAVEAT:

Legal advice includes recommending a course of action, advising the client about rights and responsibilities, and telling a client what the law is in the matter. Jennifer is right, and it is clear from the chapter that paralegals play a huge and critical role in serving clients without having to give legal advice.

Therese A. Cannon, Attorney at Law and author of *Ethics and Professional Responsibility for Legal Assistants*

Part VIII

BANKRUPTCY

CHAPTER 14

MATHEW D. LASKOWSKI

Senior Paralegal

PORZIO, BROMBERG, & NEWMAN, PC

Morristown, NJ

"Mat has been a significant resource to me in assimilating new paralegals to the firm and the practice group. He has a wealth of practical knowledge and enjoys sharing that knowledge with others. He has played an integral role in training other paralegals (and attorneys) in areas, such as electronic filing procedures and courtroom technology. Mat has also assisted me in providing other paralegals with guidance on how best to complete self-assessment forms. Other paralegals within the firm tend to rely upon Mat for information and guidance in a wide variety of areas."

Jennifer P. Allen

Coordinator of Paralegal Services

Porzio, Bromberg, & Newman, PC

EDUCATION/HONORS/CERTIFICATIONS:

- B.A. Political Science (Business Minor), Marist College, 1998
- ABA Approved Paralegal Certificate, Marist College, 1998

PROFESSIONAL ASSOCIATIONS:

- Member, National Association of Legal Assistants, 2004–present
- Member, Paralegal Association of New Jersey (PANJ), 2000–present
- Treasurer, Paralegal Association of New Jersey, 2002–present
- Website Designer, Paralegal Association of New Jersey, 2003–present
- Associate Member, New Jersey State Bar Association
- Member, Special Committee on Paralegals, New Jersey State Bar Association, 2001–present
- Member, Bankruptcy Section, New Jersey State Bar Association, 2003–present
- Member, Paralegal Program Advisory Board, Union County College, 2004–present

FIRM AT-A-GLANCE:

Porzio, Bromberg, & Newman, P.C.
Morristown, NJ
Phone: 973.538.4006
Fax: 973.538.5146
Website: www.pbnlaw.com

OTHER LOCATIONS:

New York City Office
156 West 56th Street
New York, NY 10019-3800
Phone: 212.265.6888
Fax: 212.957.3983

Brick, NJ Office
263 Drum Point Road
Brick, NJ 08723-6399
Phone: 732.262.9248
Fax: 732.262.9267

MANAGING PARTNER:

D. Jeffrey Campbell

ATTORNEYS (PERMANENT):

80

PARALEGALS (PERMANENT):

32

PRACTICE AREAS:

- Bankruptcy and Financial Restructuring
- Business Disputes and Counseling
- Corporate Law
- Dispute Resolution
- Education Law
- Employment and Labor
- Environmental Law and Litigation
- General Liability
- Governmental Affairs
- Insurance Coverage Law
- Intellectual Property Law
- Land Use, Real Estate, and Construction
- Mergers and Acquisitions
- Personal Injury
- Pharmaceutical and Medical Devices
- Pharmaceutical Marketing and Sales Compliance and Litigation
- Product Liability and Mass Tort
- Professional Liability
- Property Tax Appeals
- Securities Law
- Transportation and Motor Carrier
- Trusts and Estates
- White Collar Criminal Defense

CONSUMER BANKRUPTCY:

In 2004, Chapter 7 bankruptcy petitions accounted for slightly over 70 percent of all consumer filings ("Non–Business Bankruptcy Filings by Chapter, 1990–2004, per Quarter" http://www.abiworld.org, 28 April 2005). Chapter 7 of the bankruptcy code is generally relied upon as the most effective way to wipe out unsecured debt and, in many instances, provides unsecured creditors with little to no return on their claims.

Those who file their petitions under Chapter 13 primarily do so in an effort to preserve assets (usually a home) that would otherwise be liquidated for the benefit of creditors. Chapter 13 debtors, who make up the nearly 30 percent of the remaining consumer filings, enter into a repayment plan lasting from 36 to 60 months, whereby unsecured creditors are paid an equal percentage of their respective claims based on the debtor's disposable income. Thus, generally speaking, creditors receive a greater return on their claims, and debtors pay more to their creditors in Chapter 13 cases when compared to Chapter 7 cases.

THE NEW CODE'S GENERAL IMPACT ON CONSUMER BANKRUPTCY

In an effort to curb the number of Chapter 7 filings, the new code, entitled Bankruptcy Abuse Prevention and Consumer Protection Act of 2005 (S. 256, H. 685) purports to adopt two **means tests** to determine if a debtor may file a petition under Chapter 7. Furthermore, pursuant to Section 707(b) of the new code, the court on its own motion or by motion of the trustee may move to dismiss or convert the Chapter 7 proceeding should the debtor's income exceed the state median income (the median family income). The assumption behind Section 707(b) is that if a debtor has income in excess of the state median, the debtor's Chapter 7 filing is an abuse of the bankruptcy system. Such a debtor may convert the case to one under either Chapter 11 or Chapter 13, with a repayment plan that provides a greater distribution to unsecured creditors.

THE FIRST MEANS TEST

A complex formula is used to calculate the first means test. First, the debtor's income must be determined. Pursuant to Section 101(10A) of the new code, the debtor's income is determined by calculating the debtor's last six full months of income (prior to the filing date) from all sources (not including Social Security payments). The total is then divided by six to determine the debtor's average monthly income. Health expenses, disability insurance, and health care savings accounts are deducted from the debtor's average income. Additional expenses that may be deducted from a debtor's average monthly income include the following: (i) actual expenses for the care and support of elderly or disabled household members and (ii) certain expenses associated with elementary and secondary school up to $1,500 per dependant child less than 18 years of age. This final number is known as the debtor's adjusted income. Once the adjusted income is calculated, it may then be compared to the median family income.

The Median family income, defined in Sections 101(39A) and 707(b)(2)(A)(ii)–(iv), is calculated by reviewing the median family income by state and persons in the household generated by the United States Census Bureau, last calculated in 1999. That number must be adjusted up to the time of filing based on the Consumer Price Index. The resulting number should be reduced based upon the IRS Standards for Allowable Living Expenses by Number of Persons in Household and then further reduced pursuant to the IRS House and Utilities Allowable Living Expenses by State and County, and the Allowable Living Expenses for Transportation by Region. The allowable expenses can be adjusted over the federal level if the debtor can prove their actual costs exceed the IRS allowances.

The resulting median family income is then compared to the debtor's adjusted income. If the debtor's adjusted income is less than the median family income, the debtor will be allowed to file a petition under Chapter 7 (provided the debtor meets certain additional requirements, some of which are set forth in the following sections). Conversely, if the debtor's adjusted income exceeds the median family income, the debtor may not file a petition under Chapter 7, but may file a petition under Chapter 11 or 13.

THE SECOND MEANS TEST

Those persons whose adjusted income is over the median family income may still be eligible to file a Chapter 7 petition if they meet the requirements set forth in an additional means test determined pursuant to Section 707(b)(2). Under this calculation, the debtor's monthly expenses are subtracted from the debtor's current monthly income, thus creating an adjusted monthly income (AMI). The AMI is then multiplied by 60. If the result is less than 25 percent of the debtor's general unsecured claims, or $6,000 (whichever is greater), a debtor may file a Chapter 7 petition. If it is greater than 25 percent or $6,000, the debtor may file a Chapter 11 or 13 petition.

Additional New Requirements

The new code also requires mandatory credit counseling (see Section 111) for all individual debtors. Pursuant to Section 109(h)(1), counseling must occur within 180 days prior to the filing of a petition under any section of the new code. The counselor must be associated with an "approved nonprofit budget and credit counseling agency," as defined by Section 111(c)(2) and must develop a management plan to be filed with the bankruptcy petition. There are certain exceptions for "emergencies" or, if in the trustee's opinion, the agency could not provide proper counseling for the debtor's situation.

These emergency exceptions do not exempt the debtor from counseling. Under Section 109(h)(3)(a), the emergent debtor must complete the counseling within 30 days of the bankruptcy filing, subject to a potential court-approved additional 15-day extension to complete the counseling. Failure to complete counseling can result in the dismissal of the petition. Furthermore, debtors who are incapacitated, disabled, or on active military duty in a war zone are exempt from the counseling requirement. In addition to the credit counseling, debtors, under Section 1328(g), will now be required to complete a course in personal financial management from a program approved by the United States Trustee's office in order to obtain a discharge of their debts. Those who do not complete the program may have their discharge (the order that absolves the debt) denied under Section 727 of the code.

Under the current bankruptcy code, certain debts are not dischargeable and must be paid by a debtor, notwithstanding a bankruptcy proceeding (see 11 USC §523). The new code expands the list of items to include: (i) debts incurred 90 days prior to the filing of the petition that are owed to a single creditor and with a total of more than $500 in "luxury goods" and (ii) cash advances of $750 or more within 70 days of the filing of the petition. These changes are aimed at those debtors who allegedly "load up" their credit cards just before filing for bankruptcy, knowing that the debt is generally unsecured and likely to be discharged under the current bankruptcy code.

In addition, the nondischargibility of student loans is extended to for-profit and nongovernmental entities, whose interest is deductible for federal income tax purposes under Section 523(a)(8). Currently, only nonprofit and government-backed student loans are nondischargeable. As the code stands today, a debtor may only receive a discharge once every six years; however, once the new code takes effect, the time frame will be extended to eight years. [See Section 727(a)(8).]

In any consumer bankruptcy, attorneys for debtors will now be required to sign a verification, pursuant to Section 707(b)(4)(C), that they conducted a "reasonable inquiry to verify that the information contained" in a petition and that the schedules are "well grounded in fact." These requirements make the attorney take on an "investigative role" that will undoubtedly cause an increase in professional fees for filing such bankruptcy petitions. This "verification" requirement may also decrease the number of attorneys willing to handle these cases on a *pro bono* basis.

There will also be changes in the way that exemptions are calculated. Exemptions are statutes that allow a debtor to retain certain property in a bankruptcy proceeding. Each state, unless they participate in the federal bankruptcy exemptions (see 11 USC §522), has its own exemption scheme. The court, under Section 522(b)(3)(A), will now review where the debtor was domiciled for the 730 days immediately preceding the bankruptcy filing. If the debtor has moved within the 730-day period, the court will look back an additional 180 days. The state where the debtor was domiciled during the majority of the 180-day period will determine the exemption scheme available to the debtor.

For example, if a debtor filed for bankruptcy in Florida on April 1, 2005, they would have had to be domiciled in Florida since April 14, 2003, to be able to use Florida's exemptions. However, if they moved to Florida after April 14, 2003, the court will look back to where the debtor was domiciled from October 16, 2002, to April 13, 2003. If the debtor lived in New Jersey for the majority of this time period, then New Jersey's exemptions would have to be followed. This is to avoid situations where people relocate to another state just prior to the filing of a bankruptcy petition in order to take advantage of a particular state's exemption statutes. This is significant because some debtors have purposely filed for bankruptcy in states like Florida and Texas, where they are able to exempt an entire residence, regardless of its value. Most other states limit the amount of such exemptions.

There are also new rules affecting the automatic stay for secured creditors. The automatic stay (see Section 362) is what prevents creditors from collecting pre-petition debts from debtors. Once a bankruptcy petition is filed, creditors must cease collection efforts for the duration of the bankruptcy or the court may penalize them. All lawsuits pending against the debtor must also cease as to the debtor for the duration of the bankruptcy. Prior to the new code, a creditor was required to file a motion requesting relief from the automatic stay in order to continue collection efforts. However, under the new code [Section 521(a)(6)], secured debt (debt secured by a particular piece of property, such as a car loan or mortgage on a home) not reassumed through agreement within 45 days after the meeting of creditors (a Section 341 meeting) is subject to the lifting of the automatic stay automatically—without a motion. Should the debtor not reassume the debt, under the same section and within the same 45-day time frame, the trustee may file a motion to keep the secured property in the estate if the trustee determines that the property has consequential value.

The number of documents that need to be filed with a petition has increased under the new code. In addition to the petition, schedules, statement of financial affairs, and creditor lists, debtors must now also include proof of income for the 60 days preceding the bankruptcy filing and a certificate of credit counseling as explained previously. A court will automatically dismiss a case unless these items and others listed under Section 521 are filed within 45 days after the filing of the petition, although there is a possibility of an additional 45-day extension. Further, the most recent tax return must be turned over to the trustee seven days prior to the Section 341 meeting, and must also be made available to creditors prior to the meeting. The debtor has an ongoing duty to provide copies of tax returns filed during the course of the bankruptcy to the trustee (in both Chapter 7 and 13 cases). In addition, under Section 521(h) the trustee may require the debtor to provide photo identification as proof of identity.

Child or family support obligations have been given a higher priority. Child support takes first position in the creditor priority list (see the Section 507 priority scheme); however a trustee's administrative costs (in both Chapter 7 and 13 cases) can take priority as long as the trustee is administering assets that can be used to pay the support owed. The automatic stay does not affect the duty to pay support; in fact, failure to remain current on post-petition support is grounds for dismissal of the bankruptcy or its conversion to Chapter 7 liquidation, as per Section 1307(a)(11).

The new code will thwart consumers who try to hide assets in trusts. Under Section 548(e), trustees will now be able to look back 10 years and seize assets if (i) they were moved into a self-settled trust or similar device, (ii) the transfer was by the debtor, (iii) the debtor is the beneficiary of the trust or similar device, and (iv) the debtor made such a transfer with the actual intent to hinder, delay, or defraud any creditor.

CONCLUSION

The new code introduces significant changes. Those who practice in the bankruptcy field should not only read the bill (S. 256, H. 685), but also attend sessions sponsored by local continuing legal educators to gain further insight into these sweeping changes.

The ultimate effect of these changes remains to be seen; however, it is clear that filing for bankruptcy will become more expensive, more time-consuming, and less available for consumer debtors.

OUTLINE OF JOB RESPONSIBILITIES:

ADMINISTRATIVE DUTIES (RELATED TO BANKRUPTCY ADMINISTRATIVE WORK)

1. Serve as a mentor to new paralegals at the firm.
2. Supervise and train more junior paralegals or those new to the team, including attorneys and administrative staff.
3. Assist co-workers in joining paralegal organizations.
4. Bankruptcy team duties

DEBTOR RELATED (CHAPTER 11 OR COMMERCIAL CHAPTER 7)

1. Meet with clients to collect information needed and assist in preparation of the bankruptcy petition, schedules, and related documents.
2. Review the debtor's payment history for the 90 days preceding filing the bankruptcy to determine the potential preference suits that may be filed to bring money back into the estate.
3. Advance preference suits by reviewing creditor invoices and debtor payment history to perform New Value and Ordinary Course analysis to anticipate the creditor's defense.
4. Assist with the preparation of First Day Motions and related documents.
5. Assist with the preparation of fee applications.
6. Assist with any other projects requested by supervisors.

CREDITOR-RELATED

1. Individual Creditor
2. Assist in the defense of adversary proceedings.
3. Defend preference suits by reviewing creditor invoices and debtor payment history to perform New Value and Ordinary Course analysis.
4. Prepare proofs of claim.
5. Prepare notices of appearance.
6. Assist with any other projects requested by supervisors.
7. Assist Creditor Committee (in addition to Individual Creditor Duties)
8. Prepare fee applications and track it.
9. Assist in the research of issues of interest to the committee to help maximize the return on their debt and/or explain why the bankruptcy occurred if unclear.
10. Assist with any other projects requested by supervisors.

GENERAL

1. Use the federal CM/ECF (Case Management/Electronic Case Files) document filing system, as well as PACER, to cull filed documents and related information.
2. Attend court hearings and depositions where appropriate.
3. Participate in case strategy meetings.
4. Assist in securing records related to the bankruptcy via the use of discovery in adversary proceedings and/or subpoenas.
5. Summarize records obtained as needed.
6. Prepare for and assist at hearings and trial.
7. Prepare electronic presentations using Microsoft® PowerPoint® and the Sanction™ 2 program.
8. Prepare pleadings and discovery requests, in addition to answers to it.
9. Sheppardize cases cited in briefs and research additional cases as needed.
10. Schedule depositions.

11. Coordinate and manage document reviews both on- and off-site.

12. Manage deposition transcripts using LiveNote® software, including the summary and/or culling of specific deposition excerpts as needed.

13. Work with local counsel to file pleadings and related documents.

14. Assist with any other projects requested by supervisors.

15. Client development.

16. Assist attorneys in locating, compiling, and organizing information for use in securing of new work for the department.

17. Assist with any other projects requested by supervisors.

TYPICAL WORKWEEK:

One of the best parts of my job is that there is nothing "typical" about my workweek. I may have some duties that are part of my routine, however, each day has the potential to present new challenges. First thing in the morning and in the evening before I leave, I review the petitions filed in the bankruptcy courts, where our attorneys are admitted. I flag any case that we have expertise in, download the petition and related pleadings, summarize the case, and forward it to my team for follow-up. I also review the adversary proceedings filed to make sure our existing clients are kept aware of cases that directly affect them. I also read the Dow Jones *Daily Bankruptcy Review* to keep current on cases happening outside of our jurisdictions and/or on cases that our firm is not directly involved. I do this daily.

While I take care of some smaller tasks, I spend the bulk of my day preparing the first drafts of the voluminous fee applications that must soon be filed in three of our Creditor Committee cases. I take time reviewing the bills in order to draft the narrative of key issues we dealt with during this period. I then calculate the fees based on the tasks, followed by tracking the time spent by each timekeeper involved in the case.

I also follow up with some of the temporary paralegals working on a large-scale corporate record review project to keep track of their progress and answer any questions they may have. I do this each day.

This morning I am meeting a new *pro bono* client with one of the attorneys in my department. The client wants to file a Chapter 7 bankruptcy. We spend time with him, explain the process, and collect detailed information from him. Once the meeting is over, I go back to my desk and using my trusty Best Case® Bankruptcy software, I start the process of preparing his petition. Today, we have paralegal training. We start with a nice lunch, and we have our LexisNexis® representative coming in to show everyone how to use the various public records available from LexisNexis, including search techniques.

This afternoon I have many subpoenas that I must prepare in one of my cases. I prepare the first drafts and turn them over to the attorney on the case. She marks them up, and I make the quick revisions. The finalized subpoenas are then turned over to our processing service for delivery. This evening our firm, who belongs to a lawyers' softball league, has a game. I leave work and head for first base.

We have a heavily contested hearing in an adversary proceeding on Thursday. We meet in the morning to discuss strategy. I am given many documents to weave into our Sanction 2 presentation software in addition to preparing document binders. I have enlisted the help of the other paralegal in my department on this project. She is helping me prepare the binders and document index. In addition, she is helping coordinate with our audio/visual vendor to make sure the projector and screen are set up before we arrive, as the court is not equipped for our needs.

I call our witness to make sure they can still make court tomorrow and confirm the time and place. I spend the afternoon getting everything ready, frequently conferring with my attorneys for changes and to ensure I am preparing what they want. We do a dry run of the presentation to make sure that the "script" and documents that we have put in the presentation software is in a logical order. We work into the late evening and plan to meet early at the courthouse.

We meet early the next morning, and I set up the laptops. I take my seat at a desk next to our table so I can control the presentation. Our opening and our adversary's opening take all morning. We meet our witness for lunch and finish preparing him. Our witness takes the stand. I continue to assist with our presentation software. Our adversary starts their cross, and soon after the judge wants to end for the day.

In a normal civil case, we would just keep going; however, in this case, we will not be back in court for another two weeks. This is good and bad. You may lose momentum, but it gives you more time to prepare for the next day in court. It can be done at a slightly more leisurely pace, as opposed to going back to the office and working into the middle of the night for the next trial day.

This morning I am assisting one of the attorneys with gathering and organizing documents for a large motion we are filing in an Assignment for the Benefit of Creditors, which is a form of state court liquidation, similar to Chapter 7 bankruptcy. We represent the assignee (similar to a trustee) in the case, who is selling off the assets of the company. Once the motion is finalized, we arrange for a messenger.

I update the Web site I created for this case. As it is in state court, the documents are not available online as they would be for a federal case. On top of having general information about the case for creditors and other interested parties, I have created a document repository, and, after turning today's motion in to an Adobe® PDF file, I update the online index. By doing this we save the estate significant time and money in not having to send hard copies to everyone involved. Early in the case, we had the judge enter an order-limited notice, so in most cases we can just send an e-mail informing those who wanted notice to go to the site and download the pleading. In the early afternoon, we have our Bankruptcy Department team meeting, where we discuss potential new work, new cases that we acquired, and the status of our current workload. Work is reallocated as needed to keep everyone busy and no one completely overloaded. We discuss upcoming networking opportunities and client development plans.

In the afternoon, I assist one of my colleagues who is filing documents in the district court for the first time and needs help with the CM/ECF system. I finish the day by meeting with my coordinator to discuss my workload and to talk about a new paralegal joining the firm next week. She will be working on federal cases and will need to learn the CM/ECF system. She also expressed interest in joining a paralegal organization, and I was asked to talk to her about that as well.

GENERAL ADVICE:

1. Learn all you can about computers. Take courses. Try things out on your own computer. The more computer literate you are, the more valuable you will be.

2. If you need to prepare a pleading or related document, make sure it does not already exist somewhere else. Check your firm's systems for similar forms. If it does not exist, go look on the court's Web site. Many times I have talked to people who spent a lot of time trying to create a form by reading a court rule when the form already existed on that court's Web site.

3. Take time to visit the Web sites of courts where you tend to be involved. See what is offered on them. You never know when you can cut a corner and save time by going right to the court's Web site to find an answer.

4. Get yourself organized. It might take you a while to set up a system that works for you, but once you have it in place, you will be less likely to miss something. In addition, you'll be able to quickly provide information to those who need it.

5. Learn to anticipate your attorney's needs. People are creatures of habit. If you can have things ready before you are asked for them, based on your supervisor's record of accomplishment, you will be much more of an asset. An example is getting status reports to your supervisor before a meeting, if they normally ask for them.

6. If you use charts for organization, use Microsoft® Excel® instead of Microsoft® Word® tables. Once a Word table becomes too large, it will grow unstable. The size where it becomes unstable is related to the capabilities of the computer that the file is opened on. Unless you are putting a small table into a Word document, err on the side of caution, and only use Excel for your charting needs.

7. Ask for your own set of books. Request the "rule books" for each state and federal jurisdiction in which you file. If you do federal work, make sure you have a recent copy of the Federal Rules of Civil Procedure, in addition to any local rules you may need.

8. Make sure your files are set up in such a way that anyone could jump in, know what is going on, and where to find things. You never know when you might be switched to another project, another team, or may be out of the office. While we all have our own ways of doing things, people should be able to jump into your files when needed and retrieve information with minimal effort.

BANKRUPTCY ADVICE:

1. Learn the CM/ECF system like the back of your hand. The use of the system is mandatory in many jurisdictions. Even if it is not mandatory, learn it—it is only a matter of time until you will need it, and then you will be ahead of the curve. Further, the Federal District CM/ECF and Bankruptcy CM/ECF are slightly different in each jurisdiction. You should learn both for each jurisdiction in which you file.

2. Prepare directories on your computer that mirror the court's docket. That way you will only have to download case documents once, and it saves on page fees.

3. Make sure your firm invests in a multi-page document scanner and in multiple copies of Adobe Acrobat® (the full version, not the free reader available on Adobe's Web site). Learn about PDF files and how to work with them. Examples include learning how to move pages around and combining files.

4. If your firm does any amount of debtor work, and you do not already have petition preparation software, urge your firm to invest in it. The preparation time it will save will justify the expense. There are many great packages out there, so shop around. Our firm uses Best Case Bankruptcy. A call to the clerk's office in jurisdictions where you file documents would also be helpful, as they may be able to tell you about compatibility issues.

5. If your firm does a lot of commercial debtor or creditor work, I highly recommend a subscription to the *Daily Bankruptcy Review*. It is a Dow Jones publication, which also publishes *The Wall Street Journal* and arrives as an e-mail each morning. It summarizes recent bankruptcy news and is a tremendous resource. Knowing what is going on in the area of law you work in is just as important as knowing what is happening in the cases that affect your clients.

CAREER OUTLOOK

View your paralegal/legal assistant position as a career, not just a "job." Having the right mindset will benefit you in many ways. Viewing your job as a career helps you focus on your tasks, and most importantly, the well-being of your clients. If you begin to take it personally, that is good (within reason). It will also motivate you to get involved in your profession beyond your work duties.

CREATIVITY

Think of ways to use your creative mind in your work. Even though your firm may be used to doing something a certain way does not necessarily mean it is the best way. If you think you can improve upon a process, bring it to your attorney's or supervisor's attention. Explain why you think your idea is more efficient and how it will benefit the firm. Not everything you suggest will be adopted, but at least they know you are thinking of ways to make things better.

BE INQUISITIVE

Ask questions, especially if you are dealing with a new area of law or a task with which you have little or no experience. Although it may seem that you ask too many questions, it is better to do that than to try it on your own and possibly make mistakes. In addition, take notes when you get your answer. Nothing makes people more frustrated than to have someone ask a question over and over again because they did not write down the answer.

LOOK IT UP

Somewhere in your work, or perhaps you have already been asked, you will need to draft pleadings and related documents. If you are not sure what the terminology is, or why you are preparing something, look it up and ask about it. You can be more beneficial to your employer if you understand why you are doing something.

MAKE IT YOUR OWN

Follow the trend of the other office personnel as far as it is appropriate to personalize your space. If it is okay, fill it with things that make you feel good. It will help calm you down in those stressful situations that arise at the office. Be creative in your work area. Whether you have a cube or an office, make it your own. I'm not saying repaint the walls (I'm sure more facilities managers would frown upon that), but make sure you bring in some pictures, a plant, a drawing from your child, a diploma, or an award. "Bloom where you are planted."

ORGANIZATIONAL METHODS:

TASK AND DEADLINE LIST

Start a Task and Deadline list to organize and chart your work. Make a chart that has the task, date assigned, the person getting the work, the due date and, most importantly, the priority. You may want to add a column for the time it took you to do the work. It will help with your billing description.

Meet with the people you work for at least once a week to review your list to make sure you are on the right track and to make sure you are prioritizing your work correctly. When working for multiple people, as is often the case, make sure to deal with conflicts in priority.

Electronic Filing Cabinets

As scanning equipment, the requisite software, and computers grow faster and less expensive, you should think about ways to organize documents electronically. Those who work at the federal level should embrace these techniques now as more federal districts are switching the CM/ECF electronic filing system.

Obviously, there is still a need to hang on to original signature documents, but copies of pleadings and the like can be stored electronically, which also saves shelf space. For continuity, save all non-pleading documents in the same manner your that firm organizes hard-copy files, using directories and subdirectories instead of manila folders. It is helpful to organize in the same manner as they appear on the court's online docket for viewing on PACER or the CMJECF system. As you keep your pleadings updated, you can use the court's docket as your index. Many state courts use Verilaw™ that works similarly.

Case List

Keep a detailed case list. Your list should include the main client's name, the name of the specific case, the internal client ID number, the venue of the matter, the court's docket number, personnel assigned to the case, and the location of the main file. Organize each shelf, and give it a specific label as it appears on the case list so that files can be located easily.

Pending Files

Make sure you have a central pending filing area that mirrors your case list. All new documents should find their way into pending filing almost immediately. That way any documents not yet in the file can only be in one other place until whoever is responsible for file management can get the documents organized in its final form.

Case Charts

It is helpful in litigation to keep detailed status charts on your cases. You should keep as much information on the chart as possible; it will be useful in status meetings. In mass tort litigation, create a chart that has the case name (adversary firm contact information), your local counsel's information, the court it was in, alleged diseases, status of medical, and employment record. (See Figure 14-1: Chart 1—State Case Status.) The chart indicated discovery due dates and had a "notes" field that held recent developments in the case.

PLAYERS LISTS

This detailed chart has all of the contact information for everyone involved in the case. You should keep one for every case you have. The chart should include addresses, phone numbers (direct work number, main work number, and cell phone), their roles in the office (paralegal, associate, partner, and other staff), e-mail addresses, and what parties they represent. Keep each name in a separate field so it can be sorted in larger cases. They also help in doing mail merges that make mass mailing projects less of a headache.

TECHNOLOGY TECHNIQUES:

OFFICE SUITE

Learn how to use one the office suites, preferably Microsoft® Office®, which is the most widely used. The other programs in Office can include (depending on which version of Office you have) Microsoft® Word®, a sophisticated word processing program; Microsoft® Outlook®, an e-mail management program; Microsoft® PowerPoint, a presentation program for preparing slides and other visuals; and Excel, a spreadsheet program. Excel can also be used as a database program and for organizing documents and information.

INTERNET

Learn how to use the World Wide Web as a tool, not just for entertainment as many of us do at home. There are many valuable sites geared toward the legal community. The Web can be accessed through many search engines, such as Google (quite popular), AltaVista, AOL, Yahoo!, DogPile, Lycos, HotBot, and MetaCrawler, among others. It is also the best place to start out with investigations. You can use it to find people, doctors, experts, and information about companies. You can find nearly anything once you are proficient at searching. If your firm does not use a broadband (cable or DSL) connection, suggest that they acquire one. The increases in your productivity will far outweigh the front-end startup costs.

Figure 14-1
Chart 1
STATE CASE STATUS

(Your Firm) Staff: Partner – Associate(s) – Paralegal(s) – Chart as of MM/DD/YYYY	Additional Commonly Used Information
Local Counsel Smith, Smith & Smith 123 Main St. Anywhere, USA 12345 Website: www.smithlaw.com	Partner: Direct Dial: Email: Associate: Direct Dial: Email: Paralegal: Direct Dial: Email:

Adversary Film	Atty. Contact	Phone	Fax	E-mail	Adversary Film	Atty. Contact	Adversary Film

PLAINTIFF NAME & ADDRESS	FILE #	INTERNAL COMPUTER NUMBER	SSN/ DOB/ DOD	DOCKET	COMPLAINT FIELD	ANSWER FILED	TRIAL DATE	VENUE	PLAINTIFF COUNSEL	ALLEGED DISEASES(S) DIAGNOSIS/ DATE(S)	SMOKER	EMPLOYMENT (DATES, LOCA- TIONS, JOB)
					Total plfs: # Total Defs:#							

FREE INFORMATION

Take advantage of information available on the Internet, like state and federal statutes available, thus saving your time and money on the paid services like Westlaw and LexisNexis, by utilizing them only when you have to. Depending on your firm's agreement with Westlaw and/or LexisNexis, many times they will offer free use of their databases. Take advantage of that time to practice searching for cases. You will be more prepared when someone asks you to do research.

DATABASE

Get large repositories of information into databases, such as Microsoft® Access® or Inmagic DB/TextWorks®. Often people will create large charts in Microsoft® Excel® or Word, but when you need to run reports, or find documents, a database will be a much more efficient option. They are exceptionally good at tracking their underlying requests. You will want to track where you sent your requests, whom you have talked to, and what, if anything, has been sent. It is also effective for tracking large volumes of cases.

FIX IT YOURSELF

The more you work around computers, especially at home, the more proficient you will become at fixing them and getting around problems. If you have a small IT department, you cannot always afford to wait for them help you. Obviously, there will be some things you cannot fix, but many small problems, like missing toolbars in Word or Excel or changing printer settings, are not complicated, though they can be frequent obstacles. On your own, you may want to take a basic computing class at a community college or high school night program. Not only will it help you with your computer at home, but it will also make you more efficient and more of an asset to your office.

SYSTEMATIC PROCEDURES:

NEW TEAM MEMBER

When you are new to a department within your firm or just new to the firm, a Frequently Asked Questions (FAQ) manual or handout would be helpful. Develop one for your Bankruptcy Department that explains the basic elements of bankruptcy, and then gets into specific team procedures. This enables new people to assimilate information much faster. Ask the people in your department what they would have wanted to know when they first started, think about the questions you had, and answer them in your protocol. You will be amazed at the time it saves for someone new to fit in.

IT IS NOT A DRAFT

Any time you turn in a draft or final document to your attorney, make sure it is in its best final form. Nothing makes them more upset than to have to make easy changes to something you should have caught in the first place. Make sure your spelling and grammar checks are turned on in your word processing program. You also may want to ask a co-worker to go over what you wrote before you turn it in. Remember, the more you read something, the better it sounds to you, even if it is wrong; another pair of eyes may catch simple mistakes you do not want the attorney to see.

CONTINUING LEGAL EDUCATION (CLE)

Attend legal writing seminars to keep your skills sharp. Many of us took this class as part of our paralegal programs, but you can always improve on your writing.

DISCOVERY SHORTCUTS:

MEDICAL/EMPLOYMENT RECORDS

Make sure you secure the originals of your medical employment records in the manner they were received. Put them in a Tyvek envelope, seal, and forget about them until trial. You should only be working with copies. Reduce their size to 85 percent if you plan to put the records in a binder; that way if you punch holes in the record, you are less likely to remove important information.

DOCUMENT PREPARATION:

DOCUMENT REVIEWS/PRODUCTIONS

When attending a document review, you should make sure you have vendors ready to assist with the physical copying of documents. You may be far away from your office, so your normal vendors may not be able to help you. You should also scan documents. Often this does not cost much more because the same equipment that makes copies can also scan. This way, in the end, you have a document set on disk.

While doing the review, know your deadlines and make sure you have enough people. Make sure you keep the project managers current on your status. When removing documents to be copied, replace the documents you took with colored paper. Number the paper, then have a corresponding flag, or post it with the same number that goes with the document. That way, when you get the original back, you swap out the colored paper with the document, and you ensure you are keeping the originals in the correct order. Be over inclusive, within reason. It is easier to discard a document pulled in error then to go back and try to find one you should have pulled. If you are producing the documents, make sure the documents are Bates numbered (a hand-stamp that automatically changes the numbers on its inkpad or Bates machines and copying machines that can add the Bates label as well) and you have a thorough corresponding document index.

INVESTIGATIONS:

DIG

Use the Internet to find useful information. Sites like www.theultimates.com will help you find basic information on people, even if you start with limited information. It is linked with multiple databases that contain different kinds of information.

USE SERVICES

Use companies like DRI and the WestLaw and LexisNexis public records databases to find information. EDGAR on-line contains significant information about companies that have to file documents with the SEC.

USE OTHER FIRMS

Often your attorneys will have contacts, or you will have your own, at other firms. They may have a document you are looking for or a deposition you need. Work with your attorney in exploring these so that you may find information you could not find otherwise.

CLIENT INTERACTIONS AND INTERVIEWING:

Your clients keep the firm going; without them everyone is out of work. Depending on your duties, you may or may not have much client contact. When you do have client contact, always be professional and follow your attorney's lead; be careful not to be too casual with your clients. Your attorney may have a longstanding relationship or friendship with certain clients. Be respectful and develop your own relationship with the client. The more people working on the case the client knows and respects, the better things are all around; and it may lead to work in the future for your department.

OFFICE COMMUNICATIONS:

RESPECT

Make sure you treat everyone the same, no matter what their title is. Everyone deserves the same level of respect. The better your relationship with your co-workers, the easier your job will be.

RETURN THE FAVOR

Did someone help you out and stay late to assist with a large project you are working on? Make yourself available to return the favor the next time they ask; otherwise, you may find yourself desperately searching for help the next time you need it.

GO DOWN WITH THE SHIP

If you are working on a large project and have many people assisting you, be the last to leave. Show your responsibility to follow the project through to the end; be a good example.

SOFTWARE HINTS:

SECTION CODE

This is a simple tip, but in Microsoft® Word®, hitting the "ATL" key plus "2" then "1" on the keypad will give you the § symbol.

TRIAL POINTERS:

ELECTRONIC TRIALS

Again, as the cost drops and more people watch *CSI, Law and Order,* and the many other legal-related programs that keep popping up with each new season, jurors are starting to expect to see flashy presentations at trial. You will need user-friendly presentation software, like Sanction 2 or PowerPoint that comes with Microsoft Office, to interface with various other programs. You also need time to plan and prepare your presentation. Give yourself two or three weeks lead-time if you have it.

You can display documents, transcripts, photographs, and animations. You can synchronize videotaped testimony with a test transcript to display them simultaneously, much like a subtitle or closed captioning. Find out from the court what they have available for you. If they have projectors and screens, you are in luck; otherwise, you will need to coordinate those pieces of equipment. More importantly, find out if the judge will even let you do this. Some judges think it will clutter their courtroom or become a circus. It may take some convincing from your attorney and the IT department to warm the judge up to new technology.

Bring a portable scanner and portable printer. That way you can create and print exhibits at the courthouse, which is important for cross-examination. Make sure you have two laptops dedicated to your presentation. One you will use to show the presentation; the other you will use to find documents or testimony as your attorney needs them. Otherwise, the other side would be able to see what you are searching on the screen if you used the primary laptop. The second laptop will also serve as a backup in case the first laptop crashes.

If you are doing an electronic presentation, ask if you can bring a co-worker to help you go through the hard files, as the attorney may need documents from there; it is hard to do all at once. For larger, more document-intensive trials, where you are bringing a large number of boxes to and from the court, ask if you can have a messenger service move the boxes for you. If you do this, you should still bring the documents you will definitely need for that day in the event the messenger is delayed.

Always make sure you have enough hard copies of documents for the witness, the adversary, and the judge. You should do this even if you are doing an electronic presentation, in case it crashes on you. You should practice using the software with your attorney. Use their examination outline as a script, and identify the documents they will be referring to, being sure to note them so that when they need them, you can effortlessly put them up. Rehearse with your attorney at least twice, if time permits. This will cut down on lag time between the attorney's reference of the document and the document going up on the screen.

MASS TORT SPECIFICS

When involved in a mass tort/product liability/toxic tort case with alleged personal injury, it is extremely important to stay organized. You may find yourself managing literally thousands of cases.

To keep your facts straight and use charts. Generally, you will have status meetings to discuss the state of your cases; having the basic information summarized into charts will make the meetings go faster, and it will give your supervisors a sense that you are on top of things. Again, Chart 1 (see Figure 14-1) may be useful in mass tort cases to track the general status of your cases. If you are national counsel, you will want to set one up by state. If you are local counsel, you may want to break up your plaintiffs by the internal state jurisdiction.

Chart 2 tracks your internal firm staff involved in your cases, as well as your local/national counsel contact information. Next, chart the basic contact information for your adversary firms involved on that chart. The body of the chart will be the individual plaintiff information. When you receive your signed authorizations, send letters to record holders requesting the records listed in the authorizations. Ensure that you send two certifications, one that certifies there are records and one that certifies there are no records. Insist that this form is completed and notarized. If a provider will not send records, issue a *subpoena duces tecum* in accordance with your local rules. If the provider is out of state, you will have to have it domesticated or have your local counsel obtain the records.

When you get your records and a signed certification authenticating the records, get them copied immediately and seal the set received from the provider. Put them in a Tyvek envelope, label them, and put them in a special file away from everything else. That way, before the trial, you will know where your records are and that they are exactly what you received.

The copy set you can use in accordance with your firm's policies. Some attorneys like to have those copies Bates stamped or scanned. I like to keep a set in a binder. When you have them copied, copy the documents at 85 percent of their normal size. Many times records will take up the 85 percent and will give you enough room to punch a hole.

Binders are an excellent way to organize your documents because you can remove documents as you need them and replace them easily. It keeps them in order, which can be helpful for your attorney as he prepares for depositions or if you are sending the records to an expert.

The index you keep on the front of the binder is useful. This is where you will summarize the basic information of your records. Copies will be convenient in your case status meetings. In Chart 2 (see Figure 14-2, Chart 2), you will see what I keep at the beginning of a binder. Chart 2 has both employment and medical records, but if the file is big enough, separate the different types of records. Make sure you use *good* binders. You will be using them often. Using flimsy binders will make it hard to handle your files.

If the case is dragging on, as they often do, request updated records every six months to ensure that nothing new is in the file. In addition, when you obtain certified records from the Social Security Administration, they come riveted together and have a ribbon. Under no circumstances, should you take apart these records, or you will lose the "seal." Make sure you copy these records yourself, or make sure that the person copying them knows not to take them apart.

Use Charts, Graphs, and Forms

Use charts, graphs, and other forms to keep your facts straight. Usually, you will have status meetings to discuss the status of your cases, and having the basic information already summarized into charts will help the meetings go smoother and impress your supervisors. As shown in Figure 14-1, Chart 1 tracks the general *status* of your cases. I used this chart in defending asbestos exposure cases.

If you are national counsel, set one up by state. If you are local counsel, break up your plaintiffs by the internal state jurisdiction (again, see Figure 14-2 Chart 2), tracks your internal firm staff involved in your cases, your local and national counsel contact information. Next, chart the basic contact information for your adversary firms involved. The body of the chart will be the individual plaintiff's information.

Medical/Employment Record Collection, Organization, and Storage

The bulk of your case is going to involve the collection of records on your plaintiff. Depending on the structure of your team, you may be able to delegate this task. In some mass torts, parties will use records collection services to handle their requests. These services can be great or a nightmare. No matter what, always check the records

Figure 14-2
Medical/Employment Record Binder Tracking Chart
CHART 2
Case Name
Docket Number
Venue
Internal Client Number

Tab	Provider Name/Address	Binder Volume	Authorization	Type	Date Requested	Date Returned	Certified	Summarized	Original Secured	Notes
1	Social Security Administration	1	Yes	Employment	9/19/01	10/5/01	Yes	Yes	Yes	
2	Smith, Bob MD	1	Yes	Medical	9/19/01	9/27/01	Yes	Yes	Yes	
2a	Smith, Bob MD Supplement	1	Yes	Medical	3/14/02	3/18/02	Yes	Yes	Yes	
2b	Smith, Bob MD Supplement	1	Yes	Medical	3/30/03	4/8/03	Yes	Yes		
3	Bob's Truck Repair	1	Yes	Medical	9/19/01	3/4/02	Yes	Yes	Yes	
3a	Bob's Truck Repair	1	Yes	Employment	3/14/02	3/18/02	Yes	Yes	Yes	
4	Karl's Pipe Fitting	1	Yes	Employment	9/19/01	10/3/01	NA	NA	NA	Won't send record Subpoena sent.

you receive and make sure you track those records for new requests made for newly discovered providers. Regardless of who is collecting the records, there are steps you should take to ensure your records are in the best order.

AUTHORIZATIONS AND HIPPA

First, prepare a list of authorizations for the plaintiff's employers and medical providers. Make each authorization specific to the provider, and make sure it is signed. With all of the issues involving HIPPA (Health Insurance Portability and Accountability Act of 1996), the more specific you can be, the easier it will be get records. Congress mandated the Health Insurance Portability and Accountability Act, which creates standards for the privacy of individually identifiable health information. The privacy rule became effective on April 14, 2001. Most health plans and health care providers that are covered by the new rule must have complied with the new requirements by April 2003.

The Act gives patients more power over how their health information is used, and, further, it sets guidelines for the release and use of their health records. It forces health care providers and other record holders to create systems to protect the privacy of patients' records. The Act, in turn, creates civil and criminal penalties that violators could be subject to should they not comply.

While the Act has its positive points, it has made it extremely difficult for people involved in litigation to obtain records. Health care providers, who are worried about violating the act, tend to err on the side of caution when it comes to releasing a patient's information. In states where tight discovery deadlines exist, it can make a paralegal's job tough to obtain records necessary to the case. Further, the Act is being interpreted in different ways. This makes each experience with a record provider a potentially challenging one. In the bankruptcy realm, I'm generally not requesting too many medical records.

Obtain the provider's own form of the HIPPA request so that you do not end up wasting time if they do not accept your request form. A simple Google search will produce literally thousands of Web sites devoted to dealing with and trying to interpret HIPPA.

You can use the copy set in accordance with your firm's policies. Some paralegals like to have them Bates stamped, scanned, or you may keep a set in a binder. Binders are helpful in that you remove the documents as you need them, and it keeps everything in order, which can be helpful for your attorney as they prepare for depositions or if you are sending the records off to an expert. Again, when you have them copied, copy the documents at 85 percent of their normal size. Many times records will take up the entire page and copying them at 85 percent will give you enough room to punch a hole.

WORKLOAD:

You will most likely have workload meetings with your supervisor. If you do not have them, ask for them. It is important to let your supervisors know where you stand. Use the attached sample Chart 3 (see Figure 14-3) in your meetings. It lists the name of the states I worked in, how much of the state I was responsible for, the pending complaints, the increase since the last meeting, the total number of plaintiffs (because many mass tort complaints have multiple plaintiffs consolidated into a single complaint), and the percentage of my time I spent on that state. This chart gives your supervisor a snapshot of your workload and will aid in the reallocation of work, if necessary.

Another tool you can use to keep yourself organized is the Task and Deadline list mentioned previously. It is self-explanatory but can be useful in status meetings, workload meetings, and trial-preparation meetings. By logging all of the tasks and deadlines, you will know what you need to do, and again, it can help people decide if you have too much work.

TRIAL PREP SPECIFICS

Before you try to conduct an electronic trial, make sure you have the support of the judge and their staff. Technology intimidates some judges who fear that their courtroom may become a circus. Your office should explain to the judge, in detail, what you would like to do, and why it will not interfere with the rest of the proceedings.

When you go to trial, especially if you are out of state, you should create a list of nearby vendors, including copy services, electronic stores, computer stores, office supply stores, shipping and receiving locations, hospitals, dry cleaners, and a mall in the event you need clothing of some kind. In addition, if you are away from home, make sure you have set up "war rooms" in your hotel to work. Make sure

Figure 14-3

SUBJECT: Current Workloaded/Projects/Trial Dates

CHART 3

MEMORANDUM

TO: Supervisor
FROM: Paralegal
DATE: 01-25-07

STATES RESPONSIBLE:

State	Responsibility in State	# Pending Complaints	New Cases Since (LAST) Meeting	Total # Pending Plaintiffs	Approx. % of Time Spent on State
Louisiana	All	225	+12	1300	10%
New Jersey	All	56	+6	75	15%
New York	Split with (Paralegal)	15	+10	25	7%
Pennsylvania	All	300	+17	300	35%
Texas	Split with (Paralegal)	200	+50	275	30%
Admin	Committees, Invoice review	N/A	N/A	N/A	8% or less

Note: See individual State chart for details.

TRIAL DATES:

Date	Plaintiff Name	Plaintiff Counsel	State	Venue	Status

PROJECTS/COMMITTEE/ETC

Due date:	Description

there are enough phone and fax lines set up and high-speed Internet connections available. Do your research on these important items well ahead of the trial date, and reserve as many items as you can. This list is also applicable for out-of-state document reviews.

When involved in a mass tort/product liability/toxic tort case with alleged personal injury, it is extremely important to stay organized. You may find yourself managing literally thousands of cases.

REAL WORK EXAMPLES:

EXAMPLE 1: MASS TORT—THE PHANTOM DEPOSITION

Our Problem: In preparing for trial in one of my asbestos cases, we learned, in deposing the brother of the plaintiff in our case, that he had his own asbestos exposure suit in the 1980s. In that case, he was deposed. The brothers worked together at the same factory. We asked the plaintiff's counsel if they had a copy of it, and we were told they did not. The company that took the deposition in the 80s was no longer in business. My mission was to try to find the transcript or—as I thought—the needle in the haystack!

My Strategy for Solving Our Problem: I reviewed the file and located some copies of documents from the brother's lawsuit from the 80s previously produced by plaintiff's counsel. I was essentially looking for anything that had a list of co-defendants and their respective counsel. The best I could find was an attorney's name and firm service list attached to some interrogatory responses. LexisNexis® Martindale-Hubbell® became my best friend (www.martindale.com). I searched the names of the attorneys and started to match up the ones that were still practicing; many had changed firms. There were about 25 to 30 lawyers in all.

We then contacted everyone on the list via e-mail, as time was getting short. We started to get some responses, but unfortunately many of them told us either they didn't have the deposition or gave us names at their old firms who might be able to help us, which would take more time we didn't have.

It was turning into a wild goose chase, until I came back from lunch to find an e-mail from a paralegal at one of the firms we had contacted, who indicated that they still had the transcript in their deposition bank. It would take a day or two to get it from storage and out to us, but they had it. I shot up and ran down the hall to tell everyone of this great news. At that point, I did not know if there was even anything good in it—I was just ecstatic that we found it!

When it arrived, I immediately cracked it open and started reading. It was gold! The testimony in that transcript directly refuted what he testified to, more recently, in our case. As you can imagine, it changed the entire tone of the settlement negotiations as the case dropped in value. Our client was thrilled.

What I Learned: This case really reminded me of a principle I learned years ago—keep digging. It showed me that scraping just a little bit deeper, even when you think you have gone as far as possible can uncover that nugget of information that completely changes the landscape of your case and helps your client. It also reinforced the satisfaction that you can achieve from your work. Even before I knew what was in that transcript, I had a real personal victory in being able to find that "needle in the haystack." Looking back on that event has continued to motivate me to try hard and think strategically to find obscure information in my cases.

EXAMPLE 2: BANKRUPTCY: STATE COURT LIQUIDATION

Our Problem: No CM/ECF system to rely on... now what should we do? Recently, we had an estate with an Assignment for the Benefit of Creditors (ABC) liquidation in New Jersey. An ABC is essentially a state court-level liquidation of the estate, similar to a bankruptcy under Chapter 7 of the United States Bankruptcy Code.

In today's world, the bankruptcy courts rely on the CM/ECF system to disseminate information to creditors and other interested parties using scans of documents and sending notices to people via e-mail. As you can imagine, in some cases where you may have thousands of creditors, it would be extremely time consuming and costly to have to mail paper notices and copies of documents out via regular mail. While the system has only been in place for a few years and mandatory in most jurisdictions for even less time, it is hard to remember what is was like ... until you get into state court and no such system exists yet. What should I do?

My Strategy for Solving Our Problem: Make a CM/ECF system! I have had some experience building Web sites, so I essentially built a Web site that functioned the same way the CM/ECF site does, in terms of being able to download pleadings and other filings in the case. We also used the site as a vehicle to speak to the creditors in other interested parties in order to keep them informed about background information, events in the case, and other details. One class of creditor alone had over 50,000 people.

The site did not have to be flashy. It had to be functional and easy to navigate. Keeping the site simple and not having to farm the site out to a vendor made it extremely flexible for us. I could update the site whenever we needed from wherever I was, as I chose a company and package that included imbedded page building software. All I needed was an Internet connection and a computer that used Microsoft® Internet Explorer®. I spent a significant time "on-site" at the company's former headquarters, and if I had to use a system where I may have needed to be in front of my desktop in Morristown, it would have created some issues.

To make the site even more effective, we asked the judge enter an Order Limiting Notice so that key people would have scanned versions of the filings via e-mail, and/or were made aware of a filing via e-mail. The site also benefited the court, as the clerk's office just pointed people to our Web site who were looking for documents. Of course, there were times when we needed to send out blanket mailings, which was a challenge, but they were very limited because we used the Web site.

In being able to post answers to frequently asked questions on the site, it significantly cut down on the amount of phone calls and e-mails about the case that we had to answer. I ended up having to become a one-person customer service department for the now defunct company, and, although we had to speak with many people and answer much e-mail, I can only imagine how much harder it would have been if we did not have the Web site.

In all, the Web site has logged over 2 million "hits" and has only cost a few hundred dollars for hosting and my time to build and maintain the site. The site ended up saving the estate thousands of dollars in time and money, which in turn helps increase funds available to creditors of the estate.

What I Learned: I learned that you never know when an outside skill can become extremely relevant in one of your cases. It reinforced the importance of keeping up with the times and learning new technological skills that keep you ahead of the curve and are transferable to your work. The Web site also provided me with a template so that when we have the need to build a site for a case again, I know what worked and what did not. It has been a great and rewarding experience, and using Web sites in my cases is something I look forward to being able to do again in the future.

CHAPTER 15

MARY "BECKY" ROLLAND, CLA
Bankruptcy Paralegal
New Orleans, LA

"Becky is an experienced, efficient paralegal with a positive attitude and solid work ethic. She is definitely an asset to our firm and a pleasure to work with."

Allen J. Krouse, III
Frilot, L.L.C.

EDUCATION/HONORS/CERTIFICATION:

- B.A., English, Louisiana State University, 1983
- B.A., Sociology, Louisiana State University, 1987
- Paralegal Certificate, National Academy of Paralegal Studies, Inc., Salem State College, 1992
- Completed coursework toward M.A., English, University of Massachusetts, 1992–1993
- Certification in Business Bankruptcy Law from the Association of Bankruptcy Judicial Assistants, 2003
- Certificates of Completion in Microsoft® Word 2000, Level 2, and Excel® 2000, Level 1, New Horizons Computer Learning Centers, 2003

PROFESSIONAL ASSOCIATIONS:

- Member, American Alliance of Paralegals, Inc., 2005
- Member, National Writer's Union, 2005
- Member, National Federation of Paralegal Associations, 1991–present
- Member, Elmwood Business Association; 2003—Executive Director, 2003
- Member, New Orleans Paralegal Association (NOPA); 2005–present, Vice President and Membership Co-Chair, 2003–present
- Member, Association of Bankruptcy Judicial Assistants, 2003–present
- Member, Sokka Gakki International; 2001–2002—Women's Division Leader, 1992–present
- Member, Massachusetts Paralegal Association (MPA); 1998–2000—Chair, Bankruptcy Section, 1991–2002
- Member, Billerica Chamber of Commerce, 1999–2002; Membership Coordinator, 1999–2000
- Executive Director, 2000–2002
- Member, The Billerica Plan, 2002
- Member, Billerica Access Television, 2000–2001
- Member, Greater Boston Business Council, 1999–2001

YEARS EXPERIENCE:

15

Seminar Leader/Speaker—Massachusetts Continuing Legal Education (MCLE) and the Massachusetts Paralegal Association. Topics include bankruptcy law, **probono** work, and the freelance paralegal profession.

Pro Bono:

- First Step *Pro Bono* Bankruptcy Project MPA Board of Directors, Project of the Year, 2000
- Certificate of Appreciation, MPA, 2001–2002
- Certificate of Appreciation, NOPA, 2003–2004

FIRM AT-A-GLANCE:

Frilot Partridge, L.C.
1100 Poydras Street, Suite 3600
New Orleans, LA 70163
Phone: 504.599.8308
Fax: 504.599.8100
Web site: www.frilotpartridge.com

PARALEGALS (PERMANENT):

28

PRACTICE AREAS:

- Admiralty and Maritime
- Agricultural and Agribusiness
- Commercial Litigation
- Energy and Environmental
- Labor and Employment
- Mass Tort and Class Actions
- Medical Malpractice and Health Care
- Products Liability
- Railroad
- Transactional

OVERVIEW OF JOB RESPONSIBILITIES:

I. Bankruptcy Case Administration

    A. Set up Master File Index and corresponding file folders.

    B. Review bankruptcy court docket and claims register in main case for updates.

    C. Review civil, district, and adversarial case court dockets for updates.

    D. Review correspondence and maintain correspondence files.

    E. Maintain attorney calendar with hearing dates and/or appointments with clients.

    F. Communicate with client and creditors by telephone, e-mail, and correspondence regarding inquiries and requests for documents.

    G. Maintain creditor matrix by researching addresses for returned mail and contacting client for correct addresses.

II. Litigation

    A. Prepare bankruptcy petition, schedules, and statement of financial affairs and/or amended versions.

    B. Maintain litigation docket and attorney calendar, noting deadline dates for responsive pleadings/motions and court appearances.

    C. Review pleadings and index into pleadings binders according to court docket.

    D. Prepare attorneys by compiling legal documents needed for meetings, hearings, depositions, and trials.

    E. Draft various legal documents including motions and proposed orders.

    F. Communicate with court and opposing counsel regarding hearing dates and filings, including arranging for extensions of time to respond.

II. Proofs of Claim

    A. Review proofs of claim and index claims binder according to court register.

    B. Review proofs of claim in relation to debtor's bankruptcy schedules and note discrepancies.

    C. Prepare claims reports regarding scheduled claims and proofs of claim filed.

    D. Communicate with client regarding disputed and contingent claims.

    E. Prepare drafts of objections to proofs of claim.

III. Plan Confirmation

    A. Prepare drafts of plan and disclosure statements.

    B. Prepare and notice ballots and plan package to all creditors.

    C. Solicit ballot votes of acceptance of plan before deadline.

    D. Tabulate ballots according to creditor class and acceptance/rejection of plan.

ETHICS CAVEAT:

Remember, when communicating with clients and creditors alike to identify yourself as a paralegal and do not give legal advice, that is, do not recommend a course of action or tell clients or others what their rights and responsibilities are.

Therese A. Cannon, Attorney at Law and author of *Ethics and Professional Responsibility for Legal Assistants*

TYPICAL WORKWEEK:

I start each day by reviewing my e-mails and telephone messages. Most of my interoffice e-mails are from attorneys who are either making a request for document retrieval or asking me to check the status of a hearing or motion. E-mails from the client may contain creditor information required to either start or update bankruptcy schedules or monthly operating reports that must be filed with bankruptcy court in a Chapter 11 case.

Next, I check the firm calendar for upcoming hearings or deadlines regarding my caseload. In preparation for upcoming hearings, I make sure the attorney has a copy of each pleading on the docket for review or if necessary prepare trial binders with an index and corresponding tab for each pleading.

In bankruptcy law, you must file most pleadings electronically; therefore, if I know my week entailed filing amended schedules, motions, or monthly operating reports with the court, I make sure my service list is up to date, then electronically file the pleading and arrange for service.

A typical workweek might also entail locating documents that may be used as exhibits at trial, drafting pleadings, preparing amended bankruptcy schedules, and reviewing the court docket for objections to motions or the bankruptcy plan.

Another important aspect of my workweek is to make sure the pleadings, correspondence, and discovery files are maintained regularly. Each folder contains an index of the pleadings with corresponding tabs so that the attorney can review the case or mark a document as an exhibit for trial.

Often in bankruptcy law, the creditor will file a proof of claim stating an amount owed to them is larger than listed in the bankruptcy schedules. Upon receipt of this higher claim, I would prepare an e-mail to the client regarding the claim and inquire as to whether the claim should be disputed.

Claims reviews are essential to Chapter 11 and Chapter 13 cases because these types of bankruptcies offer to pay a dividend to the creditors. In a Chapter 11 case, the claims are usually reviewed prior to plan confirmation to ensure that each creditor is in its correct category and to give the debtor a chance to dispute claims. In a Chapter 13, a claims review must be conducted after 90 days from the date of the Section 341 creditor's meeting. In order to review all of the claims in a bankruptcy case, I first obtain a copy of the court's claim register, sort the claims according to category, and then index and update a proof of claims pleadings binder.

ETHICS CAVEAT:

Failure to communicate effectively with clients is one of the largest causes of complaints to disciplinary boards against lawyers by clients.

Therese A. Cannon, Attorney at Law and author of *Ethics and Professional Responsibility for Legal Assistants*

GENERAL ADVICE:

ETHICS CAVEAT:

Doing pro bono work is one of the most important and rewarding things that a paralegal can do and is an ethical mandate in some states.

Therese A. Cannon, Attorney at Law and author of *Ethics and Professional Responsibility for Legal Assistants*

I. How to Organize a Bankruptcy Case File

After a paralegal receives a case assignment, the paralegal is responsible for being able to retrieve a document or pleading at the attorney's immediate request. To find documents or pleadings readily, the first thing you should do is to create a Master File Index (see Figure 15-1).

Figure 15-1—MASTER FILE INDEX

MASTER FILE INDEX:

1. CORRESPONDENCE

a.	Correspondence	12/12/01– 01/31/03
		02/01/03–03/14/03
b.	Correspondence	03/15/03– 03/31/03
		04/01/03–04/30/03
c.	Correspondence	05/01/03– 05/31/03
		06/01/03–06/30/03
d.	Correspondence	07/01/03– 07/16/03
		07/17/03 07/31/03
e.	Correspondence	08/01/03– 08/31/03
		09/01/03–09/30/03
f.	Correspondence	10/01/03– 10/31/03
		11/01/03–11/30/03
		12/01/03–12/31/03
g.	Correspondence	01/01/04– 01/31/04
		02/01/04–02/29/04
h.	Correspondence	03/01/04– 03/31/04
i.	Correspondence	04/01/04– 04/30/04
		05/01/04–05/31/04
j.	Correspondence	06/01/04– 06/30/04
		07/01/04– 07/31/04
k.	Correspondence	08/01/04– 08/31/04
		09/01/04– 09/30/04

2. PLEADINGS

a. Pleadings binders 1 & 2 & 3
b. Pleadings binders 4 & 5 & 6

    c. Pleadings binders 7 & 8

    d. Pleadings binders 9 & 10

    e. Pleadings binders 11 & 12

    f. Pleadings binders 13 & 14 & 15

    g. Pleadings binders 16 & 17 & 18

    h. Pleadings binders 19 & 20 (# 662 Loose)

    i. Pleadings binders 21 &

3. EXTRA COPIES 3a & 3b & 3 c

4. DOCUMENT FILE

Initial Debtor Interview

Notice of 341 Meeting

Estimated Earning and Cash Flow

5. DRAFTS

    a. Drafts of First Day Motion/Orders

        Drafts of Pleadings

        Drafts of 20 Largest Creditors

        Drafts of Schedules

    b. Drafts of Plans and Disclosure Statements

6. FILE OPENING MATERIALS

Conflict of Interest Report/Opening Materials

Unanimous Consent of Board

Corrections to Chapter 11 Bankruptcy

Forbearance Agreement

Mortgage

Accounts Receivables

Accounts Payables

Attorney Notes

7. PROOF OF CLAIMS.

    a. 1–45 and extra copy of claims docket

    b. 46–96 and extra copy of Schedules & Amended Schedules

8. a-c APPRAISALS

9. CREDITOR MAILING LIST

General Matrix

Special Notice List

Notice of Appearance Index

Returned Mail

10. Other Litigation

Whitney v. W.	25th JDC 49-467
Whitney v.	22nd JDC 02-15759 (W/D as COR 5/15/03)
Whitney v. OB-132 Vessel	USDC 02-3454
Whitney v.	25th JDC 02-42985 (CLOSED 11/19/02)

11. DISCOVERY To and From client

a. Ltr dated 1/31/03 Jan Hayden to Whitney with enclosure of
Appraisal of Farms (Angela Lakvold)
and Marine, Inc. (Brewster Appraisal Service)

Ltr dated 2/5/03 Jan Hayden to Whitney with monthly income
statements Jan- Feb.

Ltr dated 6/12/03 Trey Roche with enclosure of financial information
to Michael Dendy UCC.

b. DISCOVERY (from Whitney to Barnett)

Ltr dated 1/31/03 from Leann Moses to Jan Hayden with enclosed
Bate Stamp #'s WNB 000001- WNB 000687

c. DISCOVERY (from Whitney to Barnett)

Ltr dated 2/6/03 from Leann Moses to Jan Hayden with enclosed
Bate Stamp #'s WNB 000688- WNB 000889

Ltr dated 4/1/03 from Leann Moses to Jan Hayden with enclosed
Appraisals of Horse Farm and Residence by Deano & Assoc.

d. DISCOVERY (Whitney's copies of tax returns & W-2)

e. DISCOVERY (Produced by Kennedy & Carr for 3/16/04)

f. DISCOVERY (Whitney's copies of ledgers & Whitney's Billing)

12. RESEARCH/ATTORNEY NOTES

**13. UCC SEARCH & Related Documents (copies of mortgages,
lien releases)**

14. a. Monthly Operating Reports

b. Monthly Operating Reports (copies)

15. DEPOSITIONS

16. APPLICATIONS FOR COMPENSATION

First Interim Application for Compensation

Second Interim Application for Compensation

Third and Final Application for Compensation

Amended Third and Final Application for Compensation

17. MISCELLANEOUS DOCUMENTS/ INVENTORIES/ ORIGINALLY SIGNED DOCUMENTS.

a. – Affidavits (originally signed)

  – Farms Financial Information

  – Abstract of Title for Vessels

  – Financial Information

  – Budgets

  – Confidentiality Agreement

  – Designated Items on Appeal

  – Equipment Evaluation

  – Financial Information (Insider pay and Accounts Payable)

  – Financial Data, Graphs, Charts

  – Non-Real Estate Inventory

  – Schedule of Proof of Claims and BTI transfers

  – Board of Directors Unanimous Consent

  – Brochures on Richie Brothers, Chiron Financial & Plant & Machinery

b. – Ballot Package

  – Certificate of Service Reports

  – Settlement Term Sheet

  – Asset Encumbered Assets

18. PREP FOR HEARINGS

a. Prep for hearings 6/16/03 (duplicates of pleadings)

  – Motion to Covert Case to Chapter 7 (US Trustee)

  – Opposition to Motion to Convert ( )

– Disclosure Statement, Amended Disclosure Statement

　　Second Amended and Restated Disclosure Statement

– Plan, Amended Plan, Second Amended Plan

– Joint Objection to Disclosure (Ad Hoc Committee)

– Objection to Disclosure (UCC)

– Amended Disclosure of Ad Hoc (Ad Hoc Committee)

– Response to Objections to Disclosure by Ad Hoc (BTI)

– Order denying approval of Disclosure (Court)

– Second Amended Disclosure (Ad Hoc)

– Comparison of First & Second Amended Disclosure (Ad Hoc)

– Second Amended Plan (Ad Hoc)

– Notice of filing of Key Terms (Ad Hoc)

– Memorandum to Record 12/18/03 (Court)

b. Prep for hearings 11/07/03 (duplicates of pleadings)

– Coastal's Motion for Order Temporary Allowing
　POC (Coastal)

– Motion for Order allowing Scheduled Claim (Assoc. Pipeline)

– Motion to File Claim late (USA Labor)

– Motion for Order Applying Proceeds of Sales

– Motion for Sanctions against BTI (Whitney)

– Joint Motion of and Riccardi

c. Duplicate of Debtors' Schedules

d. Solicitation Package Index

　　Objections to Debtor and BTI Plans

**19. Plan and Disclosure Statements
(all versions)**

20. Attorney working files

Arrange correspondence by month, allowing one Redweld per every two months of correspondence or depending on the amount received. Within each monthly file, put the latest correspondence on top.

> ### ETHICS CAVEAT:
>
> *Mark all correspondence between the law firm and the client as privileged, and store these records in separate hard-copy or electronic files so that they are not inadvertently disclosed.*
>
> Therese A. Cannon, Attorney at Law and author of *Ethics and Professional Responsibility for Legal Assistants*

II. Conducting Proof of Claims Reviews in Chapter 13 Cases

It is from viewing the court claims registry and the Chapter 13 trustee's records that a paralegal may obtain the information to conduct a thorough claims review. In approximately 49 districts, BankruptcyLink states that Casepower 13 (www.bankruptcylink.com) is available to verify basic case information, status of proofs of claim and/or disbursements on claims, and information on plan payments received from the debtor. In order to access this site, a login, and password are required, which you may obtain from the Chapter 13 trustee in your district.

If your firm represents a creditor in a bankruptcy case, the BankruptcyLink will provide you with valuable information on whether the trustee has received your client's proof of claim. In addition, the BankruptcyLink will tell you (a) the percentage of payment provided by the plan, (b) the amount allowed of the proof of claim, (c) the recorded payments on the claim, and (d) the balance remaining. Please note that the claim number, class, category, reference number, and payment sequence are codes used by the Chapter 13 office.

Finally, it is important for both debtor's and creditor's attorneys to monitor whether the debtor is making timely payments to the Chapter 13 trustee. The attorney for the debtor may have to verify whether a payment has been received to defend against a motion to dismiss filed by the Chapter 13 trustee based on non-payment of the plan or by a creditor because the debtor is delinquent in his plan payments or post-petition mortgage payments.

To determine whether a Chapter 13 plan is "feasible," you must review the proof of claims and add them up according to category to see if the plan balances. Often, the claims that the debtor lists in his bankruptcy schedules are less than those actually filed. For example, the debtor believes he owes Sears $200.00, and the proof of claim actually states that the balance due is $1,500.00. The plan will become non-feasible if the plan payment the debtor has promised to pay is simply not enough to cover all the creditor's claims filed in the case.

Figure 15-2

PROOF OF CLAIM

FORM B10 (Official Form 10) (12/03)

United States Bankruptcy Court -	PROOF OF CLAIM
Name of Debtor	Case Number

NOTE: This form should not be used to make a claim for an administrative expense arising after the commencement of the case. A "request" for payment of an administrative expense may be filed pursuant to 11 U.S.C. § 503.

Name of Creditor (The person or other entity to whom the debtor owes money or property):	☐ Check box if you are aware that anyone else has filed a proof of claim relating to your claim. Attach copy of statement giving particulars.
Name and address where notices should be sent:	☐ Check box if you have never received any notices from the bankruptcy court in this case.
	☐ Check box if the address differs from the address on the envelope sent to you by the court.
Telephone number:	This Space is for Court Use Only
Account or other number by which creditor identifies debtor:	Check here if this claim ☐ replaces ☐ amends a previously filed claim dated:_____

1. Basis for Claim
- ☐ Goods sold
- ☐ Services performed
- ☐ Money loaned
- ☐ Personal injury/wrongful death
- ☐ Taxes
- ☐ Other_____

- ☐ Retiree benefits as defined in 11 U.S.C. § 1114(a)
- ☐ Wages, salaries, and compensation (fill out below)
  Last four digits of SS #:_____
  Unpaid compensation for services performed
  from _____ to _____
  (date)   (date)

2. Date debt was incurred:	**3. If court judgment, date obtained:**

4. Total Amount of Claim at Time Case Filed: $ _____ _____ _____ _____
                                            (unsecured)   (secured)   (priority)   (Total)
If all or part of your claim is secured or entitled to priority, also complete Item 5 or 7 below.
☐ Check this box if claim includes interest or other charges in addition to the principal amount of the claim. Attach itemized statement of all interest or additional charges.

5. Secured Claim.
☐ Check this box if your claim is secured by collateral (including a right of setoff).
Brief Description of Collateral:
☐ Real Estate ☐ Motor Vehicle ☐ Other _____
Value of Collateral: $_____

Amount of arrearage and other charges at time case filed included in the secured claim, if any: $_____

6. Unsecured Nonpriority Claim $_____
☐ Check this box if: a) there is no collateral or lien securing your claim, or b) your claim exceeds the value of the property securing it, or c) none or only part of your claim is entitled to priority.

7. Unsecured Priority Claim.
☐ Check this box if you have an unsecured priority claim
Amount entitled to priority $_____
Specify the priority of the claim:
- ☐ Wages, salaries, or commissions (up to $4,650),* earned within 90 days before filing of the bankruptcy petition or cessation of the debtor's business, whichever is earlier - 11 U.S.C. § 507(a)(3).
- ☐ Contributions to an employee benefit plan - 11 U.S.C. § 507(a)(4).
- ☐ Up to $2,100* of deposits toward purchase, lease, or rental of property or services for personal, family, or household use - 11 U.S.C. § 507(a)(6).
- ☐ Alimony, maintenance, or support owed to a spouse, former spouse, or child - 11 U.S.C. § 507(a)(7).
- ☐ Taxes or penalties owed to governmental units-11 U.S.C. § 507(a)(8).
- ☐ Other - Specify applicable paragraph of 11 U.S.C. § 507(a)(_____).
*Amounts are subject to adjustment on 4/1/04 and every 3 years thereafter with respect to cases commenced on or after the date of adjustment.

8. Credits: The amount of all payments on this claim has been credited and deducted for the purpose of making this proof of claim.

9. Supporting Documents: *Attach copies of supporting documents,* such as promissory notes, purchase orders, invoices, itemized statements of running accounts, contracts, court judgments, mortgages, security agreements, and evidence of perfection of lien. DO NOT SEND ORIGINAL DOCUMENTS. If the documents are not available, explain. If the documents are voluminous, attach a summary.

10. Date-Stamped Copy: To receive an acknowledgment of the filing of your claim, enclose a stamped, self-addressed envelope and copy of this proof of claim

This Space is for Court Use Only

Date	Sign and print the name and title, if any, of the creditor or other person authorized to file this claim (attach copy of power of attorney, if any):

Penalty for presenting fraudulent claim: Fine of up to $500,000 or imprisonment for up to 5 years, or both. 18 U.S.C. §§ 1

Figure 15-3

CHAPTER **13** CLAIMS REVIEW FORM

FREELANCE PARALEGAL SERVICES

1-888-842-2493 (VOICE MAIL/FAX)

DISCLAIMER/DEFINITIONS OF TERMS

The following claims review is based on the proof of claims filed with the United States Bankruptcy Court and the Chapter 13 Trustee's Claims Register (the gold sheets). After reviewing the claims, I have given my **opinion** on whether the case is feasible or non-feasible based on the claims that have been timely filed and the amount provided for creditors in the Debtor's Chapter 13 plan.

The following are definitions of the terms that I have used in this report:

BAR DATE: The deadline set by the court for all claims to be filed in each case; 90 days following the first 341 Creditor's Meeting.

BASE AMOUNT: The term or length of the plan multiplied by the monthly plan payment. (Example: 60 months × $ 200.00 = 12,000.)

EFFECTIVE DATE OF CONFIRMATION: The effective date of Confirmation is the date the plan payments begin; the Trustee at the 341 Creditor's Meeting sets this date. This date is useful in determining how many months are remaining to complete the plan (see further explanation below).

PROVIDED FOR IN PLAN/ORDER: If the plan is pre-confirmed, I have reviewed the claim in relation to the Debtor's schedules and proposed plan, and if the plan is confirmed, then I have reviewed the claim in relation to the Order of Confirmation.

SIGNIFICANT DISCREPANCY: A discrepancy that will affect the base amount to the extent that it may impair the plan's feasibility.

VALID/INVALID: Whether there is a reason to dispute the claim, *prima facie* (on its face). An example of an invalid claim is a claim that has been untimely filed.

FEASIBLE: Based on the debtor's excess income and the plan payment as proposed, the case is feasible if the base amount covers the cost of the debtor's Chapter 13 plan and fully provides for all claims as timely filed.

NON-FEASIBLE: Based on the debtor's excess income and the plan payment as proposed, the case is non-feasible if the base amount provided to cover the cost of the debtor's Chapter 13 plan does **not** fully provide for all claims as timely filed.

ADDITIONAL NOTES:

1. The proof of claims marked with an asterisk (*) do not agree with the debtor's schedules or Chapter 13 plan. If you have cause to believe that a claim is **invalid**, you may file an objection to the claim within thirty days of the claims bar date. If you do not file an objection to claim within thirty days, the Chapter 13 Trustee will automatically provide for all claims as filed.

2. If the proof of claims as listed are valid, and the case is **NON-FEASIBLE**, it may be necessary to file an **AMENDED PLAN** to provide for the claims as filed. If the plan is not amended in a timely manner, the Chapter 13 Trustee may file a Trustee's Motion to Dismiss after conducting his/her independent claims review.

3. If you file an **AMENDED PLAN**, please note that **SCHEDULES "I" and/or "J"** must reflect that there is enough excess income to provide for a higher amended plan payment.

4. Because cities and towns rarely file proof of claims, it is generally assumed that if the Debtor has listed a real estate tax claim or water and sewerage bill, it is his/her intention to provide for this amount even though a claim has not been filed.

5. Even if the Debtor's plan calculates less than anticipated, it is the policies of the Chapter 13 Trustee offices to have the Debtor complete the plan early rather than lower the plan payments as provided.

6. If the unsecured creditor total calculates less than anticipated, then the Trustee will raise the percentage to the remaining unsecured creditors up to the base amount provided for through the plan.

   Feel free to call me to discuss the case, or if you should require my services to obtain a copy of a particular proof of claim, prepare an objection to a claim, or to prepare an Amended Chapter 13 Plan.

   Thank you for the opportunity to serve you.

   Sincerely,

   Becky Rolland
   Paralegal

CLAIMS REVIEW

DEBTOR(S) _____   DATE REVIEWED _____

CASE # _____   BAR DATE _____

BASE AMT = _____   CONFIRMATION DATE _____
(Plan Payment multiplied by   (Effective Date of Confirmation)
Term = Base)

I   SECURED CLAIMS:

NAME OF CREDITOR   AMOUNT CLAIMED   PROVIDED IN PLAN OR ORDER AS:

_____

_____

_____

_____

_____

_____

_____

II   PRIORITY CLAIMS:

NAME OF CREDITOR   AMOUNT CLAIMED   PROVIDED IN PLAN OR ORDER AS:

_____

_____

_____

_____

_____

_____

_____

III   ADMINISTRATIVE CLAIMS:

NAME OF CREDITOR   AMOUNT CLAIMED   PROVIDED IN PLAN OR ORDER AS:

_____

_____

IV   UNSECURED TOTAL: **% OFFERED**

   VS. AMT PROVIDED IN PLAN: _____

   SIGNIFICANT DISCREPANCIES: _____

_____

_____

_____

_____

_____

FEASIBILITY STUDY: _____

   TOTAL AMOUNT DUE CREDITORS : $ _____

   TRUSTEE'S FEE (10%)   : $ _____

   TOTAL COST OF PLAN   : $ _____

   LESS AMOUNT PAID TO DATE   : $ _____

   BALANCE DUE TO COMPLETE   : $ _____

   DIVIDED BY   MONTHS REMAINING = $ _____ PER _____

   MONTH. BEGINNING WITH _____ PAYMENT.

   CONCLUSION: The case is FEASIBLE/ NON-FEASIBLE _____

   NOTES: _____

_____

_____

_____

_____

_____

_____

_____

_____

_____

_____

Figure 15-4—SCHEDULES I AND J

In re _____

Debtor

Case No. _____

SCHEDULE I. CURRENT INCOME OF INDIVIDUAL DEBTOR(S) - AMENDED

The column labeled "Spouse" must be completed in all cases field by joint debtors and by a married debtor in a chapter 12 or 13 case whether or not a joint petition is field, unless the spouses are separated and a joint petition is not field.

Debtor's Marital Status:	DEPENDENTS OF DEBTOR AND SPOUSE	
	RELATIONSHIP None.	AGE

EMPLOYMENT:	DEBTOR	SPOUSE
Occupation		
Name of Employer		
How long employed		
Address of Employer		

INCOME: (Estimate of average monthly income)

	DEBTOR	SPOUSE
Current monthly gross wages, salary, and commissions (pro rate if not paid monthly)	$ 0.00	$ N/A
Estimated monthly overtime	$ 0.00	$ N/A
SUBTOTAL	$ 0.00	$ N/A
LESS PAYROLL DEDUCTIONS		
a. Payroll taxes and social security	$ 0.00	$ N/A
b. Insurance	$ 0.00	$ N/A
c. Union dues	$ 0.00	$ N/A
d. Other (Specify) _____	$ 0.00	$ N/A
	$ 0.00	$ N/A
SUBTOTAL OF PAYROLL DEDUCTIONS	$ 0.00	$ N/A
TOTAL NET MONTHLY TAKE HOME PAY	$ 0.00	$ N/A
Regular income from operation of business or profession of farm (attach detailed statement)	$ 0.00	$ N/A
Income from real property	$ 0.00	$ N/A
Interest and dividends	$ 0.00	$ N/A
Alimony, maintenance or support payments payable to the debtor for the debtor's use or that of dependents listed above.	$ 0.00	$ N/A
Social security or other government assistance (Specify) _____	$ 0.00	$ N/A
Pension or retirement income	$ 0.00	$ N/A
Other monthly income (Specify) _____	$ 0.00	$ N/A
	$ 0.00	$ N/A
TOTAL MONTHLY INCOME	$ 0.00	$ N/A
TOTAL COMBINED MONTHLY INCOME $ 0.00		(Report also on Summary of Schedules)

Describe any increase or decrease of more than 10% in any of the above categories anticipated to occur within the year following the filing of this document:

In re _____

_____
Debtor

Case No._____

SCHEDULE J. CURRENT EXPENDITURES OF INDIVIDUAL DEBTOR(S) - AMENDED

Complete this schedule by estimating the average monthly expenses of the debtor and the debtor's family. Pro rate and payments made bi-weekly, quarterly, semi-annually to show monthly rate.

☐ Check this box if a joint petition is filed and debtor's spouse maintains a separate household. Complete a separate schedule of expenditures labeled "Spouse."

Rent or home mortgage payment (include lot rented for mobile home)	$	0.00
Are real estate taxes included? Yes _____ No __X__		
Is property insurance included? Yes _____ No __X__		
Utilities: Electricity and heating fuel	$	0.00
Water and sewer	$	0.00
Telephone	$	0.00
Other _____	$	0.00
Home maintenance (repairs and upkeep)	$	0.00
Food	$	0.00
Clothing	$	0.00
Laundry and dry cleaning	$	0.00
Medical and dental expenses	$	0.00
Transportation (not including car payments)	$	0.00
Recreation, clubs and entertainment, newspapers, magazines, etc	$	0.00
Charitable contributions	$	0.00

Insurance (not deducted from wages or included in home mortgage payments)

Homeowner's or renter's . . . . $ 0.00

Life . . . . $ 0.00

Health . . . . $ 0.00

Auto . . . . $ 0.00

Other . . . . $ 0.00

Taxes (not deducted from wages or included in home mortgage payments)

(Specify) . . . . $ 0.00

Installment payments: (In chapter 12 and 13 cases, do not list payments to be included in the plan.)

Auto . . . . $ 0.00

Other . . . . $ 0.00

Other . . . . $ 0.00

Other . . . . $ 0.00

Alimony, maintenance, and support paid to others . . . . $ 0.00

Payments for support of additional dependents not living at your home . . . . . . $ 0.00

Regular expenses from operation of business, profession, or farm (attach detailed statement) . . . $ 0.00

Other . . . . $ 0.00

Other . . . . $ 0.00

TOTAL MOTHLY EXPENSES (Report also on Summary of Schedules) . . . . $ 0.00

[FOR CHAPTER 12 AND 13 DEBTORS ONLY]

Provide the information requested below, including whether plan payments are to be made bi-weekly, monthly, annually, or at some other regular interval.

A. Total projected monthly income . . . . $ 0.00

B. Total projected monthly expenses . . . . $ 0.00

C. Excess income (A minus B) . . . . $ 0.00

D. Total amount to be paid into plan each _____ . . . . $ 0.00

(interval)

Figure 15-5

EDIT TO MAILING MATRIX

Last updated 03/5/06

Deleted Creditors

Aetna U.S. Healthcare
Bud's Boat Rental, Inc.
Burlington Resources
Chauvin Bros. Tractor, Inc.
Cingular Wireless
Consolidated Electrical Dist.
Creole Chief, Inc.
Department of Environmental Quality (Financial Division)
Elmwood Dry Dock & Repair
Entergy
Fort & Schlefer, L.L.P.
Harbor Insurance Services, Ltd.
I. C. Electric Supply
New York Life
Northshore Safe & Lock
Peter A. Chopin Florist, Inc.
Southland Labor Service, Inc.
Spilsbury, Hamilton, Legendre & Paciera
The Great A & P Tea Company
Tiger Equipment & Supply Co.
Trinity Industries, Inc. (duplicate listing)
US EPA, Region 6

Returned Mail - Cannot resend

Creditor	Post Office Reason	Status
Ansa-Board, Inc. 1028 Franklin Street Harvey, LA 70058	Unable to Forward	Last mail sent 1/15/06
Con-Equip New Orleans P. O. Box 847369 Dallas, TX 75284	Closed P. O. Box	Last mail sent 1/15/06
Donovan Marine, Inc. P. O. Box 19100 New Orleans, LA 70179	Moved, left no address	Last mail sent 1/30/06
Emergency Phys- Meadowcrest P. O. Box 53007 New Orleans, LA 70153	No forwarding order on file	Last mail sent 1/30/06

Gulf Marine, Inc. P. O. Box 927 Belle Chasse, LA 70037	Box closed, no forward order	Last mail sent 11/24/06
Industrial Metals P. O. Box 10507 New Orleans, LA 70181	No longer at P. O. Box	Last mail sent 11/24/06
Land & Marine Services 6027 Chef Mentuer Highway Suite 208 New Orleans, LA 70127	Undeliverable, No forwarding address	Last mail 11/05/06
Occupational Health Solutions 1400 LaPalco Blvd. Building # 1 Harvey, LA 70058	Unable to deliver or forward	Last mail 1/15/06
Skipper Hydraulic, Inc. Post Office Box 2671 Baton Rouge, LA 70821-2671	No longer at P. O. Box no forward	Last mail 11/24/06 Barnett says out of business
South General Labor Contractor 129 Keating Drive, Suite 200 Belle Chasse, LA 70037	Unable to forward	Last mail 12/19/06
Travelers Insurance CL Remittance Center East Hartford, CT	No such office	Last mail 11/5/06
Westbank Surgical Clinic 4475 St. Charles Avenue New Orleans, LA 70072-3199	Undeliverable, no forward	Last mail 1/15/06
Don Volion Hwy45 Lafitte, LA	Insufficient address	Last mail 11/24/2006

Returned mail address changes made

Accpac International **Con-Equip New Orleans**	Forwarding sticker issued (address client provided on 2/18/06 still no good)
Cosby Tugs, Inc. Go-Cans D & M Steel Co.	Forwarding sticker issued

Donovan Marine (address client provided on 2/18/06 still no good)

Emergency Phys
Emery & James, Ltd. Ins.
Engine Parts
Gulf Coast Bank & Trust Company (address from PACER care of attorney)
Global Fabrication & Welding
Healthsouth Medical Clinic
Honeybaked Ham Co. (creditor provided by facsimile on 3/5/06)

Industrial Welding Supply (address client provided on 2/18/06 still no good

John W. Stone
Land & Marine Services (address client provided on 2/18/06 still no good)

March Laboratory Service
Nacher Corp.
Occupational Health Ser.
Premium Financing Specialists
Robichaux Equipment, Inc.
Safety Kleen Corp.
South General Labor Contractor (creditor provided by telephone 3/3/06)
Spilsbury Hamilton Legandre & Paciera
Standard Supply
Willco of Houma, Inc.
West Jefferson Medical Center

Deleted name and re-added name and address

Don Volion (Address is still incorrect)
Gulf Coast Bank & Trust Company (Changed to attorney address)
Industrial Welding (Address is still incorrect)
Regency (Client gave better address)

Figure 15-6
LETTER TO CLIENT, REGARDING RETURNED MAIL

FREELANCE PARALEGAL SERVICES
P. O. Box 2067
MANDEVILLE, LA 70470-2067
888-842-2493

February 18, 2006

Mr. William Beaux
President
Any Corporation
XYZ Road
New Orleans, LA 70130

RE: Debtor name, Case No. XX-XXXXXX-JNG

Dear Mr. Beaux,

Below is a list of creditors whose mail the U.S. Postal service has returned various reasons. Therefore, these creditors are not receiving notification from the Bankruptcy Court of Orders, Notices, etc, and may not be bound by law to abide by said Orders and Notices regarding their claim.

Please notify this office as soon as possible with correct addresses for these creditors.

1. Accpac   (Forwarding time expired)
    P. O. Box 6000
    San Francisco, CA 94160

2. Con-Equip New Orleans   (P. O. Box closed)
    Post Office Box 847369
    Dallas, TX 75284

3. D&M Steel Co.   (Forwarding time expired)
    4450 Gen Degaulle Drive
    New Orleans, LA 70131

4. Donovan Marine, Inc.   (P. O. Box closed)
    P.O. Box 19100
    New Orleans, LA 70179

5. Emergency Phys-Meadowcrest   (Addressee unknown)
    P. O. Box 53007
    New Orleans, LA 70153

6. Occupational Health Services   (No such address)
    1400 LaPalco Blvd.
    Harvey, LA 70058

7. Standard Supply   (Forwarding order expired)
    & Hardware Co.
    Post Office Box 60620
    New Orleans, LA 70160

If you have any questions, please feel free to contact me at 1-888-842-2493.

Sincerely,

Becky Rolland
Paralegal

Figure 15-7

UNITED STATES BANKRUPTCY COURT EASTERN DISTRICT OF LOUISIANA

In Re: **CASE NO.**

DEBTOR   **CHAPTER 11**

ADDITIONS TO MATRIX

Ansa-Board, Inc.
1028 Franklin Street
Harvey, LA 70058

ASAP Court Reporting Services
P. O. Box 6348
Metairie, LA 70009-6348

Binswanger Glass
2931 Lime Street
Metairie, LA 70006

Burton Marine, Inc.
P. O. Box 1418
Harvey, LA 70059

Gulf Best Electric, Inc.
4525 North Claiborne Avenue
New Orleans, LA 70117

Figure 15-8

IN THE UNITED STATES BANKRUPTCY COURT NORTHERN DISTRICT OF IOWA

In Re: **CASE NO.**

DEBTOR   **CHAPTER 11**

NOTICE OF CHANGE OF ADDRESSES TO ALL CREDITORS AND PARTIES IN INTEREST:

NOTICE IS HEREBY GIVEN that the following addresses should be corrected on the creditor matrix specified:

Old Addresses	New Addresses
Muzak, Inc. 3901 25th Street. Moline, IL 61265	Muzak, Inc. 2128 5th Avenue Moline, IL 61265-6871
Praxair Distribution P.O. Box 9213 Des Moines, IA 50306	Praxair Distribution Dept. CH 10660 Palatine, IL 60055-0660
A-I Alarm 1000 10th St. Cedar Rapids Cedar Rapids, IA 52406	A-One Alarm Co. 1000 10th St. SW Cedar Rapids, IA 52404-1908
Alliant P. O. Box 7004 Cedar Rapids, IA 52406	Alliant Utilities P. O. Box 77004 Madison, WI 53707
Coca Cola Financial Corporation Drawer 1734-NAT 5 One Coca-Cola Plaza NW	Coca Cola Financial Corp. Drawer 1734-NAT 5 One Coca-Cola Plaza NW Atlanta, GA 30301

WRITING TIPS

- Know your audience.
- Make sure you spell the recipient's name correctly.
- Use layman's terms when writing to a client.
- If you are using a term that your audience may not be aware of, make sure you define the term.
- When appropriate, include the facts and circumstances that led to the communication.
- If you are requesting documentation or eliciting a response from the reader, include the pending deadline or a follow-up date.
- Write in the active voice.
- Use clear, precise, and simple sentences.
- If you are using more than two commas, try to simplify the sentence.
- Avoid unnecessary superlatives.
- Do not use slang, contractions, or too many abbreviations.
- Maintain professionalism at all times.
- Make sure you remain within your paralegal ethical boundaries. In other words, never give legal advice.
- Double-check punctuation, especially double negatives, misspelled words, and run-on sentences.
- Mark the file location at the bottom of the document.
- Make sure you mail out the final version of the correspondence.
- Maintain a copy of all correspondence, sorted according to date.
- *Proofread.*

THREE TIPS FOR DOCUMENT PREPARATION

1. Before submitting any drafted pleadings or mailing correspondence, be sure you triple-check for the correct spelling of names, the correct use of punctuation, and for spelling errors.

2. Make sure your file name and document path are at the bottom-left corner so that the document will be easy to locate later.

3. When drafting different versions, make sure you create a new version before saving changes. In addition, when you prepare a redline version of a document, create a subversion when accepting the changes to that particular version.

> **ETHICS CAVEAT:**
>
> *I would add a fourth recommendation—always have a lawyer review documents before they are filed or submitted to the client or other interested party.*
>
> Therese A. Cannon, Attorney at Law and author of *Ethics and Professional Responsibility for Legal Assistants*

SECRETS ON CONDUCTING THOROUGH CLIENT INTERVIEWS OR BANKRUPTCY INTAKES

> **ETHICS CAVEAT:**
>
> *Paralegals are especially good at intake interviewing for bankruptcy, as they are perceived by clients as more approachable and less intimidating than lawyers. This is a great benefit to the client and the firm, but be sure not to get taken in by a good relationship and give advice, which may include predicting the outcome of the matter.*
>
> Therese A. Cannon, Attorney at Law and author of *Ethics and Professional Responsibility for Legal Assistants*

1. Most bankruptcy software programs include a client questionnaire. Not only does the questionnaire provide assistance in obtaining accurate information, but also it also serves as a record of what information the client provided at the bankruptcy intake.

2. For most individual debtors, bankruptcy is a traumatic and shameful experience.

3. It is helpful, when conducting a client intake or interview, if you can trigger his memory by using the following techniques:

   ■ If you are trying to obtain a date from the client, start by asking him which year it was, providing a range of years at first, and then narrowing it down to a season. This may perhaps trigger the date requested.

   ■ When working on Schedule B, listing the debtor's personal assets, it is helpful to go through one room of the house at a time to describe household furnishings, and then proceed to ask questions about assets that may not be readily revealed. For example, instead of asking your client if he has any collectables, you should be more specific and ask if he or she collects dolls, stamps, or baseball cards.

- On Schedule J, the debtor's expenses, it may be necessary to ask about what the debtor spends his money on besides what is listed. For example, ask about what toiletries the debtor would purchase from a drug store that may not be included in the grocery total. Ask whether the debtor makes or buys his lunch? Does the debtor smoke cigarettes or have any pets? How often does he get a haircut? Does the debtor pay for lawn service or snow removal?

4. Included are descriptions of the Statement of Financial Affairs, Schedules A–J, and the Statement of Intent as reprinted from "Preparing a Bankruptcy Petition and Plan," Chapter 15 in the *Paralegal Practice Manual* (Massachusetts Continuing Legal Education [MCLE] 1997 & Supp. 1999).

OFFICE COMMUNICATIONS

1. A new paralegal should be *proactive* in office communications, not *reactive*.

2. If you are not sure, ask questions to clarify your understanding or ask for assistance. It is better to appear foolish rather than jeopardize your career with a costly mistake.

3. When communicating with co-workers, do not take things personally if someone snaps at you. The work in law offices is inherently stressful with all of the pressures and deadlines, and usually after the deadline is met, everyone relaxes.

4. If you have an issue with a procedure or policy, do not be afraid to speak with your supervisor about it. Most supervisors welcome the input, and even if your issue is not resolved immediately, you could have planted a seed that may grow and develop.

5. Remember to make positive suggestions instead of complaints— *attitude* is everything.

SOFTWARE HINTS

1. Almost every bankruptcy court has electronic dockets available through PACER (Public Access to Court Electronic Records) or

CM/ECF (Case Management/Electronic Case Files). A paralegal may access PACER systems at http://pacer.psc.uscourts.gov, or there is a link through www.uscourts.gov. Once you arrive at the bankruptcy court Web site of your choice, you may download copies of electronically filed documents at a cost of 8 cents per page for a maximum charge for 30 pages. Please note that some PACER dockets may not have scanned images attached. If the docket number is underlined, it is a CM/ECF document and can be retrieved and downloaded electronically.

2. Most bankruptcy courts have a home page that gives information regarding CM/ECF training and how to obtain a login password in order to file documents electronically.

OTHER TIPS OR COMMENTS

Please see Figure 15-9, the Checklist for Items Required for Filing a Bankruptcy Petition. This checklist is reprinted with permission from "Bankruptcy Basics" in *Preparing Legal Documents for Paralegals* (Massachusetts Continuing Legal Education [MCLE], 2000).

Figure 15-9

CHECKLIST FOR ITEMS REQUIRED FOR BANKRUPTCY PETITION

1. Copies of mortgage statements showing creditor name, address, account #, principal balance owed, please include date you incurred mortgage(s). If you are retaining the mortgage you will need to provide a market anlysis of the real property.

2. Bank accounts, credit union accounts, safe deposit boxes, within last two years even those closed with name and address of bank, account number, current balance or balance at closing, signators and if closed, date of closing.

3. Insurance Policies with, cash value, include name, address, policy number, value.

4. Stocks, bonds, IRA, Pensions, Retirements, etc.... include name, address and value of same, you will also need to provide a statement.

5. List of autos, trucks, boats, mobile homes, trailers-provide description and value, and any mileage on same.

6. List of assets with current market value, do not list regular household goods and furnishings or jewelry, clothing unless you have something of extreme value.

7. Income tax returns for last two years with w-2 forms, specifically looking for itemized annual income two past two years. Provide year to date income for current year.

8. Tax liabilities–Federal, State, town, or city.

9. Any lease or installment sale agreements for housing, cars, furniture, etc.... provide name, address, account, lease terms.

10. All invoices and other papers covering debts—credit card accounts, medical bills, loans from relatives, utility bills, welfare debts, judgments, school debts; show name and address, account, and date of contraction of debt and balance.

11. All bank and finance company loan papers, promissory notes, installment notes, etc....

12. List name and address of any co-signers for any debts.

13. List your occupation title, your employer name and address and length of employment.

14. Last two paycheck stubs.

15. List of monthly expenses, include everything. List also any dependants; provide name and age.

16. All legal papers, law suits, divorce papers, liens, attachments, garnishments, executions, etc..., within the last year, provide case title, case number, court location, nature of proceeding and status.

17. All property that has been attached, garnished setoff, seized, repossessed or foreclosing/foreclosed within the last year, provide creditor name, address, date of action, property description, and value.

18. List any property you have transferred in the last year, provide property description, value, date of transfer, and to whom transferred with address.

19. All payments made within the last 90 days totalling more than $600.00 to any one creditor. All payments made to any inside (relatives, etc.) creditors within the last year, provide creditor name, address, payment dates and amounts and balance owed, if any.

20. List any extraordinary gifts or charitable contributions within the last year, provide value of gift, date of transfer, to whom with address.

21. List any losses from fire, theft, casualty or gambling within the last year, provide property description, value, date of loss, insurance coverage if any.

22. Any previous address within the last two years.

    BUSINESS: Sole proprietorship, partnership, or corporation.

23. List any business you have been involved with over the last six years, provide business name, address, start date, end date, nature of business, your status of involvement.

24. List any personal guarantees you made concerning any business debt.

25. List persons responsible for bookkeeping and inventory control; provide name and address and dates of involvement.

REAL WORK EXAMPLES:

CASE NO. 1: GILBERTSON—CHAPTER 11 CONSOLIDATION OF FOUR CASES

During my employment at Heller, Draper, Hayden, Patrick, & Horn, L.L.C. (Heller, Draper), both my most interesting and most challenging case was Gilbertson Restaurants, L.L.C. (the Gilbertson case). The case consisted of Burger King franchisees and was originally filed as four separate cases, Gilbertson Restaurants, L.L.C., Beaton, Inc., KC Beaton Holding, L.L.C., and Beaton Holding, L.C.; these were later jointly consolidated into one case. The case administration, electronic filing, and indexing were definitely a challenge because, originally, there were four sets of everything: court dockets, pleadings binders, proof of claim binders, and correspondence files.

After the Gilbertson case was consolidated, it became easier to manage, although it remained highly litigated. For example, when the Plans of Reorganization were filed for each of the entities, the same creditor objected to three out of the four plans. In fact, Heller, Draper filed three to four versions of amended plans and disclosure statements with the bankruptcy court before the final versions for each of the four Gilbertson entities could be distributed to the creditors with enclosed ballots for accepting or rejecting each plan.

In a Chapter 11 case, in order for the plan to be approved by the bankruptcy court, at least two-thirds of the dollar amount of claims filed and more than half of the number of claims allowed of such class held by creditors must vote to accept the plan (11 U.S.C. § 1126 (c)).

In the Gilbertson case, one of the creditors who had a high-dollar amount claim in Class 8 of Beaton, Inc.'s (Beaton) plan had voted to reject the plan. Because most of the creditors were in Class 8, the only way to gain court approval of the Beaton plan was to make sure we had more than half of the creditors in number and two-thirds of the creditors in dollar amount to vote to accept the plan.

The deadline was fast approaching, and I was given the task of calling all of the Class 8 creditors (general unsecured creditors) to make sure they received their ballots, verify that they had voted, and make sure they had returned them. Within two days, I had made contact with approximately 80 creditors. I spent the remainder of the week following up on the calls, re-sending ballots by fax and e-mail, communicating with the client which ones had been received, and then organizing the ballots into the appropriate classes of the various plans.

Finally, the United States Bankruptcy Court of the Northern District of Iowa had different local rules and requirements for submitting the ballot tabulation, and, in addition, they required a claims report, something that no one in my firm had ever done before. After many telephone calls to the case administrator and judge's law clerk, the claims report was filed, the tabulation of ballots was submitted, and the Beaton plan was confirmed.

The Gilbertson case was interesting because I had direct contact with the client and creditors; and because the case was filed in Iowa, I was able to converse with different types of people than I would encounter in Louisiana tremendous responsibility by Heller, Draper. After working on the Gilbertson case, all the pieces of the Chapter 11 puzzle seemed to fit and make sense to me.

END NOTES

First publication credits granted to MCLE.

APPENDIX

THE NATIONWIDE SEARCH FOR THE TOP PARALEGAL EXPERTS

Identifying the 15 most successful paralegals was an arduous and lengthy process. A distinguished panel of judges selected the candidates based on definitive criteria. Press releases announcing the search were sent to national and state paralegal associations, paralegal listservs, Yahoo! groups, law firms, legal publications, recruiting agencies, paralegal schools, legal-related publications, bar associations, and many other sources. Posts were made on the message boards of the National Federation of Paralegal Associations (NFPA), an organization of individual paralegal associations and their members, the National Association of Legal Assistants (NALA), an organization of individual members, and The American Alliance of Paralegals, Inc., also an organization of individual members.

The press releases invited interested paralegals to visit a Web site set up specifically for the search and submit their applications or to nominate a colleague by completing an online questionnaire. Besides the press releases and other announcements, telephone networking, and word-of-mouth that spread the word, soon the Web site was flooded with candidates. After the deadline passed for submission of applications, 50 candidates were selected and were asked to complete a second questionnaire. After these questionnaires were reviewed against the criteria, 25 candidates became semi-finalists. Each semi-finalist's file contained the following information:

1. The application
2. The first questionnaire
3. The second questionnaire
4. *Circum vitae*

5. Education

6. Experience

7. Career highlights, honors, awards, and recognitions

8. Career goals

9. Level of responsibility

10. Expertise in specialty

11. Contributions to the paralegal profession

12. Mentoring abilities

13. Challenges faced

Based on these criteria and information gleaned from questionnaires, research, and interviews, the panel of judges, who were specifically selected for their knowledge of and contribution to the paralegal profession, diligently reviewed the qualifications, experience, and forward-thinking ideas of each of the candidates and rated each of the 25 candidates on a scale of 1 to 10 for each of the above criteria. After the ratings were compiled and mathematically computed, the top 15 paralegal experts working in America's law firms, corporations, industries, schools, governmental entities, and other legal-related organizations in the country were chosen.

The compelling question and focus of this book was whether the ideas, techniques, and methods of the candidates were going to be useful for *LESSONS* readers. Could they be learned from? Can they apply these lessons to their own professional careers as paralegals?

Not surprisingly, there is no single answer or formula to follow in order to excel as a paralegal, but rather many answers. The paralegals selected for *LESSONS* differ significantly in their paths to becoming the most successful paralegals in America. Perhaps the best way for paralegals to learn how to excel is by studying the methods, tools, and techniques of the wide range of these paralegal leaders who have proven they are the *best of the best* in their profession. Throughout the pages of *LESSONS*, you can find myriad ideas to use.

Achievements that contribute to expansion of the paralegal profession and improve the efficiency of performing paralegal duties include creativity, leadership, expertise in specialty, skills, knowledge, CLE, mentoring abilities, career highlights, honors, awards and recognitions, challenges faced, and career encompassed the criteria for the selection of the top 15 paralegal experts. Because we did not receive responses in all areas of law, such as immigration and criminal law, experts in these areas were not chosen.

MEET THE JUDGES[1]

WILLIAM P. STATSKY, ESQ.

Biography

Attorney, author, and professor, William Statsky, who is currently an editorial consultant for Cengage (formerly Thomson Delmar Learning) Learning (West Legal Studies) for paralegal and law textbooks, is well known for his prolific writing for paralegals and lawyers. Professor Statsky's seminal textbooks include *Introduction to Paralegalism: Perspectives, Problems, and Skills* (6th ed., West, 2002), *Essentials of Paralegalism* (4th ed., West, 2005), and *Legal Research and Writing: Some Starting Points* (5th ed., West, 1999), and they have been used in paralegal schools, colleges, and universities for many years.

Publications

- *Family Law: The Essentials* (2nd ed., West, 2004)
- *Family Law* (5th ed., West, 2002)
- *Torts: Personal Injury Litigation* (4th ed., West, 2001)
- *Essentials of Torts* (2nd ed., West, 2001)
- *Case Analysis and Fundamentals of Legal Writing* (Statsky and Wernet, 4th ed., West, 1995)

---

[1]Reprinted with the permission of William P. Statsky, Esq., Therese A. Cannon, Esq., James S. Wilber, Esq., and Gary Melhuish, Paralegal Director, Ballard Spahr.

- *West's Legal Desk Reference* (Statsky, Hussey, Diamond, and Nakamura, 1990)
- *Legal Thesaurus Dictionary: A Resource for the Writer and Computer Researcher* (West, 1985)
- *Legislative Analysis and Writing* (2nd ed., West, 1984)
- *Rights of the Imprisoned: Cases, Materials, and Directions* (Statsky and Singer, Bobbs-Merrill, 1974; Supplements: 1976, 1978)

Since 1990, Bill has made significant contributions to NFPA as a member of its Advisory Council and as a member of the certifying board for NALA in 1995 and 1996.

Mr. Statsky's *pro bono* activities include hospice volunteer (www. pathwayshealth.org), Family Law Clinic, Volunteer Lawyers of Santa Clara County (www.probonoproject.org), tutor for jail inmates, Vision Literacy (www.visionliteracy.org), recording textbooks for the blind and dyslexic (www.rfbd.org), and food deliveries for Community Services Agency (www.csacares.org).

William P. Statsky: Q & A

Professor Statsky has been teaching paralegals and writing paralegal books on various fields of law for more than 35 years. His paralegals books were among the first in the nation. Mr. Statsky is also renowned for his law books and textbooks, which many law schools, colleges, and universities use. His responses to the following questions will help you expand your perspective of the paralegal profession and learn from Professor Statsky's seasoned knowledge.

Q. What percentage of paralegals in American law firms do you estimate perform statutory research?

A. There are two main levels of statutory research: desktop research and first-time issues research.

Desktop: You refer to a frequently used code volume or rules volume, which is usually sitting on your desk, or to an on-line site to get a brief answer. You may crosscheck an answer you already have to a brief question, for example, how many days do we have to file an answer to the interrogatories?

First-time issues: In first-time issues statutory research, you use multiple research resources (on the shelf and on-line) to answer relatively complex questions that the law firm is facing for the first time.

Percentage of paralegals that do desktop statutory research: 65%
Percentage of paralegals who do first-time issue statutory research: 5%

Q. What percentage of paralegals in American law firms do you estimate perform case research?

A. There are two main levels of case research: clean-up and issues research.

1. *Clean-up case research*: This involves getting a full citation to a case, photocopying a case, getting uncoupled information out of a case (from a citation given to you by a supervisor), and maybe using Sheppard's Citations, which is a set of red books in the law library that lists cases and their history, to Sheppardize or determine if a particular case is still valid and how subsequent cases have cited or interpreted that case. This is usually commonly called, "Sheppardizing" or key citing a case. It also helps ensure that the citation is correct.

2. *Issues case research*: This involves finding cases you do not already know the citations of, briefing them, and applying them to client issues that the office has handled before or that are new to the office.

Percentage of paralegals that do clean-up case research: 15%
Percentage of paralegals that do issues case research: 2%

Q. Why are some lawyers reluctant to let paralegals perform legal research?

A. Lawyers are reluctant only as to first-time issues statutory research and issues case research for the following reasons:

1. It is hard to supervise. (How do you know if the paralegal was comprehensive?)

2. Lawyers know from law school how extremely difficult legal research can be.

3. Many law offices do relatively little involved legal research.

Q. What obstacles do paralegals incur in performing legal research?

A. Paralegals are subject to unavailability of resources on the shelves or on-line and lack of assignments calling for legal research.

Q. Your books, *Introduction to Paralegalism: Perspectives, Problems, and Skills* and *Essentials of Paralegalism* continue to be used by paralegals. How has the perspective of paralegalism in these definitive books changed since their original editions?

A. The main difference is the wide acceptability of paralegals in the legal profession. In the 1970s when I started, we had to focus on what a paralegal was. There are still definition questions today, but they are mainly political definitional questions (e.g., when can a legal secretary switch titles to legal assistant or paralegal?).

Q. How do you think technology has changed the duties and responsibilities of paralegals?

A. I do not think the duties have changed much due to technology. What has changed is the dramatic difference in the way paralegal duties are performed. We do not have paperless offices, but we have computer-driven offices.

Q. How has technology changed legal research?

A. It is unbelievable. The biggest indication of the change, particularly in private law offices, is that law firms are canceling their subscriptions to many of the big-ticket print items, such as court reporters. Many firms are giving their old sets away. On-line legal research is almost taking over.

Q. How do you think the paralegal profession has changed since 1980?

A. The paralegal profession has changed in the following ways:

1. Greater visibility
2. More prestige
3. Increased provincialism (much effort to keep people out of the field, e.g., the California legislation)
4. More complex (e.g., paralegals need considerable computer savvy)

Q. What is your vision of the future for the paralegal profession?

A. I envision an expansion of what paralegals can do under attorney supervision, for example, conducting depositions, particularly in garden-variety cases, and an even greater expansion of independents, that is, contract and freelance paralegals offering legal services to the public without attorney supervision.

JAMES S. WILBER, ESQ.

Biography

James Wilber is a partner in Altman Weil, Inc., a law office management consulting firm with its East Coast offices in Newtown Square, PA; its Midwest office in Milwaukee, WI; and serves clients in the UK, Europe, and throughout the world from its U.S. locations. Jim works in the Wisconsin office. As one aspect of Altman Weil's many consulting services, Mr. Wilber leads consulting projects regarding paralegals and paralegal departments (i.e., paralegal development and improvement for law firms and corporations). Previously, Jim has managed law offices and has been responsible for the hiring, training, supervision, and development of paralegals. He has written articles on how paralegals can enhance profitability and the underutilization of paralegals.

Prior to joining Altman Weil, Mr. Wilber practiced law and managed law offices for 14 years. His law office management experience is extensive: as a managing attorney in both the public and private sectors, he was responsible for the hiring, training, supervision, and development of lawyers, paralegals, and law office managers. Other duties included responsibility for financial analysis, budgeting, law office technology, and computer applications.

James Wilber, a Fellow in the College of Law Practice Management, has written and lectured extensively on management issues in the legal profession. He is the Editor of the Report to Legal Management and is the Editor of the International Practice Manager of the International Bar Association. Jim has been published and quoted in numerous publications, including the ABA Journal, the *American Lawyer* magazine, the *National Law Journal*, and the journals of many state bar associations. He is an officer of Committee 10 (Practice Management and Technology) of the International Bar Association. Mr. Wilber is a *cum laude* graduate of the inaugural class of the Southern Illinois University School of Law, having served as Notes and Comments Editor of the Law Review. He has a bachelor's degree from the University of Michigan and a master's degree in English Literature.

Mr. Wilber has worked closely with law firms to develop and improve their paralegal programs. He has become an expert in increasing the profitability of paralegals. In addition, he emphasizes to his client firms the better utilization of paralegals.

James S. Wilber: Q & A

Q. Who usually calls Altman Weil for consulting services regarding paralegals or paralegal departments in a law firm or corporation?

A. In law firms, the paralegal manager or administrator might be the first to call us, or the executive director, or the executive committee may contact us. Managers are more aware of the problems with the paralegal program, and they know they can improve their program with our help. We do consult with governmental legal departments as well.

Q. What are the common problems that law firms face when contacting Altman Weil to help them with their paralegals and paralegal departments?

A. It is almost as if you can tell what the problems are before you go in. It is usually the same problem—professionalism—not every one in the firm treats the paralegals as professionals. This has an influence on the department. In addition, there is the problem of what lawyers are willing to delegate to paralegals. Some lawyers do not want to delegate work to paralegals for several reasons: they do not know what paralegals can do, they are afraid they themselves will not have anything to do, or they figure they can do it easily themselves.

Q. What other consulting does Altman Weil do regarding paralegal programs?

A. We might be asked to do various types of work. The big issue, however, is always the underutilization of paralegals.

Q. How could firms improve the utilization of paralegals?

A. Without question, the chief reason for the underutilization of paralegals in most law offices is that there are too many lawyers competing with legal assistants for paralegal-level work. This can be particularly true if there are too many inexperienced lawyers. Wherever this happens, underutilization hurts an organization's productivity and profitability. To ensure the effective utilization of paralegals, analyze the complexity and volume of legal work available in the firm or department, and if there is too little work appropriate for handling by lawyers, that fact has to be dealt with. Paralegals will never have enough challenging legal work to do if there are too many lawyers for legal work. This does not mean that a law firm or law department should willy-nilly begin laying off lawyers. A better alternative would be to quit recruiting new lawyers until the proper balance between lawyers and paralegals is achieved.

The reasons cited most often are that paralegals are not used to their capacity and that lawyers do not know what work to give paralegals, that lawyers do not know how much work to give paralegals; and that some attorneys lack confidence in the abilities of their paralegals. Often the role of paralegals is unclear. Law offices sometimes struggle with defining where paralegals fit—they are not lawyers, and they are not secretaries. This can cause confusion in work roles and delegation.

The growth of the paralegal profession has resulted in many law firms and law departments being able to deliver legal services to their clients more cost effectively. In those law offices where paralegals are used appropriately, the following characteristics are usually present. Paralegals have job classifications and salaries that are different from those of secretaries. Paralegals do not normally perform clerical or secretarial duties, although they usually work with personal computers for document drafting, database use, spreadsheet development, and so forth. Additionally, paralegals are assigned secretarial support. Usually, they share a secretary with one or more other paralegals or lawyers. Paralegals participate, with lawyers, in meetings and other practice functions and have input into the decisions made for the practice area. Paralegals participate in programs of professional development. They are given opportunities to participate in national and local paralegal organizations and professional activities.

Paralegals are bound by the same code of professional responsibility and ethics as the lawyers in the office. Paralegals are also given regular performance reviews similar to those given to attorneys. Salary increases reflect performance, experience, expertise, and each person's contribution to the smooth functioning of the office.

Q. How do you think paralegals can enhance profitability?

A. If a matter is billed by the hour, there's an anomaly, that is, if you billed a paralegal to a client for work that was previously billed by a lawyer at a higher rate, then it decreases the firm's profitability. However, there are two important things to consider about that phenomenon. First, over time, clients are not going to pay lawyer rates for services paralegals can do. Why not have the firm pass along this cost savings to the client, if you are able to do so at a reduced rate? Second, it will improve the firm's relations with clients; the firm will receive more work. However, in the long term, it will inure to the firm's benefit.

The "problem" mentioned only applies to work priced hourly. Law firms are now handling less work on an hourly basis and more on a fixed-fee basis because there is no inherent incentive for efficiency in hourly priced work, and clients do not like the uncertainty. Today, more law firms are billing on a project basis. Project work will increase profitability and encourage firms to use paralegals instead of lawyers.

Q. What do you advise your clients regarding the distribution of paralegal offices, that is, size and location?

A. We encourage law offices to treat their paralegals as professionals and provide them adequate, confidential workspace.

Q. How are your clients' paralegals trained on software? Is it through vendors, or is it through your consulting firm?

A. We do not do any software training or represent any vendors. We may consult with firms in the planning stages or on how to approach the marketplace. For example, we may help them do a request for proposal (RFP) for technology purchases, but we are not technology system integrators or trainers. We do recommend that all the professionals, including paralegals, have adequate technology to serve their clients.

Q. What did you look for in your previous positions when you were responsible for hiring paralegals and law office managers?

A. In hiring a paralegal, I considered the firm's requirements for hiring a paralegal. In some firms, the firm will not hire you unless you have a full college degree; in others you must have a paralegal certificate, and in some firms, both. In terms of hiring paralegal managers, that is, those who manage other paralegals, the emphasis must be on management. A paralegal manager may have been a paralegal, and that will increase her credibility, but in a paralegal management job, she must be a good manager first.

Q. How has the attitude of lawyers changed toward paralegals during the last decade?

A. Since the paralegal profession came into being, the utilization of paralegals has slowly increased over time, but it has increased steadily, year by year. More lawyers understand how paralegals can help them deliver legal services to clients, that is, those paralegals have a valuable role in the delivery of legal services. I cannot imagine that will ever change, with cost being so important.

Q. Given the growth of technology, what do you think is the future for paralegals?

A. There is a positive future for paralegals.

GARY MELHUISH

Biography

Gary Melhuish is the Manager for Litigation Support Services at the Philadelphia office of Ballard, Spahr, Andrews, & Ingersoll, LLP. Previously, he was the paralegal director in the Washington, D.C., office of Fried, Frank, Harris, Shriver, & Jacobson, LLP. He is the past president of the International Paralegal Management Association (IPMA) and formerly adjunct faculty at the Georgetown University Paralegal Studies Program, where he taught legal ethics and legal technology.

Gary has 28-years' experience as a legal assistant at law firms of Ballard Spahr, Fried Frank, California Federal Bank, and at the law firm of Wolf, Block, Schorr, & Solis-Cohen. He received a B.A. from the University of Maryland, an M.A. from Michigan State University, and a paralegal certificate from the Institute for Paralegal Training in Philadelphia. Mr. Melhuish is a frequent speaker at meetings of the Association of Legal Administrators (ALA), Paralegal SuperConferences, DC Bar, National Capital Area Paralegal Association (NCAPA), and IPMA training seminars and conferences (www.ipma.org).

Gary Melhuish: Q & A

Gary Melhuish is an accomplished paralegal who has advanced through the ranks. He is actively promoting the paralegal profession in his position as legal assistant manager and in his many lively motivational speeches. His activities in associations important to the paralegal profession indicate his loyalty and dedication. "Let's get one more for the paralegal profession," he says in his speeches, which are informative as well as humorous. The author had the pleasure of attending his speech at the Paralegal SuperConference in Washington, D.C. Gary had us laughing yet learning at the same time. He truly is a knowledgeable person and leader in the paralegal profession. His experience is enlightening. Read on.

Q. In your opinion, what has contributed to the growth of the paralegal profession?

A. The growth of the paralegal profession has occurred for many reasons:

1. The demand from clients that law firms deliver services in a cost-effective manner without sacrificing quality. Corporate America has embraced the demonstrated intelligence and quality of paralegals.

2. The high cost of law school has made more college graduates reluctant to invest the time and money into a degree before they have "tested the waters" to see if the legal field is the right fit for them.

3. The desire by law firms to create a position that would have greater longevity than an associate would without the expectation that the people in the paralegal position would become partners in the organization.

4. The desire by attorneys to be able to focus on the practice of law rather than the details of getting things accomplished.

5. The changes in technology that require an individual to possess specialized knowledge to efficiently complete projects—particularly litigation projects that have generated exponentially larger document sets.

Q. How would you compare the duties of paralegals today to what they were in 1980?

A. Paralegals today have to be comfortable with learning and keeping current on various technologies. Everything from Microsoft® Office® products, Westlaw and LexisNexis research tools, litigation support software, and electronic discovery programs are increasing in sophistication and applicability each year. Paralegals today must keep abreast of these changes to remain valuable. In many respects, the technology has made paralegals increasingly productive. In 1980, cite checking a brief took four hours; today using a program, it takes four minutes.

Q. What do you see as some of the common problems of paralegals today and the obstacles they must overcome?

A. The primary problem is training new attorneys on the role of paralegals. Law schools do not prepare or educate new attorneys on the role of paralegals in the legal system. In addition, the new attorneys are not taught supervisory skills, even though they will be required to supervise different levels of employees from the moment they step in the door.

Q. What would you recommend for experienced paralegals to do to advance their knowledge?

A. Write and teach—each of these activities requires that a paralegal focus their knowledge in more depth than they normally do on a daily basis. Offering to write an article for a local paralegal association or to speak at a local paralegal school will give experienced paralegals a different outlook on their experience. Getting their name out there will help advance their career.

Q. What do you think is the best way to handle evaluations?

A. Go into evaluations with the long-term view in mind. Realize that the evaluation is not a snapshot of the last two months or two weeks, but a review of an entire year. Not all years go well, and they should be ready to hear about anything that may have happened. I also recommend that paralegals should not conclude the evaluation process without setting goals for the upcoming year. Even if these goals are not offered by the person giving the evaluation, paralegals should take the time to select two or three things that they would like to accomplish during the next year.

Q. Many paralegals seem to hit a glass ceiling in law firms, and the only advancement is to become a paralegal administrator or law office manager. Do you see any alternatives for paralegals?

A. I think that the concept of "glass ceiling" is a rather dated way of looking at paralegal responsibilities. Granted, few titles may be offered to a paralegal. However, the ability to take on more project responsibilities, to try new practice areas, and to develop new skills does not end simply because a paralegal has reached the top job title available at a particular firm. Not every employee in an organization can become the CEO, not every attorney in a law firm can become the managing partner, and not every paralegal should define their career by a particular title. It is more important that we look at the job that we have and the tasks that we are performing on a daily basis and decide if these responsibilities still give us the job satisfaction.

Q. Many paralegals have difficulty communicating with attorneys. Are there any recommendations you would make to them?

A. Try to learn how the attorney communicates best and find ways to integrate that style into your communication habits. Some attorneys prefer seeing things in writing and would rather you send them an e-mail; other attorneys may want to see you in person or talk on the phone. One of the most frequent complaints that I hear from attorneys is that they often do not hear enough from a paralegal working on a long-term assignment. Paralegals need to establish the ground rules early on in a relationship with the supervising attorneys to avoid miscommunication and missing communication. Frequent updates on the progress of your project will do wonders to keep an attorney happy. Be brief and not chatty.

Q. What are the issues that paralegals face today?

A. One of the new issues that paralegals are facing is that a new group of workers is competing for work that in the past was done by paralegals—temporary attorneys, called *locus tenums*. Clients have discovered that there is a pool of talent in the marketplace who can be used for repetitive work or document review who are highly educated, motivated, and less expensive than paralegals. Paralegals must be sure to remind our employers that one of the advantages we bring to the table is a continuity and institutional memory that temporaries are not capable of providing.

> *Author's note*: Outsourcing by large and small law firms (in addition to government which dove into this service head-first) is a now an increasing and invasive reality with most of the fear of lack of client confidentiality disappearing. "Sniffing the op-

portunity, Reading-based Xansa, an IT outsourcing company in England, is extending the scope of its operations to include legal services support. The company has initiated project-based support to a big law firm it is reluctant to identify. Success of this venture, what Xansa calls a 'pilot project,' could drive its entry into a new vertical.

"We have started pilot work on some paralegal services," says Padmaja Krishnan, Director, Marketing and Business Development at Xansa's India unit, which is planning a four-fold rise in its manpower here to 10,000 people by 2007.

She says that the scope of work initially would include time-bound activity, such as processing large volumes of legal documents, and the nature of work "will essentially be supporting attorneys on the ground." (*India Courts Western Law Firms* by Rashmi Agarwal, Business Writer, India)

Q. What are your opinions on certification, specifically the Certification Legal Assistant (CLA) and the Certified Paralegal programs, sponsored by the National Association of Legal Assistants (NALA); and the PACE, Registered Paralegal (RP) program, sponsored by the National Association of Paralegal Associations (NFPA)?

A. I think that the individuals who take these exams are showing a great commitment to the profession. If given two equally qualified candidates, I would select a person with certification over a person without certification. However, I would not specifically seek out only candidates with a certification. Many highly qualified paralegals simply do not have the time to devote to studying and taking these exams.

Q. Many paralegals are overworked and do not receive overtime pay. Federal regulations regarding overtime has failed. Do you think this issue will be resolved?

A. I do not agree with the concept that the regulatory scheme has failed with regard to overtime pay. The new Department of Labor (DOL) regulations indicate that "paralegals … generally do not qualify as exempt learned professionals, because an advanced specialized degree is not a standard prerequisite for entry into the field." However, no matter how the DOL standards are interpreted (exempt or nonexempt); the regulations only tell you to whom you must pay overtime and to whom you may not pay overtime. Consequently, I expect that overtime pay will continue to be a market-driven issue.

Certain job markets will continue to pay overtime, because it makes economic sense for the firms to do so rather than to adjust the salaries of the paralegals. In other markets where overtime has not traditionally been part of the compensation package, there may be some movement to create some nonexempt positions within the structure of the paralegal programs. However a particular market operates, it is more important to look at the total compensation package offered to paralegals to ensure that they are being adequately paid for the time and value that they bring to the table.

THERESE A. CANNON, ESQ.

Biography

Therese A. Cannon is the Associate Director of the Western Association of Schools and Colleges, one of the six regional accrediting agencies in the United States. Prior to being appointed to this position, she was the former Dean of the School of Law at John F. Kennedy University. She previously served as Associate Dean of the College of Extended Learning of San Francisco State University, where she directed the Paralegal Studies program. She served as the Educational Consultant to the Standing Committee on Paralegals of the American Bar Association from 1996 to 2006. Ms. Cannon was a member of the Standing Committee, served on its Approval Commission from 1991 to 1996, the last two and a half years as chair. She also served as Educational Standards Consultant to the Committee of Bar Examiners of the State Bar of California for eight years prior to assuming the position as Dean of JFKU law school.

Cannon is the author of *Ethics and Professional Responsibility for Legal Assistants*, now in its 4th edition (2003), and *A Concise Guide to Paralegal Ethics*, both published by Aspen Law & Business. She also co-authored *Paralegals, Profitability, and the Future of Your Law Practice* with Arthur G. Greene, which was published in 2003 by the Law Practice Management Section of the ABA. She authored both editions of *ABA Approval: A Reference Manual for Legal Assistant Educators*, published by the American Bar Association in 1997 and 2004.

She is a past president of the American Association for Paralegal Education and served on its board for six years, including a term as president. She is on the advisory boards of *Legal Assistant Today* magazine and the International Paralegal Management Association and serves on the Standards Committee for the PACE of the National Federation of Paralegal Associations. She is a past member of the Certifying Board of National Association of Legal Assistants.

Ms. Cannon earned her undergraduate degree at UCLA and her law degree at Loyola Law School in Los Angeles. She is licensed to practice law in California.

Therese A. Cannon: Q & A

This question and answer portion of the chapter will give you an opportunity for you to get to know the panelists. From their expertise, your perspective on the paralegal profession will expand. Learn about their opinions on important paralegals issues.

Teri's extensive current and past involvement in paralegal-related activities gives a unique perspective of the paralegal profession and one of considerable experience, seasoned expertise, and knowledge. Read her responses carefully. You will learn much.

Q. Why do you think ethics are important to paralegals?

A. Paralegals are heavily involved in all aspects of legal work and often face with ethical dilemmas. They need a solid understanding of the rules of professional responsibility, a strong personal sense of right, wrong, and problem-solving capabilities to guide them in resolving the ethical dilemmas they may face.

Q. How do you think lawyers have changed in their attitudes toward paralegals?

A. I think lawyers have come a long way in accepting the important role paralegals have to play in the delivery of legal services. Lawyers who have worked with paralegals greatly value paralegals for their education and skills and cannot imagine working without a paralegal.

In the 70s, most lawyers did not know what a paralegal was and what a paralegal could do. They had a vague idea that a paralegal was a glorified legal secretary or a permanent law clerk. Many lawyers used to be hesitant to delegate work to a nonlawyer, but that is no longer the case. The only lawyers who do not use paralegal services now are generally in small firms and believe they cannot afford a paralegal. Even these lawyers would like to hire paralegals.

Q. Do you know of any law schools that have programs to teach law students about paralegals?

A. Some law schools teach students about paralegals in Professional Responsibility courses that are often required, but only briefly. Some law schools offer electives in Law Practice Management or Law Office Management and will mention the use of paralegal services.

Q. What obstacles did you incur in shifting from being a paralegal and going to law school?

A. I was working in a law school that had a paralegal program while attending a different law school. I did not have any problems making the shift. I think it was beneficial to have been through paralegal school first. In paralegal school, I learned how to brief cases, research and write—law practice style. I knew substantive law. This was an edge, especially in the first year.

Q. Many paralegals think about going to law school, because they feel they are doing the work anyway. What are the pros and cons you considered in making this decision?

A. Some paralegals have a difficult time making the transition, because they have demanding paralegal jobs and try to attend law school while working. Many have to change job situations to make survive. Support from employers is crucial. If a paralegal is dissatisfied with being a paralegal and wants all the responsibility that goes along with being the lawyer, I say go. However, understand law school is a challenging and time-consuming endeavor and being a lawyer carries many additional burdens but also, it has its benefits.

Q. What specific changes have you seen in the attitude of the American Bar Association (ABA) toward paralegals since the 70s?

A. The ABA has supported the utilization of paralegal services since 1968, when it created its first committee on paralegals. I am not sure I could cite an attitude change as the ABA is a member group with more than 400,000 lawyers who have many different ideas about paralegals. I think the main changes within the ABA Standing Committee on Paralegals (SCOP) and the ABA Approval Commission, which approves paralegal schools, relate to the expansion of the work of paralegals do beyond what was originally seen as routine legal work under lawyer supervision.

Q. In your current position as educational consultant of the ABA Approval Commission, you have held for eight years, and formerly five-years as its chair, what typical problems did the Commission find? What factors does the Commission consider in approving paralegal schools?

A. The ABA has extensive Guidelines for the Approval of Paralegal Education Programs, which covers organization, administration, curriculum, admissions, and students' services, including placement, faculty, program director, and library services. Each program must submit a detailed self-evaluation report and exhibits. After these are submitted, a two-day visit is held. Then a report is written that goes to the full Approval Commission. The Commission makes a recommendation to the SCOP, and then SCOP makes its recommendation to the House of Delegates, which is the entity with authority to approve.

Typical areas that delay approval are inadequate assessment, noncomplying advisory committee, lack of faculty meetings, and lack of sufficient paralegal content and practice in courses, missing library items, inadequate placement assistance, or records.

Q. Do you think other states will follow California in its enactment of the Business and Professional Code Section 6450?

A. I do not think many states will follow. California has a strong legislature that often moves into the realm of the practice of law in ways that are not tolerated in other states. I think other states may adopt court rules, like Arizona, or laws, like Maine, that define paralegal and limit the use of the title to persons working under lawyer supervision.

I do not think other states will establish a weak legislative scheme for regulating paralegals without any oversight by an entity. Most state legislatures and courts have addressed the regulation of paralegals have found that paralegals do not need to be regulated to protect consumers, because the lawyers they work for are already regulated.

Q. What do you foresee as the future for nurse consultants?

A. There will always be a need for legal nurse consultants who have expertise in nursing, medical, and legal issues. This is a small but important niche and a great career option.